ERASMUS AND CAMBRIDGE

ERASMUS

AND CAMBRIDGE

The Cambridge Letters of Erasmus
translated by

D. F. S. THOMSON

Associate Professor of Latin
University College, University of Toronto

Introduction, Commentary, and
Notes by

H. C. PORTER

Assistant Lecturer in History, University of Cambridge
Fellow and Tutor of Selwyn College

UNIVERSITY OF TORONTO PRESS

Printed in Canada

PREFACE

THIS BOOK originated in a discussion following a lecture on "Erasmus in Cambridge" given by H. C. Porter in 1958 to the Toronto Branch of the Humanities Association of Canada at Victoria College, University of Toronto. The place was appropriate; for in the library of Victoria College there is a separate Collection bequeathed by the late Dr. Andrew James Bell, Professor of Latin and Comparative Philology, which contains a large number of Erasmus items.

Thanks are due to the editorial staff of the University of Toronto Press, and especially to Mrs. Eleanor Cook, for their care in dealing with a tricky manuscript. Mr. Robin Inglis of Selwyn College Cambridge helped with the proofs.

The translations are from the text as printed by P. S. Allen. Of the thirty-one surviving letters of Erasmus from Cambridge, Allen printed only two from manuscript (Numbers 31 and 32 in our selection). The rest he took from Froben's editions of 1518 to 1521. Naturally there is a difference between the textual authority of a letter edited from manuscript, and a published letter of which no manuscript draft survives. The dates, or suggested dates, given by Allen have been accepted; though many are open to some doubt, because of the manner of compilation of the printed collections, and the degree and kind of editing such collections underwent. Compliments at the beginning and end of letters, and a few phrases of purely rhetorical importance, have been omitted from the translation. The number of each letter in Allen's edition is given in parentheses in the list on pages vii to x.

Erasmus used several Latin words to describe the vessels in which his wine was brought from London to Cambridge. The most frequent is *lagena* ("flagon"), but *uter* ("skin") appears several times, and others are used, without apparent discrimination. To avoid confusion, and unnecessary notes, the word "cask" has been adopted throughout. Sometimes in the early sixteenth century wine was carried in the cask; sometimes in a natural skin, or leather bottle; sometimes in a bottle made after the fashion of a skin or a cask; and so forth.

The book has been published with the help of a grant from The Humanities Research Council, using funds provided by the Canada Council, and from the Publications Fund of the University of Toronto Press.

H. C. PORTER
D. F. S. THOMSON

Cambridge, June 1963

ABBREVIATIONS

E.E. — *Erasmi Epistolae*, ed. P. S. Allen *et al.*, 12 vols., Oxford, 1906–58

Nichols — *The Epistles of Erasmus*, transl. F. M. Nichols, 3 vols., London, 1901–18

V.C.H. — *A History of the County of Cambridge and the Isle of Ely*, vol. III, *The City and University of Cambridge*, ed. J. P. C. Roach, London, 1959 (Victoria History of the Counties of England)

CONTENTS

LETTERS CONCERNING CAMBRIDGE

INTRODUCTION

I know with certainty that a man's work is nothing but the long journey to recover, through the detours of art, the two or three simple and great images which first gained access to his heart.

ALBERT CAMUS

"I dreamed of a golden age and the fortunate islands: and then, as Aristophanes said, I awoke."

ERASMUS, 1515[1]

I

IN THE AUTUMN OF 1499, when he was in his early thirties, Erasmus spent about two months in Oxford. He was there as a private person—a guest in St. Mary's, the college of the order of Augustinian canons, to which he belonged—being still a religious on leave from the monastery of Steyn, near Gouda; now over six years absent, first as secretary to the Bishop of Cambrai, and then (from 1494 or 1495) studying theology and teaching Latin in Paris. At Oxford he met John Colet, who was about his own age, and attended some of his public and popular lectures on the letters of St. Paul—so very unlike the biblical exegesis, dependent upon scholastic "glosses," which had irritated Erasmus in Paris.

Colet had gone up to Oxford from the city of London (where his father was sheriff) about 1483—the year in which the Beverley boy John Fisher first rode down from Yorkshire to Cambridge. After taking the arts course Colet began, about 1490, to study in the faculty of theology, but interrupted his work with a four-year grand tour on the continent (perhaps with his father and brothers), which began, most probably, in 1492, when he was about twenty-six. We know that he was in Rome during the spring of 1493.[2] And although next to nothing is known about his itinerary and studies in France and Italy—the only reference he ever made in his works to his Italian experiences was a curt English dismissal of the habits of Italian males who "shamefully give utterance to womanish outcries at the funerals of their friends and relatives"[3]—he was in his Oxford lectures to quote from Giovan Battista Spagnoli (1448–1516),[4] Carmelite friar of Mantua, the "Christian Virgil," the "good old Mantuan" invoked by Shakespeare's Holofernes; from the *Platonic Theology* (1482)

[1]*E.E.*, no. 333, lines 49–50; tr. Nichols, II, 192.

[2]Parks, *English Traveler to Italy*, 466–67; W. K. Ferguson, "A Letter of John Colet," *American Historical Review* (July 1934), 696–9. For the known and deduced details of Colet's career, see Emden, *Biographical Register*, 462–4.

[3]Lupton, *Hierarchies of Dionysius*, 138.

[4]Lupton, *Colet's Lectures on Romans*, 33.

of Marsilio Ficino (1433–99), the *doyen* of intellectual Florence at the close of the *quattrocento*, "than whose language there can be nothing finer in philosophy"[5]; and from the worthy *platonicus*[6] Pico della Mirandola, who died at the age of thirty in 1494, "in the time of lilies"; and he could have personally known all three. Colet must have seemed very grand and Italianate to Erasmus, then on his first visit to England, vaguely planning a visit to Italy which did not materialize until 1506. Oxford, for him, meant Colet. And it meant also Thomas More, twenty-one years old, a student at Lincoln's Inn, who had been an Oxford undergraduate for two years—1492–4—after leaving the household of Archbishop Morton. Erasmus met More in the late summer of 1499 in London, before the Oxford visit, and he was entirely captivated.

Those few weeks in Oxford effectively crystallized the ideas and widened the horizons of the (as yet) almost unknown Dutch cleric. It seems he was offered a teaching post at Oxford. But this he declined: partly because he did not feel himself scholar enough, partly because he sensed that such an appointment would provoke jealousy among the Oxford divines. By the first week in December he was back in London.

The brief association of Erasmus with Oxford was perhaps misleadingly emphasized in the title of a book by Frederic Seebohm published in 1867: *The Oxford Reformers: Colet, Erasmus, More*. Seebohm (1833–1912) was not a university graduate; he had studied law in London and become first a barrister, and then, from 1857, a partner in a banking firm at Hitchin, Hertfordshire, where he lived until his death. He had been working on *The Oxford Reformers* for about ten years. As soon as it was published, he was dissatisfied. For one thing, in 1867 there also appeared an edition of a treatise by John Colet, "On the Sacraments of the Church," a manuscript in the library of St. Paul's School discovered and edited by Joseph Hirst Lupton. Lupton (1836–1905) was a Fellow of St. John's College, Cambridge, and (1864–99) sur-master (under-master) at St. Paul's School. For another thing, in *Notes and Queries* for October 1868, William Aldis Wright, Librarian of Trinity College, Cambridge, published some material

[5]*Ibid.*, 32.
[6]Lupton, *Colet's Letters on the Mosaic Account of the Creation*, 170.

from a manuscript in the Trinity library concerning the early life of More. So during that October of 1868 Seebohm, in a fine patrician gesture, withdrew from sale all the remaining copies of his own book and had them destroyed. In May 1869 he put out a second edition, revised and enlarged, acknowledging the help of Lupton.

In 1869 also, Lupton published and translated commentary-paraphrases by Colet of two works by the pseudo-Dionysius. This was the second of five volumes edited by Lupton, devoted to eight works of Colet found in manuscript at St. Paul's and Cambridge. (Many other works, once listed by John Bale, have disappeared.) The fifth volume was published in 1876. Seebohm was therefore tempted to feel that *The Oxford Reformers* had outlived its usefulness. But, he wrote, "I have yielded to Mr. Lupton's pleading that the history of the fellow-work of the three friends, imperfect as it always was, and antiquated as it has now become, may live a little longer."[7] And the third edition was printed in March 1887. Later in the same year came Lupton's *Life of Dean Colet*, dedicated to Dr. John Williams, Bishop of Connecticut, "successor of Bishop Seabury," and paying tribute to the work of Seebohm:

> During the last twenty years much has been done to make Colet better known to us. Till then, his name was all but unheard of in the annals of his country. . . . The chief credit of this change is due to Mr. Seebohm's *Oxford Reformers*, which first showed Colet to us in the true greatness of his character. . . . Our fellow work, if I may presume so to call it, began just twenty years ago, and seems likely to end together, with the publication of the third edition of his *Oxford Reformers* in the early months of this year.

The third edition of *Oxford Reformers* was reprinted in 1896 and 1911; and after Seebohm's death it achieved just recognition as a classic by being reprinted in the Everyman Library (1914). Seebohm's great knowledge, conscientiousness, and skill, together with the enthusiasm and conciseness with which he told his tale, make his book worth reading still. The book reflected a corner of the Victorian conscience. Seebohm was writing "in this nineteenth century" for "those Christians who have desired, as they did, to rest their faith upon honest facts and not upon dogmas—upon evidence, and not upon authority."

[7]Preface to third edition.

Now neither Seebohm nor Lupton was an Oxford man. But the debt of the living Erasmus to Oxford was amply repaid to his shade by three sons of that university: James Anthony Froude (1818–94), Francis Morgan Nichols (1826–1915), and Percy Stafford Allen (1869–1933).

In 1892 the "fell news" reached Oxford that the Regius Professor of Modern History, Edward Freeman, had (in Lytton Strachey's phrase) "gone pop in Spain." Lord Salisbury appointed as Freeman's successor one of that scholar's bitterest enemies, J. A. Froude, who had been away from Oxford since resigning his Fellowship at Exeter College in 1849, and who was seventy-four years old. He began his public lectures in the University in November 1892 with a series on the Council of Trent, following this with a course, begun in the spring of 1893, on English Seamen in the Sixteenth Century. Also in 1893 and the early part of 1894, when he was seventy-five, Froude gave twenty lectures in his home at Oxford for undergraduates reading history; his subject was Erasmus, and the lectures were published "as they were delivered" in September 1894, with a preface written in July: *Life and Letters of Erasmus*. The proofs had been corrected on his deathbed in Devon, for the professor died in October. His last book was hugely successful. It was reprinted in October, November, and December of 1894, and January, March, and November of 1895.

The set subject for the Chancellor's English Essay Prize at Oxford in 1893 had been "Erasmus." In the summer of 1892 P. S. Allen of Corpus, aged twenty-three, had begun to work for this, finishing the essay in February 1893. He was not awarded the prize. But during his research "he realised that here lay the task for which he had been searching—to edit a new edition of the Letters of Erasmus."[8] Undeterred by his failure, he began that life-work (noting the date in his diary) on August 12, 1893,[9] when he was twenty-four. The scheme, Allen later wrote, was "undertaken with the encouragement of the late Professor Froude, at the time when he was lecturing here on Erasmus."[10] Allen was

[8]The comment is that of Mrs. Allen, in *Letters of P. S. Allen*, 11.
[9]*Ibid.*, 12.
[10]*E.E.*, I, v.

always generous in his praises of Froude; and his tributes are the more considered because as men and as scholars the old professor and the young graduate were as different a pair as even Victorian Oxford could provide. "I usually urge people to read Froude," Allen wrote in 1919, "who, with all his faults (and they have been greatly exaggerated) seems to me to have understood Erasmus as none of his other biographers have. There is a great deal of resemblance between them, in brilliance and versatility and the spirit of adventure."[11] Allen was also helped and encouraged by Seebohm, "as an historian and owner of books."[12] Seebohm had a collection of Erasmus editions at Hitchin, a library in which the Allens were to work even after Seebohm's death.

From 1897 to 1901 Allen was in the Indian Educational Service, as Professor of History in the Government College at Lahore, teaching both English and Indian history (and learning Urdu). The Erasmus work was "carried on under the gloom of Indian summers and in high valleys in Kashmir."[13] He visited England (and married) in the autumn of 1898, when the publication of the Erasmus letters was discussed informally with Bishop Stubbs, one of the delegates of the Clarendon Press. Allen at that time was thinking in terms of six volumes, on which he planned to spend fifteen years. The Press definitely agreed to undertake the series at the end of 1902, when Allen was back in Oxford, a member of the Corpus High Table, but not a Fellow. The manuscript of the first volume was delivered to the publishers in December 1904.

Meanwhile F. M. Nichols, sometime Fellow of Wadham—and owner of Lawford Hall, once the home of the Mountjoy family—had decided, in his late sixties, to undertake an English translation of those of Erasmus' letters which might seem specially interesting to an Englishman. The first volume had been published in 1901, when Nichols was seventy-five; it covered the years 1484–1509. Volume II (1509–17) appeared in 1904. Shortly thereafter Nichols was made an honorary Fellow of his college.

In September 1906 the first volume appeared of what H. W. Garrod called "perhaps the most accurate book in the world":

[11] *Letters*, 158.
[12] *E. E.*, III, iv.
[13] *E.E.*, I, v.

"one of the great monuments of English learning"—the *Erasmi Epistolae* of Allen. Allen died in 1933, having been a Fellow of Merton from 1908 (when he was thirty-eight), and President of Corpus and Honorary Fellow of Merton from 1924. Seven volumes had then been published. There were four more to come, largely prepared by Allen (who had corrected before he died the proofs of volume VIII), and completed by Mrs. Allen and H. W. Garrod. Volume XI was published in 1947. The series was completed by the index, which came in 1958.

In 1918, between the third and fourth volumes of Allen, there had been posthumously published the third volume of Nichols' translations (1517–18). This volume was prefaced by a gracious tribute by Allen to the author, who had died at the age of eighty-nine. Nichols, wrote Allen, was "an amateur in the best sense of the word. He found his work irresistibly attractive, and he gave himself to it without reserve." He concluded: "I am glad to have this further opportunity of recording that some of our work was done together."[14]

Erasmus, then, would have no cause to complain of the attention posthumously paid him by "the flourishing University of Oxford."

II

IT WOULD BE nearer the mark to describe Erasmus as a London Reformer. His affection for England was almost wholly a loyalty to London. After his return to the City from Oxford in December 1499, he wrote to Robert Fisher—not a very bright youth apparently, but a kinsman of John—who had been among his English pupils in Paris,

> But how do you like our England, you will say. Believe me, my Robert, when I answer that I never liked anything so much before. I find the climate both pleasant and wholesome; and I have met with so much kindness, and so much learning, not hackneyed and trivial, but deep, accurate, ancient—Latin and Greek—that but for the curiosity of seeing it, I do not now so

[14]Nichols, III, v, xi.

much care for Italy. When I hear my Colet, I seem to be listening to Plato himself. In Grocin, who does not marvel at such a perfect round of learning? What can be more acute, profound and delicate than the judgement of Linacre? What has nature ever created more gentle, more sweet, more happy than the genius of Thomas More? I need not go through the list. It is marvellous how general and abundant is the harvest of ancient learning in this country, to which you ought all the sooner to return.[15]

Now, it is true that those four especial friends were all Oxford men. But only Colet was still resident in Oxford—though he was also Vicar of Stepney. He was to move to the Deanery of St. Paul's in the early summer of 1504. (The Deanery was in the south-west corner of the churchyard; the palace of Bishop Richard Fitzjames of London opposite, to the north of the cathedral.) William Grocin was Vicar of St. Lawrence Jewry, hard by the Guildhall (off Guildhall Yard); Thomas Linacre was practising as a doctor in the City; Thomas More was at Lincoln's Inn. By the time of Erasmus' second visit to England, which began in the spring of 1505, the circle was more tightly knit. Thomas More had just moved into the large stone and timber house he was to own until 1520, in the area called The Barge in Bucklersbury. Bucklersbury[16] is a short street running from Cheapside to (modern) Walbrook; the More house, leased from the Hospital and grammar school of St. Thomas, was at the corner of the junction with Walbrook.[17] So More was not far east of St. Paul's and not more than ten minutes' stroll from the Guildhall and Grocin's church. If More walked east, he came in a few minutes to St. Anthony's School, where he had received his primary education, and of which Roger Wentford was now headmaster; a little farther in the same direction was the property of the Augustinian Friars, whose community included Bernard André, who was to be among Erasmus' acquaintances—not an easy relationship, for Erasmus borrowed money from the French friar and couldn't pay it back. More kept open house in Bucklersbury, at least until his second marriage in the late summer of 1511 (at about the same

[15]*E.E.*, no. 118; tr. Nichols, I, 226.

[16]Probably named after the Buckerell family, and sometimes spelt "Bucklesbury." This street specialized in grocers and apothecaries. Falstaff referred to lisping youths who "smell like Bucklersbury in simple-time" (*Merry Wives of Windsor*, III, iii).

[17]Reynolds, *St. Thomas More*, 56. Plan on page 61.

time as Erasmus went to Cambridge). Erasmus had a room *chez* More from 1509, and so did Thomas Linacre and Andrea Ammonio, the young Italian to whom Erasmus was to write his most confiding letters from Cambridge. When Ammonio moved out in October 1511, having found the new mistress of the household too much of a harpy,[18] he went only a few hundred yards: to the Hospital-School of St. Thomas, on the north side of Cheapside, just across from where that street joined Bucklersbury. The London house of Lord Mountjoy, Erasmus' patron, was between St. Paul's and the river, in Knightrider Street—a house which later in the century became the home of the "college" of Doctors of Civil Law, "Doctors' Commons." And anyone who wished to cross the river to the south bank might call upon John Fisher at Rochester House, near the future site of the Globe Theatre, almost next door to Bishop Richard Foxe of Winchester.

So when Erasmus wrote to Colet from Paris in June 1506 after his second visit to England, it was London that he praised: "this I can truly affirm, that there is no entire country which has bred me so many friends, so sincere, so learned, so devoted, so brilliant, so distinguished by every kind of virtue, as the single City of London."[19]

The "Oxford Reformers" had found a city and made of it a village.

Of course London was, in a phrase of Clarendon's, "the great and public stage of the kingdom."[20] Properly to see Cambridge and Oxford in perspective, it must first be remembered that in the England which Erasmus knew the two universities were *primarily* (though not exclusively) valued as seminaries for the training of ecclesiastics. Soon, they had changed all that. Mark Curtis has stressed that by the end of the century "the academic haunts of the medieval clergy had become a normal resort for the sons and heirs of the English gentry and nobility."[21] Second, one

[18]Letter 10.

[19]*E.E.*, no. 195; tr. Nichols, I, 412.

[20]*Miscellaneous Works* (1751 ed.), 345.

[21]Curtis, *Oxford and Cambridge in Transition*, especially chapter III, "Well-Born Successors to the Mediaeval Clerks." Although we might note that John Major, writing in 1521 (he had been at Cambridge in 1493), said that the scholars of Oxford and Cambridge were "in large part . . . of gentle birth" (*History of Greater Britain*, 27).

must bear in mind that for the "quality," even at the end of the Tudor century, and certainly at the beginning, the great finishing-school was in London, that is, the Inns of Court. "In my time," wrote William Harrison in his *Description of England* (published 1577), "there are three noble universities in England, to wit, one at Oxford, the second at Cambridge, and the third in London."[22]

Thomas More was sent to Oxford in 1492, when he was about fourteen. He left after two years to enter New Inn, one of the ten Inns of Chancery, with other "young students that come thither sometimes from one of the universities, and sometimes immediately from grammar schools" (words from John Stow).[23] The Inns of Chancery were "preparatory schools," as it were, for the four Inns of Court. Today the names of only three of the ten are well remembered: Staple Inn (the Elizabethan timber-work of which survives), Barnard's, and Furnival's; though Clement's Inn was to have fame thrust upon it for training "mad Shallow"—Robert Shallow, Esquire, Justice of the Peace for Gloucestershire. The students at the Inns of Chancery, "having spent some time in studying upon the first elements and grounds of the law, and having performed the exercises," passed on to one of the Inns of Court: Gray's, Lincoln's, the Middle and Inner Temple. Here, "continuing by the space of seven years, or thereabouts," they became Utter-Barristers (as opposed to Inner-Barristers, the junior men).[24] More was made Utter-Barrister of Lincoln's Inn in 1501.

There is a well-known description of the Inns of Court by Sir John Fortescue, written about 1470.[25] There are, wrote Fortescue, in this *studium*,

> ten lesser Inns, and sometimes more, which are called Inns of Chancery. To each of them at least a hundred students belong, and to some of them a much greater number, though they do not always gather in them all at the same time. The students are, indeed, for the most part, young men, learning the originals and something of the elements of law, who, becoming proficient therein as they mature, are absorbed into the greater Inns of the *studium*, which are called the Inns of Court. Of these greater Inns there

---

22Bk. II, chap. VI.

23*Survey of London*, I, 78.

24*Ibid.* For the Inns of Court, see W. S. Holdsworth, *History of English Law* (3rd ed.), II, 494–512.

25*De Laudibus*, tr. Chrimes, chapters 48 and 49.

are four in number, and some two hundred students belong in the aforementioned form to the least of them. In these greater Inns, no student could be maintained on less expense than £13/6/8d a year, and if he had servants to himself alone, as the majority have, then he will by so much the more bear expenses.

Now, even sixty years later a fairly well-to-do youth would spend, in all, about £5 a year at Cambridge or Oxford. By the 1550's £10 was coming to be a more usual (and much regretted) estimate.[26]

Of the thirty or so inns or hostels in Erasmus' Cambridge, very few housed so many as fifty students; although about two-thirds of the (say) nine hundred members of the university lived in such hostels (some of which had links with the colleges, some not) or in the five religious houses. A student resident in a hostel was known as a "hosteler" or "hallier." (Thomas Cranmer began his Cambridge career in a hostel, and the status of "hosteler" was later misunderstood by the "ignorant sort of Londoners," who supposed it to mean "that he had served with some inn-holder in the stable": and they "hung up bottles of hay at his gate when he began to preach the gospel."[27]) In spirit most of the hostels were probably rather like the fraternity houses in the universities of North America—the mediaeval predecessors of the Berkeley Greeks would hardly have found very attractive the austere discipline of a college. The largest of the fourteen colleges were King's, Christ's, and King's Hall, with provision, respectively, for about one hundred, sixty, and thirty-five members. The others had from five to twenty only. Not more than two or three made provision for special college teaching or for fee-paying undergraduates. Such provisions were an essentially Tudor development, until by the reign of Mary the colleges had taken over the whole student body of the University, and there were no independent hostels functioning in Cambridge—and, of course, no religious houses either. In the 1560's, a hundred years after Fortescue, St. John's had about 250 students.[28] But at the same

[26]See *Original Letters: English Reformation*, I, 190; Emmison, *Tudor Secretary*, 304.

[27]Harrison, *Description of England* (1577), Bk. II, chap. VI.

[28]There were 240—and 47 Fellows—in 1565 (State Papers Domestic Elizabeth [Public Record Office]; XXXVIII, no. 16 [i], fol. 104–5).

time Gray's Inn had 220, the Inner and Middle Temple about 190 each, and Lincoln's Inn 160.[29] St. John's was then the largest college in Cambridge. So the Elizabethan Inns of Court were still larger—much larger—than most Cambridge colleges. Again, taking Fortescue's figures as reasonable (which may be madness) the London *studium* had nearly two thousand members at the end of the fifteenth century; being twice as large as Oxford, then, where there were about one thousand students towards the end of the century, and larger still than Cambridge, which did not rival the size of Oxford until the 1520's.[30] The University of Paris, when Erasmus studied there, had about 3,500 members. In the 1560's there were nearly 1,300 students at Cambridge, and by the mid-1570's about 1,800 (including nearly 800 pensioners) and by the end of the reign of James I over 3,000 (as against less than 2,900 at Oxford).

Fortescue continued:

> there is, besides a school of law, a kind of academy (*gymnasium*) of all the manners that the nobles learn. There they learn to sing and to exercise themselves in every kind of harmonics. They are also taught there to practise dancing and all games proper for nobles, as those brought up in the King's household are accustomed to practise.

This was not just a law school, but an Academy for Gentlemen, in London.

Thomas More gave a memorable picture of the comparative status of Oxbridge when he resigned, in 1532, the office of Lord Chancellor—and his family wondered where the next meal would come from:

> "I have been brought up", quoth he, "at Oxford, at an Inn of the Chancery, at Lincoln's Inn, and also in the King's Court, and so forth from the lowest degree to the highest. . . : it shall not be best for us to fall to the lowest fare first; we will not, therefore, descend to Oxford fare, nor to the fare of New Inn, but we will begin with Lincoln's Inn diet, where many right-worshipful and of good years do live full well. Which, if we find not ourselves the first

---

29Fortescue, 197–9. In 1586 "the Inns of Court had an average of 239 students each, seven of the Chancery Inns an average of 91 each" (Aylmer, *The King's Servants*, 273).

30Rashdall, *Universities of Europe*, III, 328–33; 285. John Major wrote in 1521 (by which time he had not been in Cambridge for nearly thirty years) that "in either university you shall find four thousand or five thousand students" (*History of Greater Britain*, 26). One wonders whether Fortescue's calculations were equally exuberant.

year able to maintain, then we will the next year go one step down to New Inn fare, wherewith many an honest man is well contented. If that exceed our ability too, then will we, the next year after, descend to Oxford fare, where many grave, learned and ancient fathers be continually conversant. Which, if our power stretch not to maintain neither; then may we yet, with bags and wallets, go a-begging."[31]

To be out of London was to be out of Life.

III

SO FAR AS Oxford and Cambridge were concerned, when Erasmus came to England in 1499 Oxford was ahead. The "marvellous decade" for Cambridge was 1505–15. Not until 1516 was Erasmus able to apply to Cambridge the word which he had used of Oxford in 1499: "flourishing."[32] To the "moderns," the values which mattered tended to be Italian; and as Roberto Weiss has shown,[33] Oxford had been responsive to Italian standards since the 1470's.

Erasmus, in spite of his affection for Italy, never outgrew his honeymoon with England; he was an Italianate Dutch Anglophile –predecessor in some ways of that typically twentieth-century intellectual Ishmael, the British lover of North America. Two letters will illustrate this point. In August 1516 he wrote from Calais to John Reuchlin about the nineteen-year-old Philip Melanchthon, a recent M.A. of Tubingen:

If you send young Philip to the Bishop of Rochester with your letter of recommendation, I assure you he will be treated most courteously and promoted to a very distinguished position; and never will he secure ampler leisure for the best kind of literature. Perhaps though he is athirst for Italy? Well, in this age England *contains* Italy; and indeed she has within herself, unless I'm far wrong, a splendour that even *exceeds* the splendour of Italy.[34]

---

[31]Roper, *More*, 28–9.

[32]*Florentissima* (Oxford, 1499; *E.E.*, I, p. 247, line 60). *Effloruit* (Cambridge, 1516; *E.E.*, II, p. 328, line 235; Letter 52, *supra*).

[33]*Humanism in England during the Fifteenth Century*, chap. XII, "Humanism in Oxford."

[34]*E.E.*, no. 457 (excerpt); translated D. F. S. Thomson.

A little later, in February 1517, he wrote from Antwerp to William Latimer (1460–1545), then teaching at Oxford:

To me anyone who is excellently learned is an Italian, even though he should be Irish-born: and to me anyone who has carefully and successfully steeped himself in the Greek authors is a Greek, even though he has no beard. I myself am well-inclined to the glory of Italy, just for the reason that I find this country more congenial than my own. But to express my frank opinion, if I were to obtain Linacre or Tunstall (to say nothing of yourself) as my tutor, I shouldn't miss Italy. Therefore (I repeat) do consider seriously whether it is not a rather unwise course of action to seek abroad for something which exists at home. Why, was it not in England that Grocin, whom you cite as an example, first learnt the rudiments of Greek? He did, afterwards, go to Italy and sit at the feet of the great masters; but for the present it was to his advantage to have learnt beforehand what he did learn, from such teachers as might be found.[35]

But whatever Italian tone there was in English academic circles was felt first, as Erasmus implied in the letter to Latimer, at Oxford. There was a printing press there, for example, by December 1478—thirteen months after Caxton, at Westminster, had printed the first English book; though this press, run by Theodoric Rood of Cologne (in conjunction from 1481 with an English stationer), published mainly elementary text books, its products proved "the growing demand for humane literature, and the change in taste which was taking place in Oxford during the latter part of the century."[36] (Pietro Carmiliano of Brescia, later to be discussed in Erasmus' Cambridge letters, was among those concerned with Oxford printing in the 1480's.[37]) Thomas Linacre,

[35]*E.E.*, no. 540 (excerpt); translated D. F. S. Thomson. Augustin Renaudet has argued that although Erasmus was "le premier écrivain qui ait, en homme moderne, subi la séduction de la vie romaine" he remained in spirit a Northerner: "Il restait un enfant des Pays-Bas, riverain des grands fleuves et des mers grises du Nord. Il avait grandi, il était venu à l'âge d'homme dans les plaines de l'Overyssel et de la Hollande. Il savait et il aimait l'art flamande et gothique; nous ignorons ce qu'il put éprouver devant les fresques de Florence, de Sienne ou de Rome, les bronzes ou les marbres de Ghiberti, de Donatello ou de Michel-Ange. Sa religion demeurait fidèle aux images de la piété médiévale. Au cours d'un controverse avec Lefèvre d'Etaples sur un texte de l'Epître aux Hébreux, il apparut que le Christ d'Erasme demeurait l'Ecce Homo couronné d'épines sanglantes, le Dieu de pitié des ateliers de Flandre et de Bourgogne, tandis que le Christ de Lefèvre demeurait le Dieu métaphysique de Marsile Ficin." (*Erasme et l'Italie*, ix and xi.)

[36]Weiss, *Humanism in England*, 175. See Duff, *Fifteenth Century English Books*, 132–3.

[37]Weiss, 170–2.

a Canterbury boy, had learned some Greek in the 1480's when he was a Fellow of All Souls; he then, about 1487, went to Italy for six years, for part of the time in company with Prior William Selling of Canterbury (whose third Italian trip this was, the first being in the 1460's), and met such shining stars as the Professor of Latin and Greek at Florence, Angelo Poliziano (1454–94), whose Latin poems Samuel Johnson, age twenty-five, was to wish to print, whose play *Orfeo* (1472) had been the first secular drama in Italian, whose translation of Homer into Latin, begun when he was barely seventeen, had won him the appellation *omerico giovinetto*, and whose fame, by the second decade of the sixteenth century, was known to such Cambridgeshire schoolmasters as William Gonnell of Landbeach. Linacre returned to Oxford in the 1490's. William Grocin was teaching Greek (and divinity) in the Oxford of the early 1490's, having also studied at Florence under Poliziano from 1488–90. All this, and Colet too. Colet's Italianate references in his lectures from 1497, no less than his especial reliance on Jerome and Augustine, made a singular contrast to the lectures of the first Lady Margaret Professor of Divinity in Oxford, who took as his text in 1497 a work by the British Franciscan Duns Scotus (c. 1264–1308), who had taught at Oxford and Paris, and whose name Erasmus habitually used to symbolize the over-subtle and trifling: those "bawling Scotists" who "hug themselves in their happiness, and are so taken up with these pleasant trifles that they have not so much leisure as to cast the least eye on the Gospel or St. Paul's Epistles."[38] That was the sort of lecture Erasmus had heard in Paris.

Colet's intention was to "follow the mind of St. Paul."[39] "Think what a man he was! godly minded and thoughtful beyond all others: one in whom was the Spirit of God and the mind of Christ; in whom Christ himself spake."[40] But he followed Paul in his own original, almost eccentric, way. What Paul actually said: what he really meant. But Paul as seen through the eyes (c. 400) of Augustine; of (c. 1490) Ficino and Pico della Mirandola (it is

[38] *Praise of Folly*, 97–8.
[39] *Corinthians*, 119.
[40] *Ibid.*, 51.

appropriate that Colet's monument in St. Paul's was to be by the Florentine Pietro Torrigiano); and (c. 500) of the Greek philosopher Dionysius, whom Colet supposed to be the member of the Areopagus converted by Paul in Athens and taught by Paul "the interpretation of the divine word."[41] A Paul at once Augustinian, Athenian, and Florentine. Colet's world picture was Dionysian in its stress on light, on the "mystical mathematics of the City of Heaven": the ninefold order of all creation reflecting the harmony of God; Christ as incarnate light and order; faith as infused light; the church as the ordered community, the priesthood as the prophetic guardians of the secret things of God—his impetus as a "reformer" should be set in the Platonic context of the nature of a holy community, undistracted by *meum* and *tuum*. Philosopher kings: and the shadows—grace as the enemy of nature; human reason and learning as the contradiction of divine truth. Here Colet was a gloomy Dean indeed. For the Cambridge Platonists of the mid-seventeenth century (following Hooker and Aquinas), grace perfected nature; for Colet, Oxford Platonist, it destroyed it. The link between reason and law was broken; and his theology of predestination was nearer to the later Augustine than that of Hooker was to be. An Augustinian theologian of the Renaissance, then. But with all this an "Erasmian" emphasis on the simple, the brief, the sincere, the "truly spiritual"; on the primacy of charity; on Christian courtesy; and—we catch a pre-echo of Whitgift—on the circumstances of time and place. Such was the *philosophia Christi* in the exposition of which John Bale was to find Colet's claim to inclusion among the illustrious authors of Great Britain.[42] Such was the mind—high-powered, off-beat—Erasmus encountered at Oxford. And Erasmus' own *Enchiridion Militis Christiani*, which he wrote in 1502, owes more to Colet than is usually realized. It is not without significance for the English Reformation that the *Enchiridion* was to be translated into English, in the early 1520's, by a Gloucestershire private tutor called William Tyndale. We may also note that in his exposition of the Epistles Colet did

[41]Lupton, *Hierarchies of Dionysius*, 19.

[42]*Illustrium Scriptorum Summarium* (1548), 214–15 ff.; *Scriptorum Illustrium Majoris Britanniae*, Part One (1557), 648–9; Bale's notebook, printed by R. L. Poole and M. Bateson, as *Index Britanniae Scriptorum* (1902), 195.

not quote very much, except from the New and Old Testaments —on at least one occasion discussing the Greek.[43] In his *expositio* of the first chapters of Romans (not the Oxford lectures) Colet commented:[44]

We must here remark, how simple was the mode of citation followed by the Apostles, when they quoted any passage from the Old Testament. This way of ours which is now in vogue both with modern theologians (*recentiores theologos*) and lawyers, of citing authorities of every quarter so minutely by the chapter had its origin in the ignorance of men who mistrusted themselves and their own learning. . . . And in process of time this painful and over-scrupulous alleging of authorities has risen to such a pitch that many devote themselves to it for the mere commendation of memory.

The "good scribe" (and lecturer)

proceeds in a bolder and more dignified way. His quotations from other sources, if at times he makes any, are both fewer and simpler, and drawn from a remoter antiquity. He uses them without self display, without any servile deference to the judgment of others. This is what was done by St. Paul and the other Apostles and by a host of grave divines for eight hundred years after their time.[45]

Colet had no time for *disputatores.*[46]

When he attended some of those lectures at Oxford in the autumn of 1499, Erasmus wrote to Colet:[47]

In saying that you dislike this modern school of divines, who spend their lives on mere subtleties and quibblings of sophistry, you are quite of the same way of thinking as myself. It is not that I condemn their pursuits; for there is no literary pursuit that I do not approve of.[48] But when these

---

[43]*Corinthians*, 136.

[44]*Letters on the Mosaic Account of the Creation, etc.*, 63–4.

[45]In the St. Paul's statutes, Colet implied that the "later blind world" followed hard upon Jerome and Augustine. Milton had a similarly rather vague notion of when began "the times of ignorance that God winked at": his estimates varied from 200 to 500.

[46]*Hierarchies of Dionysius*, 44. Colet, according to Lupton's note, was referring to Aquinas and Lombard. Colet disliked Aquinas—who for More was "the very flower of theology" (*Confutation*, cccxiv).

[47]*E.E.*, no. 108; tr. (slightly amended) by Lupton, *Colet*, 110–11.

[48]Compare a passage written two or three years later. "Of the interpreters of scripture choose them above all other that go furthest from the letter"; Origen, Ambrose, Jerome, and Augustine. "The divines of later time stick very much in the letter and with good will give more study to subtle and deceitful arguments than to search out the mysteries, as though Paul had not said truly our law to be spiritual." "I say this not because I despise these new divines, but because I set more by things more profitable and apt for the purpose" (*Enchiridion*, tr. Tyndale, 67).

pursuits of theirs are isolated, and not seasoned with more ancient and polite literature [*antiquioribus elegantioribusque litteris*], they are only qualified, in my opinion, to make a man a contentious smatterer: whether they can render him wise, let others determine. For they drain the intellect dry with their hard and barren refinements, and neither invigorate nor inspire it. Worst of all, while Theology, the queen of all the sciences, was enriched and adorned by the eloquence of former writers, they disfigure it in the way we see by their want of power of expression, and by the solecisms of a barbarous style. While it was made clear by the intellects of the old race of scholars they now entangle it with thorns, and confuse everything in their very efforts to find a solution, as they call it, for everything. And so you may behold her that once was the most dignified and majestic of all the sciences, now wellnigh speechless, and destitute, and in rags. Meanwhile we are being drawn on by a sweet and seductive, but morbid, passion for insatiable disputes. . . . Then, lest it should be thought that we have made no addition to the discoveries of older theologians, we have, confidently enough, prescribed certain fixed rules according to which the Almighty performed his wonderful works. And yet there are times when it is nearer to perfection to believe the fact of God's working, but to leave the mode of it to His omnipotence.

Erasmus continued:

we find those as a rule applying themselves to Theology, the highest of all literature, who, from their dull and feeble intellect are hardly fit for any literature at all. I would not speak in such terms of the learned and estimable professors of theology, whom I look up to and revere in the highest degree; but of this vulgar and conceited herd of divines, who, in comparison with themselves, despise all the learning of the scholars that ever lived. In having undertaken to do battle with this doughty race of men, that you may do your best to restore to its pristine beauty and dignity the old and true Theology, beset and hampered as it is by their thorny subtleties, you have chosen a department, my dear Colet, in many ways most excellent.

And Colet was not neglected in his own university.

Among theologians themselves there are a good many who have both the will and the power to assist these honourable efforts of yours. Nay rather, there is none but will give you the right hand of fellowship; seeing that in this renowned university there is no Doctor even, but has listened most attentively to your public lectures on St. Paul.

(Unfortunately we do not know how attentively Cambridge was to listen to Erasmus' public lectures on Jerome, thirteen years later.) So when Erasmus wrote to Colet from Cambridge in August 1511, he referred naturally enough to "your own St.

Paul."[49] And after he had been in Cambridge for less than a month he was doing "battle on your behalf against the Thomists and Scotists."[50]

Erasmus was to hear from John Fisher stories of the curriculum at Cambridge in the 1480's, and he used those reminiscences to sketch some features of the unregenerate university—so different, he said, by 1516.[51] So far as the arts course was concerned, Erasmus mentioned the *Parva Logicalia*[52]—the "small logicals," a potted compendium of Aristotelian logic, part (probably) of the *Summulae Logicales* composed in the thirteenth century by the Paris-trained Portuguese divine, Pedro Giuliano (Petrus Hispanus), who ended his days as Pope John XXI (1276–7). (Erasmus was in favour of logic as a subject for boys; but, he wrote in 1512, "I refuse to go beyond Aristotle, and prohibit the verbiage of the Schools."[53]) But he was more concerned with the course in theology, taken after graduation as Master of Arts. Here he naturally named the standard, basic theological textbook, on the whole of which prospective Doctors of Divinity were required to have lectured: the *Books of Sentences* written in the early 1150's by the Bologna-educated Italian, Pietro Lombardo, who had been teaching in Paris since about 1139 and who was to be Bishop of the city for the last year of his life (1159–60). This was a reasonably brief work—about 220 pages in Migne's edition[54]—though as time went on it was swelled by commentaries; "there be almost as many commentaries upon the Master of Sentences," commented Erasmus in 1518, "as be names of divines."[55] It was divided into four books: concerning the Trinity, the Creation, the Incarnation, and the Sacraments. Pietro was much influenced by the treatise

[49]Letter 1. [50]Letter 3.

[51]Letter 52.

[52]Hythloday, in his account of education in Utopia, commented that the Utopians "have not devised one of all those rules of restrictions, amplifications, and suppositions, very wittily invented in the small logicals which here our children in every place do learn" (83).

[53]Woodward, *Erasmus Concerning Education*, 165: from *De Ratione Studii.*

[54]*Patrologia Latina*, vol. 192, cols. 521–964. For Peter Lombard, see J. de Gellinck, S. J., *Le Mouvement Théologique du XIIe Siècle* (2nd ed., 1948), 213–49. Peter was born at Novara, Lombardy; in 1953, the eight hundredth anniversary of the *Books of Sentences*, celebrations were held there; from these there sprang the collection of essays in his honour, published in 1956, *Miscellanea Lombardiana.*

[55]*EE.*, III, 858. New Preface to *Enchiridion*, Tyndale translation, 4.

on the law of the church by the monk Gratian of Bologna:[56] the *Concordia Discordantium Canonicum* (to be known as the *Decretum*), which appeared about 1140. This was an arrangement from materials covering all of a thousand years—papal decrees, canons of councils, opinions of the Church Fathers. It was systematically arranged into *distinctiones*, *causae*, and *quaestiones*: a problem was stated, and all the relevant authorities arranged—first one side, then the other, then the considered verdict of the compiler. In similar manner, the *Books of Sentences* were an attempt at a complete, synthesized theological exposition, broken down logically into "distinctions" and "questions," based on and buttressed by quotations from the Bible and the Fathers. The work was a signal example of that move, from the middle of the twelfth century, away from "old-fashioned biblical studies." Beryl Smalley has written:

> This one-sided development was quite natural. The innumerable problems arising from the reception of Aristotelian logic and the study of canon and civil law, the new possibilities of reasoning, the urgent need for speculation and discussion, all these produced an atmosphere of haste and excitement which was unfavourable to Biblical studies.[57]

One of these many teachers who were to write commentaries on the *Books of Sentences* was Duns Scotus. Another—also Franciscan, also British—was Alexander of Hales (c. 1170–1245), or, correctly, Hailes, in north-east Gloucestershire, near Winchcombe. They had both, in addition, compiled their own books of theological "Questions," for use, originally, in class debate. Erasmus held them both up to scorn in his 1516 letter about Cambridge.

Colet, in his lectures on Paul at Oxford in the late 1490's, and Erasmus, with his lectures on Jerome in Cambridge during the early 1510's, were out of step with the mediaeval traditions and statutory requirements of the divinity faculties. Erasmus died in

[56]Milton was to discuss them as two of a kind: "those two misbegotten infants, and for ever infants, Lombard and Gratian, him the compiler of canon iniquity, the other the Tubalcain of scholastic sophistry, whose overspreading barbarism hath not only infused their own bastardy upon the fruitfullest part of human learning, not only dissipated and dejected the clear light of nature in us, and of nations, but hath tainted also the fountains of divine doctrine, and rendered the pure and solid law of God unbeneficial to us by their calumnious dunceries" (*Doctrine and Discipline of Divorce*, 1643, chap. XXII).

[57]*Study of the Bible in the Middle Ages*, 77.

July 1536. And in October 1535, under the new Chancellor Thomas Cromwell (Fisher having been executed in June), Cambridge had received a set of Injunctions which would have gladdened his heart.[58] All divinity lectures were to be "on some part of the Scripture" and it was ordered "that no authors hereafter be publicly read who have written on the Master of the Sentences" and that there should no more be used "the frivolous questions and obscure glosses of Scotus," etc. Further, "it should be permitted to all freely to read God's word in their private studies." In addition, the study of canon law was abolished. Mullinger took these injunctions as "the line that in university history divides the mediaeval from the modern age."[59] It should be noted, however, that so late as 1652 young Cambridge divines were advised, with respect to their private reading, that "when you are of ripe understanding" the Schoolmen might be studied, "with some judgement." The Schoolmen specifically named included Pietro Lombardo and Alexander of Hales.[60]

In his two months' visit Erasmus saw that Oxford in 1499—or at least that Oxford group he found sympathetic—was up to date, not second-hand or stale.

IV

THE CAMBRIDGE OF 1500 was comparatively provincial. "There are in England," wrote in 1521 the Scot John Major (who had been a contemporary of Erasmus at the Collège de Montaigu in Paris), "two illustrious universities: of which one—I mean Oxford—is famous even among foreigners."[61] Major had spent a year at Cambridge, about 1493, when in his early twenties, at Godshouse —which, fresh from Scotland, he had chosen because it was in the

[58] *Letters and Papers Henry VIII*, IX, no. 615. Summarized in Fuller, *University of Cambridge*, 216–21.

[59] *University of Cambridge*, I, 631.

[60] Costello, *Curriculum*, 122. William Perkins, for example, knew some scholastic works well. He also used an unpublished treatise of Thomas Bradwardine, found in Corpus library.

[61] Major, *History of Greater Britain*, 22.

parish of St. Andrew. In a passage praising the sweet and skilful bells of England he gave a memorable little glimpse: "when I was a student at Cambridge, I would lie awake most part of the night, at the season of the great festivals, that I might hear the melody of the bells. The university is situated on a river, and the sound is the sweeter that it comes to you over the water."[62] The reminiscence, unlike the bells, rings slightly false. But the fact remained: Cambridge was "somewhat inferior to Oxford, both in the numbers of its students, and in reputation for letters."[63]

For one thing, Cambridge had no printing press until 1520. And, writes Professor Weiss, of the fifteenth century, "If we compare Cambridge with Oxford from the standpoint of *belles-lettres*, we cannot but realise its inferiority. We do not find there that taste for Italian learning already present in Oxford by the middle of the century."[64] Yet Cambridge had its Italian visitors—the Franciscan, Lorenzo di Savona, for instance, "who, while in residence at Cambridge, compiled in 1478 the *Nova rhetorica* that was printed almost immediately by both Caxton (c. 1479) and the printer of St. Albans."[65] Lorenzo lived in the Cambridge house of the Grey Friars, on the present site of Sidney Sussex College; but he appears also to have lectured on Aristotle and Augustine in the divinity faculty of the university. And some Cambridge men, after all, had been to Italy. John Doget studied canon law at Padua and Bologna as early as the late 1460's, when he was in his early thirties; he was Provost of King's from 1499 to 1501. John Argentine, his successor as Provost (1501–8), who had gone up to King's at the age of sixteen in 1458, travelled in Italy in the 1470's; back in Cambridge, he wrote Italian, a little self-consciously perhaps, inside some of the books he owned.[66] At King's, in fact, "the Renaissance of classical studies had taken firm and early root";[67] some of the famous library of manuscripts collected

[62] *Ibid.*, 110. [63] *Ibid.*, 25.

[64] Weiss, *Humanism in England*, chap. XI, "The Beginnings of Cambridge Humanism," 160.

[65] Knowles, *Religious Orders in England*, III, 53.

[66] See four articles in the *Transactions of the Cambridge Bibliographical Society*: D. E. Rhodes, "Provost Argentine and his Books" (1956); A. N. L. Munby, "Notes on King's College Library in the 15th Century" (1951); W. Cargill Thompson, "King's Library 1500–70" (1954); J. C. T. Oates and H. L. Pink, "Three 16th Century Catalogues of the University Library" (1952).

[67] John Saltmarsh in *V.C.H.*, 394.

by Humphrey, "the good Duke of Gloucester," brother of Henry V, were given to King's after his death in 1447, his nephew Henry VI having founded the college in 1441.

The founding of Godshouse in 1439 as a training school for schoolmasters displayed an interest in the education of youth which looked forward, not back. And it must be pointed out that of the three great colleges founded in England in the 1440's, Magdalen, Oxford, was the brainchild of a bishop, but King's, Cambridge, that of a king, and Queens', Cambridge, of his queen. It may be that Cambridge was deliberately promoted by the rulers of the fifteenth century, against Oxford, with its Wycliffite past. After 1448 there were no colleges founded in Oxford until 1509 (Brasenose). That barren period saw in Cambridge the establishment of St. Catharine's (1473), Jesus (1497), and, in 1505, the transformation of Godshouse into Christ's College, the foundation of the Lady Margaret Beaufort, mother of Henry VII, great-grand-daughter of John of Gaunt, "time-honoured Lancaster," and self-styled "heir to all Henry VI's godly intentions." According to Professor Weiss, it is from the end of Edward IV's reign that Cambridge began "to study the humanities from a less rigidly mediaeval standpoint than it had hitherto."[68] Edward IV died in 1483. And in that year John Fisher went up to the small college of Michaelhouse.

Fisher was elected Master of Michaelhouse in 1497. At that time Erasmus was living in the English Hall of Residence in Paris. He had moved there in the autumn of 1496, about two years after going to the Collège de Montaigu to study for the degree of Bachelor of Theology. One of the English boys living in the hall was Robert Fisher. In the spring of 1498, when Erasmus was living in private lodgings in Paris, he took as a Latin pupil William Blount, Lord Mountjoy, just turned twenty, and a Cambridge man—probably Queens'. With him was Richard Whitford, Fellow of Queens'. So before he ever came to England, Erasmus had some personal contacts with Cambridge. And when he came to the country for the second time in 1505 he met John Fisher, now Bishop of Rochester, President of Queens', and Chancellor of the University.

68Weiss, *Humanism in England*, 167.

In April 1506, there was a royal visit to Cambridge by Henry VII, aged forty-nine, his mother, Lady Margaret Beaufort (who had been to Cambridge many times before), and members of the Court. The mayor and aldermen and the sheriff of the county rode out two or three miles to meet the royal party; the group, thus escorted, was met first, a quarter of a mile from the university, by the four orders of friars, and the other religious, who held up a cross for the king to kiss; next stood all the graduate members of the university, in their appropriate robes; and beyond them, the elaborate, heavy, and valuable University Cross, held by the cross-bearer (a regular university officer). Here, in Preachers' Street (now Emmanuel Street), near Christ's, the party dismounted, to be received by Fisher, who made a welcoming speech lasting about fifteen minutes. We had come, he said, "almost to desolation": there had been lengthy and killing plagues, difficulties with the town,[69] a shortage of benefactors. But now, the King and his mother having turned a favourable eye upon Cambridge, Cambridge could once more go forward. The speech over, the royal visitors rode with Fisher down past the Dominican Friary (where Emmanuel now stands) and across to Queens'. In Queens' the King changed into more formal attire, rested for an hour, and went to a service in the (unfinished) Chapel of King's. The party spent the night in Queens'. The next day, there was a requiem mass in King's for the founder, at which Fisher was the celebrant. After which the royal party left Cambridge for Walsingham.[70]

Now, it is very likely—though not absolutely certain—that Erasmus was also a guest of Fisher at that time. It is certain that there is in the university Grace Book for the year 1505/6 an entry allowing Erasmus (a Bachelor of Divinity of Paris) to take the Degree of Doctor of Divinity at Cambridge—after suitable academic exercises, including two "responses" in a disputation in the Schools, preaching two sermons to the university, and giving some lectures on Romans.[71] No doubt this action of the

[69]There had been a "treaty" between the university and the town in 1503, after the report of a board of arbitrators, including Fisher. Such a board had been recommended by the Lady Margaret.

[70]Fisher's speech is in Lewis, *Life of Fisher*, II, 263–72.

[71]See Allen, "Erasmus at Cambridge in 1506," *E.E.*, I, appendix VI.

university was taken at the suggestion of Fisher. Erasmus had been very anxious to "take the title of Doctor" since the beginning of 1501, at least.[72] But in fact he did not take it at Cambridge; he left England for Italy at the beginning of June 1506, and received the degree at Turin in September (characteristically saying that he accepted it "contrary to my own sentiment and by the compulsion of friends, who thought this title would confer on me some authority").[73] However, the approach had been made.

When Erasmus came officially to Cambridge, five years later, the building work at Christ's was just completed. The court and the chapel were almost finished by the end of 1506; the final touches to the chapel stonework were made in the early summer of 1510; and the building was consecrated in June 1510, just one year after the death of the Lady Margaret; joiners and carpenters worked on the woodwork until the spring of 1511. In that same spring, in March, the remaining Augustinian canons of the Hospital of St. John were rowed away down the river to Ely, and work was begun (repairs to the old, construction of the new) on the first court of St. John's College, the charter of which was granted in April, four months before Erasmus arrived in Cambridge. (A pity he could not have seen the exodus down the Cam of the Cambridge members of his own order!) Almost precisely during the period of Erasmus' stay in Cambridge, work continued at St. John's, and the chapel, the hall, and the master's lodge were ready by the beginning of 1514, when Erasmus rose from his sickbed to go to London, never to return. There were no students at St. John's, however, and no academic activity, until 1516: the college was formerly opened by Fisher in July of that year. There were five Charter Fellows in 1511, who appear to have been given a living allowance to maintain themselves elsewhere in Cambridge. The first Master was Robert Shorton, a friend of Fisher, but he was away from Cambridge a great deal, and in 1515 Fisher appointed a President, who was in effective control until July 1516, when Alan Percy, son of the fourth Duke of Northumberland, was made Master. So in Erasmus' time there was only a caretaker government at St. John's.

[72] *EE.*, no. 145; tr. Nichols, I, 296.
[73] *E.E.*, no. 201; tr. Nichols, I, 418.

The amount of new building going on in Cambridge must have been either exhilarating or annoying, according to taste. Erasmus, on his horseback rides round the town, would have had a good deal at which to look. We know about the rides because of a chance comment by Roger Ascham. Ascham went up to St. John's in 1530, when he was fifteen; and in 1544, when he was twenty-eight, Fellow of the College and lecturer in Greek, he wrote his *Toxophilus*, or *The School of Shooting* (a book about archery), in which he made use of one of the reminiscences of Garrett Godfrey, the Dutch bookseller who lived in Cambridge:

> pastimes for the mind only, be nothing fit for students, because the body which is most hurt by study, should take away no profit at all thereat. This knew Erasmus very well, when he was here in Cambridge: which when he had been sore at his book (as Garrett our bookbinder hath very often told me) for lack of better exercise, would take his horse, and ride about the Market Hill.[74]

Would he have enjoyed the sights and smells? Cambridge was largish, about twenty-ninth in ranking among provincial towns, Oxford being about twenty-seventh (in wealth and population Oxford had been declining for 150 years).[75] The Cambridge market was older than the university: with its fruit and vegetable stalls in the middle; its milk market towards Great St. Mary's; the stalls for butter, cheese, eggs, and poultry; the cookshops in Petty Cury, *parva cokeria*; and the meat in Butchery Row (Guildhall Street). Cambridge was well provided with fish, freshwater fish especially—pike, tench, perch, roach. But then Erasmus didn't care for fish. Riding down the High Street, he would have seen the work in progress on the porch and vestry of Great St. Mary's. Rebuilding of that church had begun in 1478, and the roof of the nave was finished thirty years later, in 1508; Henry VII had given some money to spur along the work in 1507. Great St. Mary's was complete by 1519, except for the tower, which came later. But better, perhaps, in the High Street, to look at King's. In 1508 there had begun the third and final period of work on the chapel, under the direction of the master-mason John Wastell, "its last and greatest architect."[76] The foundation stone of the

[74]Ascham, *English Works*, 18.
[75]Hoskins, *Local History*, 176–7.
[76]Saltmarsh, *King's College and Its Chapel*, 6.

chapel had been laid in 1446, but after the deposition of the "royal saint" in 1461 things did not go so smoothly. However, by 1483 the five eastern bays of the chapel were finished and roofed in timber. In 1499 the Provost and Fellows took occasion to remind Henry VII "of his uncle's great work abandoned, the splendid building left to stand an unsightly fragment,"[77] but the King does not seem to have done anything until after his visit to Cambridge in 1506, when he gave King's £100. Then his generosity made up for any procrastination. In 1508 he gave £4,000, and in March 1509, three weeks before his death, a further £5,000. In 1512 his executors paid another £5,000. Fisher's speech had had its effect! When Erasmus arrived in Cambridge, the stonework of the chapel was nearing completion: "the shell was complete by 1512; in the same year the outer roof of timber and lead, begun under Edward IV, was carried westward and finished by the master-carpenter Richard Russell; the great fan-vault beneath it, designed by John Wastell, was finished by 1515."[78] The contract for the vault was drawn up in April 1512, nine months after Erasmus began his stay.[79] He saw it developing, then, that "notable pile":

> . . . this immense
> And glorious work of fine intelligence! . . .
> that branching roof
> Self-poised, and scooped into ten thousand cells,
> Where light and shade repose. . . .

The frustrating fact is, however, that there is no hint of a mention of any of this in Erasmus' Cambridge letters.

Of the fourteen colleges, three were new, the paint still fresh, so to speak: St. John's, Christ's, Jesus. Then, working backwards, came St. Catharine's (1473), Queens' (1448), King's (1441), Clare (which received its statutes in 1359), Corpus (1352), Trinity Hall (1350), Gonville Hall (1347), Pembroke (1347), King's Hall (formerly established by Edward III in 1337, though

[77] Saltmarsh, *V.C.H.*, 389.

[78] Saltmarsh, *King's College and Its Chapel*, 6.

[79] It has been argued (not too convincingly) that there is a portrait of Erasmus in one of the windows of King's College Chapel, dating from the late 1520's (James Wood, in the *Cambridge Review*, March 1, 1940). The figure in question is reproduced on the cover of Kenneth Harrison's *Illustrated Guide to the Windows of King's College Chapel* (1953).

tracing its history to a writ of Edward II in 1317), Michaelhouse (1324), and Peterhouse (1284). (Note that there had been a "university" at Cambridge for at least seventy-five years, probably more, before anyone thought of founding a college; and that a further forty years passed before there was another.[80]) Queens' had fourteen Fellows (some being what we should now think of as senior scholars). And it was to Queens' that Erasmus came. As he later said, Queens' was one of the three colleges favoured by Fisher—the other two being Christ's and St. John's—

> in which the things to be taught are not those which fit men for sophistical contests, making them dull and witless in serious matters, but studies such that from them they may proceed forth well versed in true learning and in sober discussion, men who can preach the Word of God in a serious and evangelical spirit.[81]

Colleges "out of which could proceed theologians not so much fitted for battles of words as equipped for the sober preaching of the Word of God."[82]

Erasmus' first two surviving Cambridge letters are specifically dated from Queens', *ex collegio Reginae*—the letters of August 24 and 25, 1511. In that of the twenty-fifth, Erasmus said: "I expect I shall stay at this college for several days, anyway." He was certainly still there on September 16; a letter to Ammonio on that date (number 5) has the address. After that he made a short trip to London; and after his return the letters, if they have a dateline at all, merely have "Cambridge." It has sometimes been assumed that after his return from London he no longer lived in the college.

Some hints might seem to support the idea that Erasmus moved into private lodgings in the town of Cambridge. He later referred to Garrett Godfrey, who lived near Great St. Mary's, as "my host of old time."[83] Also, he had developed, we know, a great dislike in general of collegiate or community life. Here, for instance, is a note written in 1498: "I wish for nothing but that leisure may be given me, in which I may live wholly to God, bewail the sins of

[80]Unless one counts the House of Studies of the Gilbertine canons, established in the 1290's: St. Edmund's, on the present site of Addenbrooke's Hospital.

[81]Letter 47 (1529).

[82]Letter 46 (1535).

[83]Letter 52.

my thoughtless age, busy myself with the holy scriptures, and read or write something: I cannot do this in a college or a retreat, as I am in extremely delicate health"; *id in secessu aut collegio non possum.*[84]

That note was written when Erasmus was about thirty. He had spent six years, probably, in the monastery of Steyn (1487–93). Then, after a year or so in the service of the Bishop of Cambrai, he had gone to study in Paris in 1494 or 1495. And there, at first, he lived in the Collège de Montaigu, the Master of which, Jan van Standonck of Malines, was a friend of the Bishop of Cambrai. Now Standonck had been educated at Gouda by the Brethren of the Common Life and had become a Reformer of passionate austerity. He was appointed Master of the College (founded in 1314 by Gilles Aycelin de Montaigu, Archbishop of Rouen) in 1493, after six years on the staff. It was a hostel for the well-to-do, but in a bad state when Standonck took charge; he converted it into a community for poor clerics, living under a strict monastic discipline—a discipline which was greatly to influence Loyola, who was attached to the college in the late 1520's and early 1530's. When Erasmus moved into the college, there was a faculty of twelve (representing the apostles), and seventy students; by 1503 there were two hundred. In 1495 new buildings were completed, the staff having individual cells on the second floor and the students a communal dormitory on the third. No meat was eaten, no wine drunk; the régime was one of frugality, abstinence, corporal exercises, silences. The spirit of Steyn, but perhaps more so. Marcel Godet has written that the basic diet at the reformed Collège de Montaigu was cheap eggs and herring.[85] After a year or so, Erasmus became so ill that he left Paris and returned to the Bishop and then to Steyn. In his own words: "At Paris, in the College of Montaigu, from the bad eggs and an infected bedchamber, he contracted a disease, that is, an ill condition of body, having been before free from

[84]*E.E.*, no. 75; tr. Nichols, I, 157–8.

[85]Godet, *La Congrégation de Montaigu.* For Standonck and the Collège de Montaigu see also Hyma, *The Christian Renaissance*, chap. VII, "The Christian Renaissance in France"; and Renaudet, *Humanisme et Renaissance*, chap. VIII, "Jean Standonck : Un réformateur catholique avant la Réforme." Standonck also founded colleges at Cambrai, Valenciennes, Mechelen, and Louvain.

taint."[86] The experience was recalled in the dialogue "On the Eating of Fish," written in the 1520's. As Master of the College, says a Fishmonger to a Butcher, Standonck,

> what with lying hard, by bad and spare diet, late and hard studies—within one year's space, of many young men of a good genius and very hopeful, some he killed, others he blinded, others he made run distracted, and others he brought into the leprosy, some of whom I know very well; and in short, not one of them but what was in danger by him. Was not this cruelty against one's neighbour? Neither did this content him, but adding a cloak and a cowl, he took away the eating of flesh altogether. . . . Whosoever uses such engines, uses force. Neither did this cruelty only destroy mean persons, but many gentlemen's sons too, and spoiled many a hopeful genius. It is indeed the part of a father to hold in youth that is apt to grow lascivious, by restraint. But in the very depth of winter, here's a morsel of bread given them when they ask for their commons. And as for their drink, they must draw that out of a well that gives bad water, unwholesome of itself, if it were not made the worse by the coldness of the morning: I have known many that were brought to such an ill state of health that they have never got over it to this day. There were chambers on a ground floor, and rotten plaster: they stood near a stinking 'house of office,' in which none ever dwelt but he either got his death or some grievous distemper. I shall say nothing of the unmerciful whippings, even of innocent persons. This they say is to break their fierceness, for so they call a sprightly genius. And therefore they thus cow their spirits, to make them more humble in the monasteries. Nor shall I take notice how many rotten eggs were eaten, nor how much sour wine was drunk. Perhaps these things may be mended now. But however, tis too late for those that are dead already, or carry about an infected carcass. Nor do I mention these things because I have any ill will to the college, but I thought it worth while to give this monition, lest human severity should mar inexperienced and tender age under the pretence of religion. How much civility, or true piety, may be taught there at present, I don't determine. If I could but see that those that put on a cowl, put off naughtiness, I should exhort everybody to wear one. But besides, the spirit of a vigorous age is not to be cowed for this sort of life; but the mind is to be formed for piety.[87]

That is, basically, an attractive protest: "lest human severity should mar inexperienced and tender age, under the pretence of religion." The Collège de Montaigu was not in fact a Dotheboys Hall; but the "savage indignation" of Erasmus sprang from a Dickensian heart.

And when he returned to Paris at the end of 1496, Erasmus lived at first privately and then in the Residence Hall for English

[86]From the *Compendium Vitae* (1524). *E.E.*, I, 50; tr. Nichols, I, 10.
[87]*Colloquies* II, 90–2.

students. A passage written in 1515 shows the depth of his dislike of the community life as it actually was, though he chooses to criticize not austerity but idleness:

Perhaps it would be to the advantage of the state if the number of monasteries were limited, for in them is found a peculiar form of idleness, especially among those whose lives have little to be said for them, and are spent in a lazy and sluggish fashion. What I say about monasteries is also true of colleges.[88]

Perhaps he had found his Cambridge colleagues sluggish. The inmates of the Collège de Montaigu were hardly that. Rashdall has confirmed that the austerity of Standonck's statutes "would repel everything short of the direst poverty and the most intense devotion to duty."[89] Queens', one assumes, would cater a little more to academic weakness: the eggs, at least, were fresh.

Erasmus (like Milton) was in favour of temperance rather than abstinence. He wrote to Thomas Lupset in 1521: "As to your wholly abstaining from suppers, after Colet's example, I do not approve of it, any more than I approved of it in his case. If you feel that at your age the bodily energies need curbing, you will effect this more successfully, in my opinion, by temperance in eating and drinking than by severe and prolonged abstinence."[90] But what of Lent? Erasmus (he himself said) "has been much subject to fever, especially at the season of Lent, on account of the fish diet, the mere smell of which was always offensive to him."[91] In 1502, when he was staying in the Benedictine house of Saint-Omer, about thirty miles from Calais, he had a conversation which he was to recall in 1521:[92]

I was then staying with Anthony of Bergen, Abbot of St. Bertin, at whose table dinner was not served until after mid-day; and as my stomach could not brook so long a fast (it was then Lent) especially as I was very busy with new studies, I used to stay my stomach before dinner with a warm cup of broth, that I might keep on till dinner time. When I consulted him

88*Education of a Christian Prince*, 226.

89Rashdall, *Universities*, III, 413. Rashdall has a list of the Paris colleges (I, 536–9).

90*E.E.*, no. 1229; tr. Lupton, *Colet*, 150. Cf. *E.E.*, IV, 516; Lupton, *Vitrier and Colet*, 25. Colet had a frugal "dinner" in the early afternoon.

91From the *Compendium Vitae* (1524). *E.E.*, I, 51; tr. Nichols, I, 11–12.

92*E.E.*, no. 1211 (IV, 511); tr. Nichols, I, 348.

whether this was permissible, having first glanced at the lay companion who was with him, from some apprehension that he might be offended, "Yes, indeed," said he, "you would sin if you omitted to do so, and for want of a little food hindered your sacred studies and injured your delicate constitution."

Queens' was, of course, a clerical community, and one might wonder how strictly it enforced a Lenten discipline upon its infirm guest—were it not for the interesting fact that, of Erasmus' surviving Cambridge letters, not one was written in Lent. It may be assumed that he spent the Lents of 1512 and 1513 in London; the Lady Margaret Professor was not required to lecture during Lent. So perhaps he would not have found the collegiate life at Queens' too intolerable. The reference to Godfrey as his "host" may mean, obviously, that on occasion Erasmus was entertained by him; or he may sometimes have stayed with him (the fact that Godfrey knew about his working and riding habits, and later told Roger Ascham about them, suggests that this may have been the case). Erasmus also stayed out at Landbeach with the Gonnell family, especially in the autumn of 1513 when the plague in Cambridge was especially dangerous.

There are two pieces of evidence, moreover, which decisively confirm the connection of Erasmus with Queens'. First, in a letter to William Gonnell in October 1513—within three months of his leaving Cambridge forever—Erasmus wrote: "Once again there has been a death not far from the college"; *non longe a collegio.*[93] So at the end of his stay, as at the beginning, Erasmus was living in Queens'. Second, Robert Aldrich of King's wrote to Erasmus in 1525 and called to mind the time when "I personally read with you some books by Seneca and Jerome, at Queens' College"; elsewhere in the letter he mentions "those six months of reading I enjoyed when you took me to your side and bade me attend on you."[94] That period must have been in 1512 or 1513.

Finally, it is significant that in his first will, made at Basle in January 1527, Erasmus directed that from the "not less than fifteen hundred copies" of an edition of all his writings, twenty sets, "specially adorned with care," were to be set aside as presen-

[93]Letter 31. [94]Letter 63.

tation copies; of the twenty sets, six were to go to England, and one "to Cambridge, for deposit at Queens' College in the public library of that college."[95] The other five English sets were for John Fisher, William Warham, Cuthbert Tunstall, Thomas More, and Bishop John Longland of Lincoln; of the remaining fourteen, three were to go to cathedral or monastic schools; seven to private persons; and four to colleges: the "Trilingual College" at the University of Louvain;[96] the university at Tournai (which had a short life, both founded and dispersed in the 1520's); the College of Lille; and the University of Alcala, near Madrid. This idea of twenty presentation copies was dropped from Erasmus' final will (February 1536), perhaps because the collected edition showed no signs of appearing. In fact, the Froben firm decided to push forward such an edition soon after Erasmus' death in July 1536. Of the nine-volume edition, one volume appeared in 1538, two in 1539, and six in 1540. There is a copy of this Basle *Omnia Opera* in the library of Queens', with a note inside, written by a later librarian: "left in his will by Erasmus to Queens' College." As there is no contemporary record of bequests to the library, it is not known how the set arrived there. It may have been among the books bequeathed by Thomas Smith (1513–77), author of *De Republica Anglorum*, Fellow of the College in the 1530's.

It is a pity that the Queens' buttery books do not survive from before 1560.

The President of Queens' during Erasmus' time was Robert Benkenshaw, who, however, was not very often there. The effec-

[95] 1527 Will in *E.E.*, VI, 503–6.

[96] The Trilingual College (Greek, Latin, Hebrew), endowed by Jerome Busleiden, and opened in 1518, the year after his death, had its own buildings from 1520. It was part of the University of Louvain and was very small—three professors, and about twenty students, at first. Its objects were, of course, very dear to Erasmus' heart, and he mentioned the college in the last sentence of his last surviving letter. Roger Ascham was to visit the college in 1550, and he said it was the St. John's or Trinity of Louvain—though he hastened to add that both the college and the university were much less distinguished than Cambridge (quoted in Allen, *Erasmus*, 162). A description of the University of Louvain by another Johnian has survived—Nicholas Darynton, in the 1520's: "in one way it is easier to study here than in Cambridge; for there are none of those tiresome visits of formality, none of the backbiting and discussion of others, the canvassing for offices and pursuit of votes by all means fair or foul, while the conduct of the university is neglected" (*ibid.*, 161).

tive head of the college was John Fawne. Of the fourteen Fellows, Erasmus was later to mention four as valued friends: Fawne, John Vaughan, Humphrey Walkden, and his dearest Cambridge friend, Henry Bullock, who had been elected Fellow at the age of nineteen in 1506 (did Erasmus meet him then?). Richard Whitford had resigned his Fellowship in 1504. So his especial ties at Cambridge were with Queens', not to mention his friendship with Fisher (who had resigned as President in July 1508).

The first full statement of the "Erasmus tradition" at Queens' appears to be that made by Thomas Fuller, who went up to the college in 1621. Fuller wrote, in the 1630's, of Erasmus' "having his abode in Queens' College, where a study on the top of the south-west tower in the old court still retaineth his name."[97] That court stands today almost as it did then, one of the brick glories of Cambridge. It was built in 1448 and 1449, the charter of foundation of the college by Margaret of Anjou, Queen to Henry VI, being dated April 1448; the other Queen in Queens' was Elizabeth, wife of Edward IV. The president's quarters were in the north-west corner of the court (that is, to anyone entering by the main gate, the far right-hand corner): a study and a bedroom (now the Dockett room, Andrew Dockett being the first President) over the Senior Combination Room, with a small gallery, supported on brick walls, towards the river. The present gallery, the main feature of the Cloister Court, was to be built during the sixteenth century.[98] The actual cloisters of the Cloister Court were there in Erasmus' day, having been built in the mid-1490's. The river range, the far end of this court, dates from about 1460. Queens', it is not surprising to learn, was the second wealthiest college in Cambridge. King's was the first.

Fuller continued:

> Queens' College accounteth it no small credit thereunto that Erasmus (who no doubt might have picked and chose what house he pleased) preferred

---

[97] Fuller, *University of Cambridge*, 175.

[98] Nikolaus Pevsner, in his Cambridgeshire volume in the Penguin Buildings of England series, wrote (1954): "The gallery cannot accurately be dated but must have been built about 1540" (115). The Royal Commission on Historical Monuments volume, *The City of Cambridge* (1959), suggests, however, that it is perhaps more convincingly thought of as belonging to the second half of Elizabeth's reign (II, 168).

this for the place of his study for some years in Cambridge. Either invited thither with the fame of the learning and love of his friend Bishop Fisher . . . or allured with the situation of this college, so near the river (as Rotterdam his native place to the sea) with pleasant walks thereabouts.[99]

Erasmus would not have been amused by the reference to Rotterdam. It was really more like Venice; but that too would have been an unfortunate spur to memory—a college in the damp obscurity of the fens could never revive the happiness Erasmus had felt in Venice, five years before, drinking Aldo Manuzio's malmsey in the house near the Rialto Bridge. The walks, however, were certainly pleasant. To the north, on the present site of Friars' Court, there was the property of the Carmelites,[100] and below that, down to the river, the college garden. Across the river, on the island where the Fisher Building now stands—land which the college had bought from the town in 1475—there were among the trees a garden and an orchard, which were properly hedged in Erasmus' day (1512). (Much later, in the reign of Charles II, a walk was to be planted on the north-east of that island, towards King's, to be known as the Erasmus Walk.[101]) Beyond, there was open country: along the backs (or, as they were then more picturesquely called, the backsides), or across to Newnham, or down the river towards Grantchester.

Andrew Paschal, who went up to Queens' in 1647 and was Fellow from 1653 to 1663, gave a more detailed guess-work about Erasmus' study in the tower.[102]

[99]Pp. 165–6.

[100]The remains of the Carmelite house were visible in the summer of 1957, when the college was trenching for the new building: the Erasmus Building (opened in 1960).

[101]There is a late mediaeval pine chair at Queens', "as fine a turned chair as exists in Europe," which is known, by a disarming leap of the imagination, as the Erasmus Chair. See Frank Davis in *Illustrated London News* (December 15, 1934). P. S. Allen, in a letter of July 1908 after a visit to Cambridge, said that at Queens' "the most grotesque traditions were afloat, even among the servitors. The butler showed us Erasmus' corkscrew, and the scout who let us into the rooms he is said to have occupied told how 'in one of his letters he mentions having seen 2 rivers from his windows, i.e. the Granta and the Cam, which were in view before that mill was built'. The letter is a figment, but where can the story have come from? Ascham in 1544 gathered oral tradition about Erasmus and his horse: but can tradition of this sort have lasted orally nearly 400 years?" (*Letters*, 77.)

[102]Quoted in Searle, *Queens' College*, 154.

The stairs which rise up to his study at Queens' College in Cambridge do bring first into two of the fairest chambers in the ancient building; in one of them, which looks into the hall and chief court, the Vice President kept in my time; in that adjoining, it was my fortune to be, when Fellow. The chambers over are good lodging rooms; and to one of them is a square turret adjoining, in the upper part of which is the study of Erasmus, and over it, leads. To that belongs the best prospect about the college: viz., upon the river, into the corn fields and the country adjoining. So it might very well consist with the civility of the house to that great man (who was no Fellow and I think stayed not long there) to let him have that study. His sleeping room might be either the Vice President's, or to be near to him, the next. The room for his servitor that above it; and through it he might go to that study, which for the height and neatness and prospect might easily take his fancy.

There is a great deal of "might" about the description. But if Paschal was correct, Erasmus had an extensive suite: a bedroom above the kitchen and the buttery, the "good lodging rooms" on the floor above–three rooms, probably, one of them being in the tower; and, up the stairs, the tower study, the room with the view. Reconstruction and alterations on the "lodging room" level were made in 1911, and so nowadays it is impossible to work out the exact geography of the apartment.

The Erasmus tower inspired one of the best rhetorical passages in James Bass Mullinger's great history of Cambridge University. In the first volume, published in 1873, there is called up before us (p. 506)

a solitary, isolated scholar, prematurely old with anxiety and toil, weighed down by physical suffering, dejected by disappointment, and oppressed with debt; rarely venturing beyond the college gates, and then only to encounter hostile or indifferent glances; while all around there waited for him an invisible foe–the pestilence that walketh at noonday; often by night, in his study high up in the south-west tower, "outwatching the Bear" over the pages of St. Jerome, even as Jerome himself had outwatched it many a night, when transcribing the same pages in his Bethlehem cell, some eleven hundred years before. Then winter came on, and, towards the close of each shortening day, Erasmus could mark from his window the white fogs rolling in from the surrounding marshes, reminding him of the climate he most of all disliked–the climate of his native Holland; while day after day, the sound of footsteps, in the courts below, grew rarer and rarer. At last the gloom, the solitude, the discomfort, and the panic, became more than he could bear; and, one night, the customary lamp no longer gleamed from a certain casement in the south-west tower.

V

AT WHAT did Erasmus toil in the tower?

First, at the beginning of October 1511 he began his lectures on the Greek language. For this he had been invited to Cambridge. He referred to the lectures in a letter of October 16: "Up to this moment I've been lecturing on Chrysoloras' Grammar, but the audience is small; perhaps more people will attend when I start Theodore's Grammar."[103] Erasmus was probably using the 1507 Paris edition of the Greek grammar by Manuel Chrysoloras. Chrysoloras (1355–1415) was a Byzantine, born at Constantinople itself, who had taught Greek at Florence in the late 1390's. He visited England in the first years of the fifteenth century and is known to have looked through the library of Salisbury Cathedral for Greek manuscripts. His brief, simple grammar—the earliest in use in the West—was first printed in Venice in 1475. By now it was rather out of date. Erasmus wrote, at about the same time he came to Cambridge: "Amongst Greek grammars that of Theodore Gaza stands admittedly first; next to it I rank that of Constantine Lascaris."[104] The Gaza grammar had been printed by Aldo Manuzio in Venice in 1495. Theodore Gaza (1400–75) was another Byzantine in Italy; he had gone there in the 1430's. His grammar was in four books. Erasmus was to publish a Latin translation of Book One in 1516 (Martens, Louvain) and of Book Two in 1518. An edition of Book Four by Richard Croke appeared in 1516.

It will be recalled that, at the time Erasmus was instructing his small class in Cambridge, Raphael Hythloday, the Portuguese ancient mariner, was teaching Greek to the inhabitants of the island of Utopia—so well that "in less than three years' space there was nothing in the Greek tongue that they lacked."[105] Raphael had neglected (he told More, Peter Giles, and John

[103]Letter 8.

[104]*De Ratione Studii* (1511); tr. Woodward, *Erasmus Concerning Education*, 163. Cf. 170: "in all that concerns Greek constructions we should do well to follow the guidance of Gaza's grammar."

[105]*Utopia*, Bk. Two, 95.

Clement) to pack the grammar of Theodore Gaza; he used that of Lascaris.

Apart from that brief reference in October 1511, Erasmus in his Cambridge letters tells us nothing about his Greek lectures. Who attended them? Henry Bullock, we can be sure, and some other Fellows of Queens'. Bullock's personal copy of Theodore's grammar, his name on the cover, is now in the Cambridge University Library.

At Padua, in the winter of 1508, Erasmus had greatly admired the pluck of a professor in his seventies for whom "no winter weather was so cold as to prevent his going at seven o'clock in the morning to attend the Greek lecture of Musurus, who scarcely let four days pass in the whole year without reading. Some of the lads could not bear the severity of the season, but neither shame nor winter kept that old man from the lecture room."[106] (Marcus Musurus, 1470–1517, was a Cretan who professed Greek at Padua from 1503 to 1510.) It would be pleasant to think that some of the reverend seniors of Cambridge had a similar passion.

In that same letter of October 16, 1511, Erasmus wrote from Cambridge: "Perhaps also I will undertake lecturing in theology, for that's under discussion at present. The stipend is too small to tempt me."[107] In fact he did deliver such lectures, for writing in 1514, after he had left the university, he said, "I taught Greek and Divinity for a great number of months at Cambridge."[108] It had been traditionally assumed, though there is no direct contemporary evidence for this, that he was given the Lady Margaret Professorship of Divinity. Detailed regulations for such a chair were drawn up in 1503, but this "lecture of the king's mother" dates back to 1497, when Henry VII granted the licence for the founding of divinity lectureships at Cambridge and Oxford. The known professors before 1511 were John Fisher (1502), Thomas Cosyn, Master of Corpus (1504), and William Burgoyne of Peterhouse (1506). In a letter of November 26, 1511, Erasmus told Ammonio that he had "undertaken to expound" St. Jerome;[109] and John Caius, later in the century, said that Erasmus lectured

[106] *E.E.*, no. 1347; tr. Nichols, I, 449.
[107] Letter 8. [108] Letter 43. [109] Letter 18.

in Cambridge on the letters of St. Jerome and on the three short books of the *Apology* against Tyrannius Rufinus.[110] Such a lecture course would have tied in fruitfully with his research programme; and it would have been approved of by Fisher, for whom Jerome was "the most learned of Scriptural scholars."[111]

Erasmus had been familiar with the works of Jerome (340–420) since his days at the monastery of Steyn. In 1489, when he was in his early twenties, he mentioned that he had copied out for himself some of Jerome's letters[112]—the first, casual announcement of a great theme, to resound through his life for thirty years. After his return to France from England in 1500, he listed the things he most wanted to possess: clothes; Greek books and a Greek tutor; and "the whole works of Jerome, upon whom I am preparing commentaries."[113] In December 1500 he set forth a "grand design":[114]

> I have long ardently wished to illustrate with a commentary the epistles of St. Jerome, and in daring to conceive so great a design, which no one has hitherto attempted, my heart is inflamed and directed by some divine power. I am moved by the piety of that holy man, of all Christians beyond controversy the most learned and most eloquent; whose writings, though they deserve to be read and learned everywhere and by all, are read by few, admired by fewer still, and understood by scarcely any. Good heavens, shall the names of Scotus, Albertus and writers still less polished be shouted in all the schools, and that singular champion, exponent and light of our religion, who deserves to be the one person celebrated—shall he be the only one of whom nothing is said?

If such an author could be presented with a sympathetic and perceptive commentary, then his genius would stand revealed in all clarity; the task of a "humanist" was so to present him.

> I am not unaware of the audacity of my project—what a task it will be, in the first place, to clear away the errors which during so many ages have become established in the text; and in the next place what a mass there is in his works of antiquities, of Greek literature, of history. And then what a style, what a mastery of language, in which he has not only left all Christian authors far behind him, but seems to vie with Cicero himself. For my own part, I may be led astray by my partiality for that holy man, but when I compare the speech of Jerome with that of Cicero, I seem to miss something in the prince of eloquence himself.

---

[110] *Annals*, 125.
[111] *Defence of the Sacred Priesthood*, 68.
[112] Nichols, I, 75.
[113] *E.E.*, no. 138; tr. Nichols, I, 283.
[114] *E.E.*, no. 141; tr. Nichols, I, 289.

What Erasmus did not know was that the Basle printer, John of Amorbach, was planning, by then, an edition of Jerome; and that during this same year 1500 Amorbach had taken into partnership a younger Basle printer called John Froben—who, sixteen years later, three years after Amorbach's death, was to publish a nine-volume edition of Jerome, of which the first four volumes, devoted to the letters, owed most to the editorial work, over a period of almost two years, of Erasmus.

Cambridge was quite rich in Jerome manuscripts: the University Library, for instance, had a volume of the letters, and there were at least seven volumes of Jerome MSS at Peterhouse. Robert Aldrich, then a young scholar of King's, was to remember in 1526 the months he had spent in Queens' reading aloud books of Jerome to Erasmus.[115] In May 1512 Josse Bade, the Paris printer, mentioned in a letter to Erasmus the possibility of an edition of the Jerome letters.[116] And in a letter four months later Erasmus said he was about to "finish off St. Jerome's letters"[117]—just over a year after he had come to Cambridge. The work went slowly, however, because he had so many other irons in the fire. To Colet he wrote in July 1513 that he was "starting on" the final checking for the work.[118] He worked at his hardest through the month of August, helped by his young assistants. By September 1[119]

> My mind is so excited at the thought of emending Jerome's text, with notes, that I seem to myself as if inspired by some god or other. I've already almost finished emending him by collating a large number of ancient manuscripts, and this I am doing at enormous personal expense.

He was still at work on Jerome at the end of November, less than two months before leaving Cambridge for good. It was the most sustained effort of his Cambridge years. And so, in July 1514, writing to the prior of his own monastery, he counted this among his achievements: "In the last two years I have (among many other things) revised St. Jerome's letters; I have slain with daggers the corrupt and interpolated passages, while I have elucidated the obscure parts in my notes."[120]

[115]Letter 63.
[116]*E.E.*, no. 263.
[117]P. 151.
[118]Letter 26.
[119]Letter 28.
[120]Letter 43.

By August 1514 he was in Basle. The house of Froben, he decided, was the publisher for him. And so, as it were, he pooled his resources with the members of the Froben-Amorbach editorial staff who had been working on an edition of Jerome for some six years: Basil and Bruno, two sons of John of Amorbach (who had died in December 1513); Beat Bild (Beatus Rhenanus) from Alsace, who had joined the firm in 1511; and such special consultants as John Reuchlin of Stuttgart, an old friend of John of Amorbach, a correspondent of Erasmus, and a noted Greek and Hebrew scholar. Erasmus took over the supervision of the projected four volumes of letters. Beat Bild later wrote that, "whenever he was consulted, his judgement being required on account of some variation in the manuscripts, he was always ready to give his opinion. But the volumes of Epistles were specially claimed by him as his own."[121]

In May 1515 he made a quick trip to London. One of the motives for the visit, probably, was to do some final work on the Jerome manuscripts there. A letter from London on the fifteenth gave some account of the work:[122]

I have long been trying, at vast expenditure of nightly labour, to achieve what I may call the rebirth under our eyes of the whole St. Jerome. We of the Latin tradition consider him the prince of theologians, to such a degree, almost, that he alone merits the name of theologian; yet his text is so spoiled, disordered and impure that, even though there's nobody so well worth reading, he above all others is the hardest to read, let alone to understand. Accordingly I began by putting in order all his works, especially those in the form of letters. (This was the hardest task of all). Next, with the help of some old manuscripts and my own wits, I removed the blemishes with which the text was blotted—or rather, blotted out. I have added summaries; also notes, as appropriate, whenever the passage so required. The result should be that, whereas previously Jerome evaded the understanding of even the most learned scholars, he can now be read without much difficulty by men of quite modest scholarship. Though this may be an arrogant claim to advance, still—it's true! And let me add that, just as old Romulus was as remarkable for his boasts about the splendid feats he did as for his doing them, so also in St. Jerome himself there is visible, combined with original and wide learning, a sort of holy ostentation.

I have most carefully restored the Greek and Hebrew parts of the text, which either were missing or had been added by hand in such a fashion that they had been better left out. The spurious and corrupt passages

---

[121]From his 1540 *Life*. *E.E.*, no. IV; quoted Nichols, I, 34–5.
[122]*E.E.*, no. 334, lines 99–119; tr. D. F. S. Thomson.

(which indeed make up a large proportion of the text) I have banished to a separate volume, in order that the reader whose appetite exceeds his learning might not feel he was cheated of anything, while on the other hand there might be no further currency in ignorant twaddle promulgated under the name of so incomparable an author as Jerome.

(Erasmus also took occasion to point out the fiendish expense of the whole undertaking!)

The four volumes devoted almost exclusively to the letters were published in April 1516; the remaining five volumes of Jerome (four volumes of Old Testament commentaries, one of New) in September.

The extraordinary fact is, that in the first week of March 1516, less than two months before the publication of the Jerome letters, the Froben press had issued the *Novum Instrumentum*, Erasmus' edition of the New Testament, in double column—the Greek text on the right of the page, to the left a Latin translation substantially (though not completely) different from the Vulgate. There were nearly 550 pages of New Testament text, followed by 450 pages of notes, and preceded by some explanatory and apologetic material, including the *Paraclesis*, an enlarged version of which was to be translated into English in 1529 (*An Exhortation to the Diligent Study of Scripture*). This was the first Greek text of the New Testament ever published, though not the first to be *printed.* In January 1514 a Greek text had been printed, with the Vulgate, at Alcala, near Madrid, part of the project under the patronage of Ximenes, Primate of Spain, for a printed Bible in Hebrew, Greek, and Latin; but the sheets were stored away unbound, not to be published until 1522.[123]

In the summer of 1504, when Erasmus was exploring the library of a monastery near Louvain, he came across a manuscript volume of notes on the New Testament written in the 1440's by the Roman humanist, Lorenzo della Valle (Valla: 1407–57). The name of Valla was not new to Erasmus. When he was in his late teens, at the monastery, he had made for a local schoolmaster a paraphrase of the Italian's *Six Books on the Elegancies of the Latin Language*, written in the late 1430's or early 1440's and first published in Rome in 1471. Lorenzo's aim was to restore the

[123]See Letter 60, note 210.

"glory of Latinity," which had been allowed "to decay in rust and mould."[124] In 1489 Erasmus wrote of Valla as "a man who with so much energy, zeal and labour refuted the stupidities of the barbarians, saved half-buried letters from extinction, restored Italy to her ancient splendour of eloquence, and forced even the learned to express themselves with more circumspection";[125] "with what zeal he exerted himself to expose the absurdities of the barbarians and to bring back into use the observances of orators and poets long covered with the dust of oblivion."[126] That work of Valla's ran through fifty-nine editions between its first printing and the year of Erasmus' death. Erasmus' early paraphrase was published (without his permission) in Cologne in 1529; he put out an authorized edition, based on a fuller paraphrase he made in Paris in the 1490's, at Freibourg in 1531. (Rather ironically, Luther was to quote Valla against Erasmus in the exchange of books on the subject of the freedom of the will.[127])

Erasmus had received a training which made him receptive to such Italian "moderns" as Lorenzo della Valle. Between 1475 and 1484 (probably) he had been educated in the school at Deventer controlled by members of the devout and learned Brethren of the Common Life, whose founder had been a native of Deventer: Gerard Groote (1340–84). By 1500 there were a dozen or more of these excellent schools in the Netherlands and Germany, and the teaching was better than at most universities. Deventer in the 1470's was not so good as that; its distinction began in 1483, when Alexander Hegius was appointed headmaster. Hegius taught Greek to the senior boys, and Erasmus attended his classes; Hegius was a friend of the great Italianate Dutchman Rudolph Agricola (1444–85), born near Groningen, whom Erasmus once saw (and he never forgot it). Agricola had

[124]Translated in *Portable Renaissance Reader*, 134. The article on Valla in the *Enciclopedia Italiana* (1937) is by Delio Cantimori. Valla is perhaps best known for his "exposure" of the Donation of Constantine: English translation in 1534 (the year of the Act of Supremacy).

[125]*E.E.*, no. 26; tr. Nichols, I, 71.

[126]*E.E.*, no. 23; tr. Nichols, I, 67.

[127]Valla's short *Dialogue on Free Will* is translated, with an introduction, in *Renaissance Philosophy of Man*. Luther claimed Augustine, Wycliffe, and Valla as his "authorities."

spent the year 1468 to 1479 in Italy, being a pupil of Gaza at Ferrara. In some ways he represented the northern Renaissance better than Erasmus: classical scholar, but fluent also in German, French, and Italian; philosopher of education, and also accomplished musician, sportsman, and artist, interested in anatomy and architecture; and, moreover, very impressive and grand in appearance, "a man goodly to look upon," a Dutch *cortegiano.*[128] Erasmus often remarked that he was the inferior of his compatriot. The works of Agricola were to be recommended for study for arts students at Cambridge in the Royal Injunctions of October 1535.

To continue: the Valla notes on the New Testament greatly excited Erasmus, and he published them at the Paris press of Josse Bade in April 1505, just before his second visit to England. In the prefatory letter of that edition, to the English ecclesiastic Christopher Fisher (kinsman of John?), Erasmus touched on many points which later, and not least at Cambridge, were to be elaborated and defended.[129] "Tell me," he wrote,

what's so shocking about Lorenzo Valla's action in making a number of annotations on the New Testament after comparing several Greek copies both ancient and emended. After all these are the sources from which the whole Testament unquestionably comes; and Valla's notes had to do with internal disagreements or slipshod and seemingly inadequate renderings of the meaning or things that might be more intelligibly expressed; or finally, with anything in the text that has come down to our day in a corrupted form.

Valla's work with the Greek texts of the New Testament would have won applause from such scholastics as Roger Bacon of Oxford, who in the late thirteenth century had lamented the neglect (increasing, as he rightly thought) of scientific biblical study, of research into the sources.[130] Few of the Schoolmen knew enough Greek to tackle the New Testament in its original; nor did Colet or Fisher. But by 1505 Erasmus felt himself at home in Greek, which he had begun intensively to study in 1500. He was better equipped than his predecessors. Also—and this is

[128] Woodward, *Education during the Renaissance*, chap. V.
[129] *E.E.*, no. 182, lines 119–25, 132–40, 192–202; tr. D. F. S. Thomson.
[130] Smalley, *Study of Bible in Middle Ages*, 329–33.

always the key to the importance of Erasmus—he had at his service the printing press. He continued:

But I hardly suppose that even Theology, the queen of sciences, will think it outrageous for Criticism, her humble attendant, to pay attention to her while showing a proper degree of reverence. Though Criticism is below some other sciences in recognised status, assuredly none has a more important function. To be sure it deals with minute matters, but matters no man who is destined for greatness can ignore; or (to put it another way) I admit that it bandies trifles about, yet these trifles have consequences of real importance. Now if a protest is raised that Theology is too august to be bound by the rules of Criticism, and that the whole business of interpreting Scripture depends on the wind of the Holy Ghost and the blowing thereof—why, in that case the theologians have a quite new claim to distinction, and I'll tell you what it is: they alone have licence to talk ungrammatically.

Five years later Erasmus' *Folly* was to laugh at the divines who "say 'tis beneath the dignity of divine mysteries to be cramped and tied up to the narrow rules of grammarians: from whence we may conjecture the great prerogative of divines, if they only have the privilege of speaking corruptly."[131] A final quotation from 1505:

Therefore it's true to say (as you so often do, my learned Christopher) that those who venture to write on Scripture (and not only Scripture, but any ancient books at all) without a reasonable command of both languages and literatures in question, have neither modesty nor intelligence. For when men like these strain their hardest in an endeavour to show themselves as learned as the best of scholars, it is precisely then, as you see, that they become objects of supreme derision to those who really know the languages, and all their fuss and alarm can be laughed out of court when a single Greek word is cited. But even the man who has not time to learn Greek thoroughly and completely will be vastly helped by Valla's labours, because Valla has on the one hand employed remarkably good judgement in his thorough discussion of the New Testament as a whole.

Valla was one influence on Erasmus' biblical studies. The other was Colet's enthusiasm for Paul. Three years ago, wrote Erasmus to Colet in 1505, shortly before the publication of the Valla, "I did venture to write something on St. Paul's Epistle to the Romans, and finished with a single effort some four rolls, which I should have continued if I had not been hindered, my principal hindrance being my constant want of Greek."[132] By the time of

[131] *Praise of Folly*, 100.
[132] *E.E.*, no. 181; tr. Nichols, I, 375–6.

the second visit to England (April 1505 to May 1506) this gap had been filled. And during that year Erasmus began to prepare a new Latin translation of the Gospels and the Epistles, for which Colet lent him Greek and Latin manuscripts from the library of St. Paul's. Copies of Erasmus' Latin version of Matthew and Mark are contained in two manuscripts written for Colet about 1509, later presented by Archbishop Parker to the Cambridge University Library; a slightly later copy of Luke and John survives in a British Museum manuscript.

During his time in Cambridge, Erasmus worked over and completed this Latin version. (He lent his only copy of the Matthew to Fisher in 1513 and was very worried when it went astray.[133])

Also—and more important—while he was at Cambridge Erasmus began systematic work on the Greek text of the New Testament. In his very first Cambridge letter, to Colet, he said, "I may even begin to tackle your own St. Paul." At first he had in mind just an edition of the Greek text, with notes. There were at least four important manuscripts in Cambridge which he used for collating. One of them, now known as the Leicester Codex, he borrowed from the library of the Cambridge Franciscans. "Presently," he wrote to Peter Giles from London in the autumn of 1512, "I shall have finished my revision of the New Testament."[134] And in July 1513 he wrote to Colet from Cambridge that he had "finished the collation of the New Testament."[135] At the same time he was preparing notes on the text, in the manner of Valla. In a letter of July 1514 he summed up his Cambridge work: "I've revised the whole of the New Testament from a comparison of the old Greek manuscripts and have annotated over a thousand places with some benefit to theologians. I have begun a series of commentaries on Paul's Epistles, which I'll finish when I have published this other work. For I have made up my mind to die in the midst of Holy Writ."[136]

By the summer of 1515, after the brief visit to England in August (his fourth), Erasmus had decided to incorporate some of his Latin translation and to have the volume printed by

[133]Letter 33.
[134]See p. 151. [135]Letter 26. [136]Letter 43.

Froben. (He used his own Latin translation in full, discarding the Vulgate, in the second edition of the New Testament, March 1519.) The printing took about six months; the volume was out by the end of the first week in March 1516.[137] In the middle of August Henry Bullock wrote to Erasmus from Queens' about "this newly published work of yours on the New Testament: great gods, how clever it is, how clearly reasoned, and to all men of sound judgement how pleasing and how indispensable."[138] And how much—as Bullock no doubt knew—the result of Erasmus' labours in that college.

What else was he working at, in Cambridge? Pick out another quotation from his letter to Peter Giles in the autumn of 1512: "I have got ready my work on Adages; I've expanded it to such an extent that I've quite changed it into something new—but much better, unless I'm mistaken, though it wasn't particularly bad before."[139] This was the *Adagia* of which he had written over twelve years before, in April 1500: "I am devoting all my strength to the preparation of my Adages, which I hope will be made public soon after Easter, a work of some length and demanding an infinity of pains. We have collected some 800 Proverbs, part Greek and part Latin."[140] The book was printed in Paris in June 1500 and dedicated to Lord Mountjoy. Apart from a slim volume of verse printed in Paris in 1496 and a letter in a history of France in 1495, this was Erasmus' first published work. His public career began then. The *Adagia* was constantly on his mind; he collected, everywhere he went, additional proverbs and pithy sayings from the classics, so that the book might be as R. R. Bolgar has described it in our own day: "the handbook to the past for which five generations had waited, which made the wisdom of the ancients accessible and ready for use."[141] In 1508 a new edition was printed in Venice by Aldo Manuzio,[142] a much enlarged version, containing over 3,200 proverbs, as against the 800 of 1500. Copies of this Aldine edition were still on sale in

[137]For the making of the New Testament, see Allen in *E.E.*, II, 164–6 and 181–4.

[138]Letter 51.

[139]P. 151.

[140]*E.E.*, no. 124; tr. Nichols, I, 236.

[141]Bolgar, *Classical Heritage*, 300.

[142]For Manutio and his press, see Norton, *Italian Printers 1501–20.*

Paris in the spring of 1511, when Erasmus was there—being sold at a discount rate too! But the work of revision and expansion went on, in Cambridge as always. In the autumn of 1512 there was enough material for another issue, to be printed (so Erasmus then thought) by Bade of Paris, who had been responsible for the second edition of the work in 1506. However, John Froben now came on the scene. For one thing he reprinted the 1508 *Adagia* at Basle in August 1513 without Erasmus' knowledge or permission. For another, the revised manuscript of the work, which Erasmus entrusted to a German book-agent called Francis Berckman, was delivered not to Bade in Paris but to Froben at Basle; Erasmus, in a letter from Cambridge written in December 1513, pretended to be very cross about this.[143] But, even if the switch had been made without his consent, it is doubtful whether he was too indignant. At all events, the little comedy of mislaid copy began his connection with the firm of Froben, which was a happy union indeed. The revised *Adagia* was published at Basle in May 1515. There were to be seven more editions of the work before Erasmus' death—the sixteenth century, it has been said, was "soaked in proverbs."[144]

Next, Erasmus continued his translations of Greek into Latin; the authors to be mentioned here are St. Basil, Plutarch, and Lucian.

One of the first works Erasmus mentioned after arriving in Cambridge was his Latin version of a little commentary on the Book of Isaiah by St. Basil (330–79), a treatise running to only thirteen pages in its final printed form. Erasmus had probably borrowed the Greek text from the library of William Grocin, at St. Lawrence Jewry. By the middle of September, a month after his arrival in Cambridge, he was at work on the translation, which was finished by the beginning of October. He sent it to Fisher. The Chancellor, however, was not very impressed, suspecting,

143Letter 38. The revised version included more of Erasmus' own comments and essays: of which Mrs. M. M. Phillips is preparing a study.

144Janet Heseltine, introduction to *Oxford Dictionary of England Proverbs*, xlv. Some of Erasmus' proverbs were translated into English in 1539 by Richard Taverner of Corpus. See also Tilley, *Dictionary of Proverbs in the Sixteenth and Seventeenth Centuries.*

apparently, that it was not a new and direct translation from the Greek, but a warmed-up version of a previous Latin translation. However that may be, this *In Esaiam Commentariolus* was to be printed at Basle in 1518.

The next Greek author was a particular favourite of Erasmus': Plutarch (46–125), a writer the Utopians also "set great store by."[145] Erasmus was especially strongly to recommend the study of Plutarch in his *Education of a Christian Prince* (Basle, May 1516—yet another product of that Erasmian year). "I've translated a good many books of Plutarch," he wrote in the autumn of 1512, "which I will send subsequently after revising the text."[146] We know of two specific translations at that time: the "Precepts of Good Health" (*De tuenda bona valetudine precepta*), which was published in London by Richard Pynson in July 1513, the one book of Erasmus' to be first printed in England; and the *De discrimine adultatoris et amici*, which Erasmus mentioned in a letter from Cambridge to Thomas More in July 1513: "I'm translating a book by Plutarch, 'On how to tell a flatterer from a friend' —*rather* long, but I like it the best of them all."[147] This was among the manuscripts which Francis Berckman took to the Froben press at Basle; and the *Plutarchi Opuscula* were printed there in August 1514, hard upon Erasmus' arrival.

Third, there was Lucian (125–200) of Samosata on the Euphrates, the Syrian satirist whose dialogues had delighted and inspired Erasmus since 1499 at least, and which he had been translating into Latin since 1503 when Aldo Manuzio printed some of them in Venice. He wrote of Lucian in 1504: "With what humour and with what quickness does he deal his blows, turning everything to ridicule, and letting nothing pass without a touch of mockery."[148] More was equally pleased; the Utopians were "delighted with Lucian's merry conceits and jests."[149] In 1507 Bade printed in Paris a collection of translations from Lucian, some by More, most by Erasmus.[150] This particular partisanship of Erasmus and More was unsympathetic to those who thought, disapprovingly, in terms of "lewd Lucian." For John Frith, of Eton

[145]*Utopia*, 95.
[146]P. 151.
[147]Letter 27.
[148]*E. E.*, no. 193; tr. Nichols, I, 371.
[149]Everyman ed., 95.
[150]See Thompson, *Translations of Lucian by Erasmus and More.*

and King's, More was to seem "another Lucian, neither regarding God nor man."[151] (Divergent sense of humour provides one explanation of differences in doctrinal emphasis.) By the winter of 1513, after two years in Cambridge, Erasmus had ready several new titles, which he sent over to Paris; they were published in May 1514. These were all short works, the longest being "Icaromenippus: an Aerial Expedition," which has about twenty pages. This dialogue is of particular interest because it was dedicated to Andrea Ammonio. Erasmus sent a copy of it to his young Italian friend in November 1511, three months after arriving in Cambridge.[152] This satirical sketch was one of his consolations, then, in that first chilly autumn. A glance at the "Icaromenippus," written about 165, will make clear why Erasmus found Lucian a kindred spirit.[153]

Menippus, the hero, troubled about life and the universe, consults some scientists, who do nothing but fill him up with technical terms and contradict each other; so he gets a pair of wings and flies up to heaven (with a stop *en route* on the moon, from where he observes the human comedy); in heaven Zeus addresses a general meeting, and complains about the philosophers, the human race having "split up into various schools of thought based on various tortuous arguments"—"a clear case for a thunderbolt": "liquidate the philosophers"—but not yet, for it is still vacation time!

It is pleasing to think of Erasmus sitting in Queens' relishing such sharp nonsense, in the same autumn in which he wrote to Colet of his battles with the Cambridge Scotists. But his *Folly*, whose oration had been published in the previous spring, had brought Menippus to her aid:[154]

> if a man like Menippus of old could look down from the moon and behold those innumerable rufflings of mankind, he would think he saw a swarm of flies and gnats quarrelling among themselves, fighting, laying traps for one another, snatching, playing, wantoning, growing up, falling, and dying. Nor

---

[151]Frith, *A Mirror to Know Thyself* (1532): *Works*, 267. Cf. Grindal on Lucian as a "blasphemer" (1564: *Remains*, 8). Grindal, though, was an admirer of Erasmus, and inherited a portrait of him from Parker (*ibid.*, 459).

[152]Letter 19.

[153]Translated by Fowler, *Works of Lucian*, III, 26–44. And lately by Turner, *Lucian: Satirical Sketches*, 111–132.

[154]*Praise of Folly*, 83.

is it to be believed what stir, what broils, this little creature raises, and yet in how short a time it comes to nothing itself; while sometimes war, other times pestilence, sweeps off many thousands of them together.

Folly had dealt with the same theme a little earlier:

Suppose a man in some lofty high tower [would not the tower of Queens' do?], and that he could look round him, as the poets say Jupiter was now and then wont. To how many misfortunes would he find the life of man subject? How miserable, to say no worse, our birth, how difficult our education; to how many wrongs our childhood exposed, to what pains our youth; how unsupportable our old age, and grievous our unavoidable death? As also what troops of disease beset us, how many casualties hang over our heads, how many troubles invade us, and how little there is that is not steeped in gall? To say nothing of those evils one man brings upon another, as poverty, imprisonment, infamy, dishonesty, racks, snares, treachery, reproaches, actions, deceits—but I'm got into as endless a work as numbering the sands—for what offences mankind have deserved these things, or what angry god compelled them to be born into such miseries is not my present business. Yet he that shall diligently examine it with himself, would he not, think you, kill himself?[155]

"What would become of the world if all men should be wise?" The answer: "it were necessary we got another kind of clay and some better potter."

Apart from Jerome, the Latin author most on Erasmus' mind during the Cambridge years was Seneca (3 B.C.–65 A.D.), "whose writings are wonderfully stimulating and excite one to enthusiasm for a life of moral integrity."[156] By the autumn of 1512 he had decided to "correct Seneca," "if I can find the time."[157] He did find the time and some helpers as well, such as young Robert Aldrich of King's, who also worked with him on Jerome.[158] We know that Erasmus consulted two manuscripts in the library of King's, one containing some aphorisms attributed to Seneca, and also the moral essay *De beata vita*, some fifty pages long; the other having the letters which Seneca wrote to his young friend Lucilius, the *Epistulae Morales*, of which 124 survive. Erasmus also used Seneca manuscripts from the library of Peterhouse. The Erasmus *Seneca* was published at Basle in the summer of 1515. In 1526 Erasmus, in process of preparing a second edition, wrote

[155] *Ibid.*, 48–9.
[156] *Education of a Christian Prince*, 200.
[157] P. 151.
[158] Letter 63.

to Robert Aldrich to ask him to check the Cambridge MSS. This correspondence (Letters 62 to 64) gives us the most information about the details of Erasmus' working habits at Cambridge.

Last, but absolutely not least, may be placed those books by Erasmus which were intended for use in schools.

The first to be mentioned was a little book "upon the right method of instruction," *De Ratione Studii*, which Erasmus sent to Colet from Cambridge in September 1511.[159] Erasmus had been at work on this treatise since his Paris days. Indeed in the very next month, October 1511, there was to be printed, without his permission, an earlier draft. In defence of his "right method of instruction" Erasmus claimed: "I undertake by its means to carry forward youths of merely average intelligence to a creditable standard of scholarship, and of conversation also, in Latin and Greek, at an age when, under the common schoolmaster of today, the same youths would be just stammering through their primer" (p. 178).

What was required, first, of a good teacher of Latin and Greek? Those who wish to teach, so wrote Erasmus, being "competent to recognize the best," must "go straight to the Greeks: to Plato, Aristotle, Theophrastus, and Plotinus; to Origen, Chrysostom, Basil" (p. 167). As for the Latin Fathers, he continued, "Ambrose will be found most fertile in classical allusions. Jerome has the greatest command of holy scripture" (p. 167). The teacher should also know "the legends of gods and heroes" (p. 167): from Homer, Hesiod, Ovid, Boccaccio. He must have some geography (p. 167):

> This subject includes two parts, a knowledge, first, of the names, ancient and modern, of mountains, rivers, cities; secondly, of names of trees, plants, animals, of dress, appliances, precious stones, in which the average writer of today shews a strange ignorance. Here we gain help from the works which have come down to us upon agriculture, architecture, the art of war, cookery, precious stones, and natural history.

---

[159] Letter 3. An abbreviated paraphrase of *De Ratione* was published by Woodward in 1904: *Erasmus Concerning Education*, 162–178. Baldwin discussed it in *Shakespeare's Small Latin and Less Greek* (1944), I, 75–93. I have not seen the theses by Baldwin's pupil J. F. Larkin: a critical edition and translation (Master's thesis, 1941); and "Erasmus' *De Ratione Studii*: Its Relationship to Sixteenth Century English Literature" (Doctorate thesis, 1942). My quotations are from Woodward's version.

Archaeology is important too—for which material "is to be found not only in literary sources but in ancient coins, inscriptions and monuments." Also "astrology—futile as it is in itself—must be understood for the sake of many poetical allusions." Finally, the study of history is "of special importance": "for its own sake as well for the reason that it is the key to many references in other writings"; for instance, "to understand such a poet as Prudentius, the one Christian poet of real literary taste, a knowledge of sacred history is indispensable" (p. 168). How many early Tudor schoolmasters could possibly have lived up to this? One who could was the Cambridgeshire schoolmaster, William Gonnell of Landbeach, later tutor in the family of Thomas More; but he, of course, was exceptional.

Now for the actual teaching of the boys. Erasmus is concerned first to stress the importance of language: "defective knowledge of language reacts upon our apprehension of the truths expressed. We often find that no-one is so apt to lose himself in verbal arguments as the man who boasts that facts, not words, are the only things that interest him" (p. 162). So, "the elements of Greek and Latin should be acquired early," under a "thoroughly skilled master"; if such a one is not available, then the student may "fall back upon self-teaching by means of the study of classical masterpieces" (p. 163). The able teacher "must select certain of the more necessary rules of accidence and syntax, and state them simply, arrange them in proper order, and dictate them for entry in note-books" (p. 169). So far as Latin is concerned, this is to be a revised method of teaching; as regards Greek, the *De Ratione Studii* was prophetic, not descriptive, Colet's foundation of St. Paul's being the first English school to include Greek in the curriculum. The Latin teacher, said Erasmus, should introduce "devices for increasing fluency . . . as, for instance, a game of forfeits and prizes for faults and corrections, the master choosing the judges from among the top boys" (p. 169). This is to be no Dry-as-Dust education (pp. 163–4):

I must make my conviction clear that, whilst a knowledge of the rules of accidence and syntax is most necessary to every student, still they should be as few, as simple and as carefully framed as possible. I have no patience with the stupidity of the average teacher of grammar who wastes precious years in hammering rules into children's heads. For it is not by learning rules that we acquire the power of speaking a language, but by daily intercourse with those accustomed to express themselves with exactness and refinement, and by the copious reading of the best authors.

There were other, more visual, aids advocated in *De Ratione Studii* (p. 166):

Verbal memory may with advantage be aided by ocular impressions; thus, for instance, we can have charts of geographical facts, genealogical trees, large-typed tables of rules of syntax and prosody, which we can hang on the walls. Or again, the scholar may make a practice of copying striking quotations at the top of his exercise books. I have known a proverb inscribed upon a ring, or a cup; sentences worth remembering painted on a door or a window.

(Proverbs again!)

In the class-room, the important things are composition and conversation (p. 169).

Care must be taken to propound "themes" not only worthy in subject but suitable, as being within the range of the boy's interests. For in this way he may acquire not only training in style but also a certain store of facts and ideas for future use. For example, such a subject as the following would prove attractive: "The rash self-confidence of Marcellus imperilled the fortunes of Rome: they were retrieved by the caution of Fabius." Here we see the underlying sentiment, that reckless counsels hasten towards disaster.

Surtout, pas de zèle. Of these "themes," says Erasmus, "my book *Adagia* will supply you with instances enough" (p. 170). By such means the boy will attain "a certain facility in speaking and in writing Latin" (p. 170). (The same would apply to Greek, once the basic constructions had been learned from Gaza's grammar.)

Such use of the "direct method" must be controlled by the example of the great authors (p. 171):

. . . when once the simpler rules of composition, in prose and verse, and the commoner figures of speech have been mastered, the whole stress of teaching must be laid upon a close yet wide study of the greater writers. Fortified with this, the student can produce original work in prose, under the criticism (this is most important) of a thoroughly skilled instructor.

For acquiring a working knowledge of the languages, the best authors are the Greeks Lucian, Demosthenes, Herodotus, Aristophanes, Homer, Euripides, and Menander; and the Latins Virgil, Horace, Cicero, Sallust, Plautus ("carefully chosen comedies" only), and Terence, who "for pure, terse Latinity has no rival" (p. 164). A good guide for the Latin writers is the *Elegantiae* of

Lorenzo Valla (p. 165). When the boy is technically fairly proficient in the language, he should devote "his attention to the *content* of the ancient literatures." Especially to the Greek: "I affirm that with slight qualification the whole of attainable knowledge lies enclosed within the literary monuments of ancient Greek. This great inheritance I will compare to a limpid spring of whose undefiled waters it behooves all who truly thirst to drink and be restored" (p. 164). This was a favourite image of Erasmus'; he had written, for instance, in 1501, while he was himself perfecting his Greek: "Latin erudition, however ample, is crippled and imperfect without Greek. We have in Latin at best some small streams and turbid pools, while they have the clearest springs and rivers flowing with gold."[160]

Greek was, so to speak, everything the Middle Ages was not. John Colet was not a Greek scholar, but in the statutes of his new school he wished that the boys "were taught all way in good literature both Latin and Greek," that the two masters "instruct the children in Greek and reading Latin, in reading unto them such authors that hath with wisdom joined the pure chaste eloquence." The High Master should be "learned in the good and clean Latin literature, and also in Greek—if such may be gotten." The statutes of many Tudor grammar schools were to repeat that condition. The clean Latin literature, the true and old and very Roman tongue, later corrupted, was that of Cicero, Sallust, Virgil, Terence; of Jerome, Ambrose, and Augustine; and of six specified Christian Latin poets—four from the fourth century (Lactantius, Prudentius, Juvencus, Valeria Faltonia Proba), one from the fifth (Sedulius), and one contemporary, Colet's acquaintance, Battista Spagnoli of Mantua (Mantuanus). They were the authors emphasized in the St. Paul's statutes;[161] and that, as well as the provision for Greek (and, we might add, the fact that the government of

[160]*E.E.*, no. 149; tr. Nichols, I, 313. Cf. More's description of Raphael Hythloday in *Utopia* (1516): "very well learned in the Latin tongue, but profound and excellent in the Greek language, wherein he ever bestowed more study than in the Latin, because he had given himself wholly to the study of philosophy; whereof he knew that there is nothing extant in Latin that is to any purpose, saving a few of Seneca's and Cicero's doings" (15).

[161]The statutes have been much criticized as in fact ignoring much of the best Latin literature, and distrusting "the spirit of the classical writers"; C. S. Lewis condemns Colet for a "distrust of pagan literature," as well as for his animosity

the school was settled in a city company and that the masters were laymen) has led a recent authority to write that "the year 1509, in which St. Paul's School was founded by Colet, may be taken as the date of the introduction of humanism to English education."[162]

A word about St. Paul's school. Colet had come into money on the death of his father in 1505; and in 1508 he began to construct at the east end of St. Paul's churchyard a stone schoolhouse to house 153 children, who would be taught free. The buildings were fully finished by 1512. It was—so far as numbers went—a larger school than Winchester (founded 1382) or Eton (1440). The first High Master was William Lily (1468–1523), an Oxford man. Colet had asked Erasmus to find an Under Master for him at Cambridge: salary, £17.6s.8d. The first Under Master was in fact to be John Rightwise, who had gone up from Eton to King's in 1509 and was thus beginning his third year when Erasmus arrived in Cambridge. We may assume that Erasmus had some influence in his appointment. It is doubtful whether boys were in fact taught in the new school (as distinct from the older cathedral school) until 1512.

To continue with Erasmus' course of study. Every schoolboy should be taught to write original letters in Latin, to turn prose into poetry and poetry into prose, to study the oratory of Cicero and Quintilian, and to translate Greek into Latin. In this latter (and most novel) exercise (which Roger Ascham was to think too difficult for boys under any but a "perfect master"),

> we are committed to three distinct operations: first, we have to analyse the construction of the passage in the older tongue; next we are forced to appreciate carefully the peculiar genius of each language and to note the

towards mediaeval Latin (*English Literature in the Sixteenth Century,* 160). Compare the young Macaulay on Johnson's criticism of Milton's Latin verse: "Johnson had studied the bad writers of the middle ages till he had become utterly insensible to the Augustan elegance, and was as ill-qualified to judge between two Latin styles as a habitual drunkard to set up for a wine taster" (*Essays,* Everyman edition, I, 156).

[162]Clarke, *Classical Education in Britain,* 4. See Foster Watson, *English Grammar Schools,* chap. XXX, "The Teaching of Greek." The St. Paul's statutes are printed in Lupton's *Life of Colet,* appendix A; abridged version in *Thought and Culture of the English Renaissance,* ed. Nugent, 37–41. For St. Paul's, see Clark, *John Milton at St. Paul's School.* J. H. Rieger has written on five poems published by Erasmus in September, 1511, intended to be sung as hymns: "Erasmus, Colet, and the Schoolboy Jesus," *Studies in the Renaissance,* IX, 1962, 187–93.

principles which are common to both; thirdly, in producing an accurate rendering from the Greek we are exercising in moving freely amidst the resources of Roman vocabulary and sentence structure. (pp. 171–2)

Erasmus ends with some advice on how the class should be taken through a text. "In reading a classic, let the master avoid the practice, common to inferior teachers, of taking it as the text for universal and irrelevant commentary. Respect the writer, and let it be your rule to rest content with explaining and illustrating his meaning" (p. 173). The boys should first be told something about the author; then about the type of work under study—what, for example, comedy is; next, an outline of the plot or theme, and some comments on the language; and finally, an elaboration of the "broader significance" of the work, the "moral applications"—for example, the second eclogue of Virgil should be treated, says Erasmus, as a parable of unstable friendship: "the lesson finally left on the mind of the pupil is that it is the prudent part to choose friends among those whose tastes and characters agree with our own." "Such methods of treating a classical story, by forcing attention to the moral to be deduced from it, will serve to counteract any harm which a more literal interpretation might possibly convey. After all, it is what a reader brings to a passage, rather than what he finds there, which is the real source of mischief" (pp. 175–6).

The Cambridge version of *De Ratione* was printed in Paris, in July 1512. At the same time Josse Bade printed a more substantial educational work, running to over 140 pages, *De Duplici Copia Verborum ac Rerum Commentarii Duo*; usually known briefly as *De Copia*: concerning fullness of expression.

This work is mentioned many times in the Cambridge letters. Erasmus had begun to gather material when he was teaching Latin in the Paris of the 1490's; in a letter of December 1500, after his first visit to England, he mentioned that he was still "struggling with" it;[163] Colet spurred him on after his return to England from Italy in 1509; indeed Colet suggested that Erasmus should dedicate the book to St. Paul's School and offered (so Erasmus later said) to give him a financial advance.[164] In fact

[163]*E.E.*, no. 136; tr. Nichols, I, 279. [164]Letter 26.

Colet assigned the book for study, in his statutes for the school;[165] and his example was followed in many Tudor grammar schools, for example, at Rivington, near Bolton, Lancashire, founded in 1566 by James Pilkington, Bishop of Durham and sometime Master of St. John's.[166]

In the sixteenth century, both in England and Europe, the *De Copia* was to be among the leading school-books dealing with the principles of Latin composition for themes and orations, an early variation on a favourite sixteenth-century theme, the Art of Rhetoric (a treatise of that title [1553] by Thomas Wilson, who was at King's in the 1540's, was to be one of the most popular things of its kind in English, and Wilson included among his examples of "what to say and how to say it" a long letter by Erasmus in praise of matrimony [probably written in fun for Lord Mountjoy in Paris in the late 1490's]). Thomas Elyot in *The Governor* (1531), discussing the teaching of rhetoric to noble youths of about fourteen, felt himself bound to recommend Quintilian and Cicero; but

> in good faith, to speak boldly that I think: for him that needeth not, or doth not desire, to be an exquisite orator, the little book made by the famous Erasmus (whom all gentle wits are bounden to thank and support) which he calleth *Copiam Verborum et Rerum*, that is to say, plenty of words and matters, shall be sufficient.[167]

Elyot, who was born about 1490, may have known Erasmus slightly, for his father was friendly with More and some other of the London humanists.

Bishop Pilkington also recommended another book of Erasmus' for his Lancashire lads: *De Conscribendis Epistolis*. The two works, said the Bishop, "will give a great light, and make the way more easy, if they be not so much tarried in, as laid before them like a pattern to learn by, and to follow."[168] This latter essay in "the gentle art of letter writing" also dates from Erasmus' Paris days. It was originally written in 1498 for Robert Fisher; Erasmus

[165]Lupton, *Colet*, 279.
[166]Kay, *History of Rivington and Blackrod Grammar School*, 186.
[167]Everyman edition, 1962, 34.
[168]Kay, *loc. cit.*

worked over the manuscript when he came to Cambridge, and gave a copy to Henry Bullock; and in October 1521 John Siberch printed the book in Cambridge, probably from Bullock's manuscript. This act of piracy did not make Siberch popular with Erasmus. Erasmus had Froben print an official version at Basle in August 1522, with a preface condemning the Cambridge edition.

The fourth school-book Erasmus worked on in Cambridge was an edition of the moral precepts in couplets (such as Polonius would have delighted in) dating from the third or fourth century A.D. and attributed to a certain "Cato." (The origins of the *Disticha Catonis* are rather obscure.) There had been over thirty printed editions of this work by 1500. Erasmus' version (with his comments) was first printed at Louvain by Thierry Martens in September 1514. This was the work which John Watson of Peterhouse (soon to be Master of Christ's) found in the summer of 1516: "A few days ago I came across the small *Cato* that you have furnished with explanatory notes; and you'd be more than amazed to know what delight these same notes have given me, while I marvelled at the view of a harvest so sweet and so rich garnered out of a field so modest in extent."[169] The collection, whether in Erasmus' edition or not, was used for beginners in Latin in many Tudor grammar schools. J. H. Brown, a leading English authority on Elizabethan schools, has written of the distichs:

> improving, no doubt, but dull reading. No book was more commonly used in schools in the sixteenth and seventeenth centuries, when not to "know one's Cato" was a synonym of the most complete ignorance. It was frequently prescribed in the statutes, Mulcaster alone raising his voice against it, on the very reasonable ground that it was "too serious for little ones, who mind nothing but their toys."[170]

Bishop Pilkington assigned it for the boys of Bolton; perhaps nothing was too serious for them.

Finally, of these contributions of Erasmus during his Cambridge years to English grammar school education, there must be

[169]Letter 48.
[170]*Elizabethan Schooldays*, 75.

discussed his revision of William Lily's draft *Libellus de Constructione Octo Partium Orationis*, first printed with no author named, by Richard Pynson in 1513, and to appear in at least two hundred editions throughout western Europe before the end of the century. This was a short Latin syntax, in Latin: a more advanced work–for use perhaps in the sixth form–than Lily's syntax in English, the *Rudimenta*, which may have been printed as early as 1509.[171] This was a period of a plethora of Latin grammars, and Colet was much concerned to have a new and suitable one for his boys. Thomas Linacre had drafted a version, but Colet had rejected this by the autumn of 1511.[172] For the very small boys, there was the *Rudimenta* and Colet's own accidence, in English, the *Aeditio*, written about 1509 and first printed (so far as we know) in 1527.[173] Lily's *Libellus de Constructione* was compiled to complete the series. And Erasmus worked over it in Cambridge in 1512.

The committee which drew up in 1540 an authorized Latin grammar "generally to be used in the king's majesty's dominions" drew upon this Lily-Erasmus syntax, as well as upon Erasmus' own paraphrase of the *De Elegantiis Linguae Latinae* by Lorenzo Valla. They used also the *Aeditio* of Colet and the *Rudimenta* of Lily.[174] "King Henry's Grammar," which came to be popularly known as Lily's Grammar, was last printed (heavily edited and revised, for schoolboy use) in 1858. Its reputation survives today because Shakespeare had some sport with it: Holofernes in *Love's Labour's Lost*, Hugh Evans in *The Merry Wives of Windsor*, and Sir Toby Belch were addicted to their Lily. In holding up that particular comic mirror Shakespeare, for all his small Latin, was reflecting just a little the Cambridge work of Erasmus.

171Excerpt in Nugent, *Thought and Culture*, 121–2.

172Letter 3.

173Excerpts in Lupton, *Colet*, 290–2; and in Nugent, *Thought and Culture*, 119–21.

174The authoritative account of the formation of "Lily's Grammar," and its relation to the work of Colet-Lily-Erasmus for St. Paul's, is a paper read to the Bibliographical Society (London) by C. G. Allen in 1953, and printed in the *Library* (June 1954), 85–100. There is a photographic reprint of the 1567 edition, with an introduction by V. J. Flynn in *Scholars' Facsimiles and Reprints*, New York, 1945. Baldwin, *Shakespeare's Small Latin*, II, 690–701, is an earlier discussion of the "Formation of the Authorised Grammar."

VI

THE THIRTY-ONE surviving letters written from Cambridge by Erasmus were to six of his friends in England. Much the largest group—seventeen letters—went to Andrea Ammonio. There remain also six to John Colet, four to William Gonnell, two to Roger Wentford, one to Thomas More, and one to William Warham.

Ammonio was Erasmus' most valued friend in London because he was a member of the papal "diplomatic corps"; he and a fellow-citizen of Lucca, Silvestro Gigli, Bishop of Worcester, were Erasmus' best propagandists to the papal Court. Gigli (1463–1521) had gone to Rome as English agent at the Court in 1498; he was in England from 1504 (when Ammonio came to the country with him) until the early part of 1512, when he returned to Rome to attend the Fifth Lateran Council.

Why did Erasmus need such allies? The answer emphasizes the fact that for twelve years, from 1505 to 1517, two of his besetting worries were his illegitimate birth and his monastic vows. Erasmus had been ordained priest in April 1492 when he was between twenty-two and twenty-five. But by canon law a bastard was incapable of the priesthood. Now, Erasmus came to England for the second time in the latter part of 1505, and there was talk of his being presented to a benefice; such talk continued until March 1512, when Warham in fact arranged for him to become rector of Aldington, Kent. But if his "defect of birth" invalidated his priesthood, it would make it impossible for him to accept such a position, which of course he valued not as a spiritual charge but as a source of income. So at the end of 1505, with the help of Ammonio and Gigli in London, he had his case argued in Rome; and, by a letter of Julius II dated January 1506, he was absolved from the penalties incurred by a bastard priest and given permission to accept ecclesiastical livings.[175] That was one worry for the moment shelved. But in addition, Erasmus had taken the vows of an Augustinian canon at Steyn, after a year's

[175] *E.E.*, III, xxix–xxx. Addressed "Desiderio Erasmo, Canonico Monasterii de Steyn in Hollandia, ordinis Sancti Augustini." Erasmus had first used the additional name "Desiderius" in 1496. The form "Desiderius Erasmus Roterodamus" first appeared on a title-page later in this very year of 1506.

probation, in 1488, when he was between nineteen and twenty-two. He left the monastery in 1493 (probably) and thereafter he returned to Steyn only for visits, the last being in 1501. His argument was that he "in his boyhood was by those that had charge of him presented to a monastery of canons regular, wherein, more by reason of threats, shame and want, than of his own free will, he remained until he made the profession."[176] In 1503, when he was in Louvain, Erasmus received episcopal permission to wear a modified version of the habit of the order of Augustinian canons.

John Dickinson has emphasized that in the Augustinian order "there was probably no complete uniformity of wardrobe."[177] But the outdoor dress of a canon seems to have been a black cassock (maybe lined with fur); a white surplice or rochet over the cassock; and over that a cloak or cope, sometimes black, sometimes white, with a hood. This outdoor cloak, or *pallium* (as distinct from the black *cappa*, worn in church) was one of the distinguishing marks of the Augustinian canon. At Louvain Erasmus wore his black cassock with a linen scapular—a sort of hood, worn from the shoulders, which could cover the head. When he went to Italy in 1506 he made further changes in his dress to suit the custom of the country, wearing the scapular with the black cloak. In Bologna, however, probably in 1507, he was almost involved in an incident because of the scapular, which some hoodlums mistook for the white scarf worn by plague inspectors; such an inspector should have carefully avoided walking through crowded streets. (This is the story Erasmus told;[178] it has been doubted.) So he asked Julius II "for permission either to use the habit of my order or to refrain from using it, at my discretion, provided only that I dressed like a cleric." And Julius, in a letter, gave him "a full pardon" for "any faults I had previously committed in this respect." So in Italy he wore the costume of a secular priest. When he returned to England in the summer of 1509

[176]Phrase from the letter of Leo X to Ammonio, January 26, 1517. *E.E.*, no. 517; tr. Nichols, II, 461–3.

[177]Dickinson, *Origins of the Austin Canons*, 185. See particularly Clark, *Observances in Use at the Augustinian Priory at Barnwell*, lxxiii–lxxxii. Clark printed a drawing, from a brass, of a canon of St. Frideswide's, Oxford, who died in 1515 (lxxvi).

[178]The material in this section is based on Letter 43 (1514).

he decided (so he said) to wear again the modified Augustinian habit. Julius' dispensation probably applied only to Italy. But some of Erasmus' English friends (not all) advised him that the habit would be found offensive in England. (Allen noted that "English Austin canons, when not domiciled in houses of their order, had ceased to wear the strict habit."[179]) So he packed away his Augustinian garments in a trunk and dressed as an ordinary priest. He was so dressed throughout his Cambridge stay. Did he, we wonder, visit the Augustinian priory at Barnwell, outside Cambridge?

But this was all very uncertain; and in his first letter to Ammonio from Cambridge Erasmus made satirical reference to the expenses involved in attempting to have his position regularized at Rome.[180] When he was given the living of Aldington in March 1512, worth about £40 a year, he immediately resigned it for a pension therefrom, of about £24 a year. One of the reasons for this action was his doubt about his priestly status. In 1514, at about the time he left Cambridge, the prior of Steyn reminded him of his obligations to that community. And so Erasmus tried to accelerate the efforts to have a complete dispensation from Leo X (who had become Pope in 1513). Gigli was in Rome from 1512, and in June 1515 Ammonio was appointed deputy collector of papal revenue in England (in succession to Polydore Vergil) —in a letter to Leo in August 1516 Erasmus referred to Ammonio as *tuae sanctitatis apud Anglos nuncius*.[181] The dispensation finally came in January 1517.[182] Erasmus, the papal letter to Ammonio ran, has incurred "apostacy and other sentences, censures and penalties ecclesiastical," because he has been promoted to the priesthood "although he labours under a defect of birth having been begotten of an illicit, and, as he fears, incestuous and forbidden intercourse"; and because "he did first cover and then altogether put off the habit usually worn" by the Augustinian canons "and hath for several years gone about in the habit of a secular priest and so goeth at present." These things were "not of

179*E.E.*, I, 571.
180Letter 2.
181*E.E.*, II, 289.
182January 26, 1517. Leo to Ammonio, *E.E.*, no. 517. Leo to Erasmus, *E.E.*, nos. 518, 519.

his own fancy," but because he was "constrained by circumstances." By the papal letter Ammonio was given "licence and faculty" to "absolve him from apostacy and the aforesaid sen-
stances." By the papal letter Ammonio was given "licence and
penances according to his offence, if he has contracted any by celebrating mass or other divine offices"; to "dispense that he may lawfully dwell without the monasteries of the said order"; to allow him to "carry the sign only of his canon's habit under the dress of a secular priest"; and to "receive and lawfully retain whatsoever ecclesiastical benefices shall be conferred upon him." That was exactly eleven years after the first letter of Julius II. Ammonio had commended the cause to Leo so that Erasmus "may apply himself with a calmer mind to the common cause of learning."[183] At Cambridge, Erasmus must often have anticipated the assurance of Miss Flite, expecting a judgement shortly from the High Court of Chancery—on the Day of Judgement!

And Erasmus surely exhibited what has been described as the hallmark of a Christian spirit: the divided mind, the uneasy conscience, the sense of personal failure.

No one could claim that the Cambridge letters are among the most important products of Erasmus' pen. Some of them will seem inordinately trivial. That is their charm. They show the private man, not the public figure. The letters to Ammonio, especially—two immigrants saying things about their adopted home which they would never have dared reveal to their distinguished English friends—have a spontaneity which makes them more attractive than the set pieces, intended for publication, which Erasmus came more and more to write as his fame grew. Renaudet has written:[184]

The correspondence between Erasmus and Ammonio is confiding, secret, and full of fun. Ammonio is revealed as a charming soul, with enormous delicacy and verve, at times a little melancholy and discouraged. In the Cambridge letters we have an intimate Erasmus, who loves friendship and long conversations in writing, who talks about everything and understands everything, worries easily, and—already seriously ill—does not neglect the creature comforts: he shows himself to us in slippers. . . .

[183]Tr. Nichols, II, 389.
[184]Renaudet, *Erasme et l'Italie*, 111.

These very personal letters, a little gossipy and facile, do not give the impression, quite, of being the work of a great man. It is necessary to listen carefully; and not to forget that if his thought was by nature serious, since his going to Paris he had made a habit of expressing himself, with his Italian friends, in a frivolous way.

In spite of the minor quality of the letters, the major themes run through, implicit or muted more often than not, but sometimes soaring out with an engaging directness and force. The effect, sometimes, is as if the letters of Horace Walpole had been ghost-written by St. Paul!

Some of the typically Erasmian themes, as they sound in his Cambridge letters, may be discussed here.

First, there was his impatient interest in Italian affairs. Erasmus, led on by Lord Mountjoy (among others) had hurried from Italy to London on the accession of Henry VIII; and he was conscious, often with some bitterness, that England was "this country, which I have chosen in preference to Rome."[185] By February 1512, after his first Cambridge winter, he was "tortured" by his longing for Rome, with its "climate, countryside, libraries, walks, and delightful scholarly conversations."[186] (There was always in Erasmus an element of the "grass is greener.") This nostalgia was one of the threads through his relationship with Ammonio, for the Italian, too, was an uneasy *émigré*, and for him Rome was the true *sedes fortunae.*[187] In Cambridge Erasmus apparently kept up his contracts with such Italian friends as Paolo Bombace of Bologna.

And he constantly pestered Ammonio for news of the political situation in Italy. During October and November 1511 Ammonio sent to Cambridge three quite detailed reports on current Italian events. *The Prince*, we remember, with its fine final "Exhortation To Liberate Italy from the Barbarians," was written in 1513 and Erasmus was moved, like Machiavelli, by the "present condition" of Italy—"more enslaved than the Hebrews, more oppressed than the Persians, and more scattered than the Athenians; without a head, without order, beaten, despoiled, lacerated and overrun."[188] Such was the *calamitas Italiae* of which Erasmus wrote

[185]Letter 36.
[186]P. 143. [187]Letter 17.
[188]*The Prince*, tr. Ricci and Vincent, chap. XXVI.

in November 1511.[189] (But Erasmus did not hope for a "liberator.")

One key to Erasmus' approach to Italian politics was his hatred of Julius II, Guiliano della Rovere, who had been elected Pope in 1503. Erasmus made fun of him in his second surviving Cambridge letter (to Ammonio) at the end of August 1511. And the recently printed *Praise of Folly* contained criticism enough of the successors of Peter:[190]

> though those words in the Gospel, "We have left all, and followed Thee," were his, yet they call his patrimony lands, cities, tribute, imposts, riches; for which, being inflamed with the love of Christ, they contend with fire and sword, and not without loss of much Christian blood, and believe they have then most apostolically defended the Church, the spouse of Christ, when the enemy, as they call them, are valiantly routed.

And so Erasmus disapproved of Julius' attempts to "liberate" Italy from the French, to drive them across the Alps bag and baggage. "not because I love the French but because I hate war."[191]

The question was not at all academic in England, for during November 1511, less than three months after Erasmus went to Cambridge, Henry VIII allied himself with the Pope. This was the "Holy League," the other members being the Republic of Venice (once Julius' great enemy, but now, for the moment, brought to heel); the Duke of Milan; and Ferdinand, Henry's father-in-law, King of Aragon, Governor of Castile (on behalf of his insane daughter Joanna), and ruler of the Italian South—the Kingdom of Naples and Sicily. The "great powers" were squaring up to each other, with the Italian peninsula as their testing ground. For Erasmus this "brinkmanship" was too dangerous; "when every day we see the most trivial of raids taking several years to end (and not easily, at that), what will be the prospect if such an extensive war once breaks out?" (this from Cam-

[189] Letter 12. Compare Guicciardini's comment on the years 1492–1532 as seeing "le calamità d'Italia" (Quoted Hay, *Italian Renaissance*, 39).

[190] *Praise of Folly*, 118–19. Compare a modern judgement: "finding it necessary to play off the principal sovereigns one against the other in succession, Julius II turned Italy into a battlefield for a long time and drew down upon his country those 'barbarians,' as he termed them, whom he earnestly wished to destroy" (R. Aubenas in *New Cambridge Modern History*, I, 81).

[191] Letter 14.

bridge, November 1511).[192] There was, moreover, in the musings of this self-styled armchair strategist, a King Log–King Stork sort of pessimism. "Suppose the French driven out of Italy," he wrote to Ammonio, "and then reflect, please, whether you prefer to have the Spaniards as your masters. . . . I fear Italy is to have a change of masters, and, because she can't endure the French, may have to endure French rule multiplied by two."[193] But the French, while Erasmus continued at Cambridge, were losing ground. Julius had a famous victory in June 1512. "We have won Paris, we have won," said the Pope. "May God give your Holiness joy of it," answered his confessor. "And to all the faithful souls whom He has at last deigned to deliver from the yoke of the barbarians."[194] The French were again beaten in 1513; in Italy by the Swiss troops paid by the Pope, and in the Netherlands by Henry VIII (Ammonio was on this campaign, as royal secretary and chaplain, and he kept Erasmus fully informed). The change of masters, however, did in fact come about. Within ten years Italy was overshadowed by the power of Charles V, Emperor, Archduke of Austria, Count of Habsburg, King of Spain, King of Naples and Sicily, King of the Balearic Islands—as well as (among other things) King of the Indies and Lord of Asia and Africa. The Holy League of 1526 was against him—and it was led by a now allied Pope and King of France! *Calamitas Italiae.* Ammonio did not comment on these opinions of Erasmus. One wonders how far he was stirred by notions of *patria oppressa*—to use a phrase not irrelevant over three hundred years later, when Verdi had it sung by his Scottish army in *Macbeth.*

A second theme may somewhat tire the reader. That is, Erasmus' obsession with his "beggarly role,"[195] his "grinding poverty."[196] In his first Cambridge letter he took occasion to point out to Colet: "On the subject of gain, I see nothing in prospect. What can I filch from people who haven't a rag to their backs?"[197] His friends, too, became at times a little weary of this. Even Ammonio told him that he was, in fact, rather lucky, because of

[192] *Ibid.*
[193] Letter 18.
[194] Pastor, *History of the Popes*, VI, 416.
[195] Letter 3.
[196] Letter 4.
[197] Letter 1.

his powerful patrons.[198] But the image of Diogenes persisted; and it was for Erasmus a fearful (if funny) thought.

In 1518 Erasmus said that he considered £200 a year an adequate income, which would just about cover his expenditure.[199] By then, of course, he was living at quite a rate. In Cambridge his expenses were not so great. In November 1513 he wrote to Ammonio that he had got through about £24 in about twenty weeks; [200] an annual expenditure of, say, £75. That was at the end of his Cambridge stay. In the beginning, he had lived less cheaply. During the summer of 1511 he had almost £30 put by, all of which had gone by November; annually, at that rate, he would have spent up to £120. It is probably safe to estimate that his average expenditure in the Cambridge years was about £100 a year.

Now, what was his income? He came to Cambridge lured by the prospect of salaried employment, as a special lecturer in Greek. Unfortunately we do not know what he was paid. We get a hint from a letter of the university to Mountjoy, which probably relates to this subject:[201]

> Even were there not a present hope of help for Greek Letters in your Lordship's distinguished person and supreme character as our great patron, yet our very necessity at this time must needs prompt us to supplicate repeatedly for your Lordship's support; inasmuch as we stand in a situation from which it cannot be that we should advance without the active assistance of yourself and some others. The salary we have promised to a teacher of Greek is extraordinarily high: but the resources of our scanty and all-but-exhausted treasury cannot retain the services of a professor, except by means of ready payment; and how are we, lacking those means, properly to effect the said payment? In such a case we must choose either to abandon Greek letters or to burden our friends, trusting whose favour (not, as we hope, in vain) we have burdened our credit with a sum greater than it can bear. And unless your Lordship, above all others, shall be ready to add lustre to the magnificence of your subvention by quickness in furnishing the same, our promises are presently upon the point of dissolution.

"Extraordinarily high," then. This can be linked with Erasmus' remark that the stipend of the divinity lectureship offered him

[198] Letter 17.
[199] See *E.E.*, XI, 363. In this, the gold florin has been taken as worth about 4*s*. 6*d*. sterling.
[200] Letter 37.
[201] *E.E.*, I, appendix X; tr. D. F. S. Thomson.

was too small to be tempting[202]—if this was in fact the Lady Margaret Chair, that paid £13 6*s.* 8*d.* a year. We may note also that the Professor of Greek at Venice and the Professor at the language college founded in the University of Louvain in 1518 both got paid well over £20.[203] It seems not unlikely that Fisher had promised Erasmus a similar sum. If so, it was a very special concession; for in 1520 the stipend of a university lecturer in Greek is quoted at £10,[204] though the Regius Professor of Greek, when the Chair was founded in 1540 got £40.

For his two lectureships, then, Erasmus may have been paid as much as £33. For comparison, we remember that the average Cambridge don got £5 or £6 a year, plus his food and keep, or some of it. The Master of the new College of Christ's got £6 13*s.* 4*d.* and an allowance of about £3 10*s.* 4*d.* The only financial "plum" in Cambridge was the Provostship of King's— no less than £66 13*s.* 4*d.*[205] How admirable if Erasmus could have been Provost!

However, £33 a year was only a third of Erasmus' expenditure.

His lectures were free; that is, in fact if not in theory he got almost nothing from his students; he once mentions a payment of about eight shillings, which he said he took unwillingly.[206] The only fixed source of income he had, apart from the university salary, was the pension from the rectory in Kent to which he was presented in March 1512. This was for life; but in the period before he left Cambridge early in 1514 Erasmus probably made no more than £12 from this English benefice.[207]

And so Erasmus had to rely for more than half his income on those powerful patrons Ammonio praised. The trouble was they were sometimes slow about dipping into their pockets. Mark Twain once noted that "the holy passion of friendship is of so sweet and steady and loyal and enduring a nature that it will last through a whole lifetime, if not asked to lend money." The observation was pessimistic (as befitted a man who thought there

[202]Letter 8.
[203]*E.E.*, XI, 363.
[204]*Letters and Papers Henry VIII*, III, 1540.
[205]These Cambridge figures are from the *V.C.H.*
[206]Letter 37.
[207]Pp. 146–7.

would be no humour in heaven); but it was not unduly false. "I am–," wrote Erasmus in November 1511, "so far as *promises* of gold are concerned–unmistakably wealthy; apart from which, I live in stark hunger!"[208] Warham, at this time, was giving him about £30 a year–his most generous benefactor.[209] Lord Mountjoy had arranged to pay him an annual pension of about £25, but this was rather slow in coming, especially at the beginning of the Cambridge stay, when Mountjoy was in Belgium.[210] Erasmus also got money from Colet and Fisher (not much); and at the end of 1513 Bishop Ruthall of Durham gave him about fifty shillings.[211] If Mountjoy was prompt, then, Erasmus might expect to receive from his patrons about £60 a year.

In all, his income at Cambridge, then, was not more than £95 a year; perhaps considerably less. His expenditure, as we have seen, was not less than £100; perhaps considerably more. A little arithmetic (howbeit somewhat hypothetical) puts the grumbling in some perspective. It was always the same. In 1518 he received £130 and spent £200. "Annual income twenty pounds, annual expenditure nineteen nineteen six, result happiness. Annual income twenty pounds, annual expenditure twenty pounds ought and six, result misery. . . ."

Often, the reader will be reminded of nothing so much as the Cambridge letters of Thomas Gray. "This silly dirty place"[212] with its "quiet ugliness"[213] and a "spirit of laziness"[214] roused Gray, from his undergraduate days, to rhetoric:

> Surely it was of this place, now Cambridge, but formerly known by the name of Babylon, that the prophet spoke when he said, "the wild beasts of the desert shall dwell there, and their houses shall be full of doleful creatures, and wolves shall build there, and satyrs shall dance there; their forts and towers shall be a den for ever, a joy of wild asses; there shall the great owl make her nest, and lay and hatch and gather under her shadow; it shall be a court of dragons; the screech owl also shall rest there, and find for herself a place of rest." You see here is as pretty collection of desolate animals, which is verified in this town to a tittle.[215]

But all this grumbling was more or less affectionate. "I would certainly avoid giving offence," wrote Gray in 1765, "to a set of

208Letter 15.
209Letter 43.
210*Ibid.*
211Letter 36.
212Gray, *Letters*, III, 32 (1764).
213*Ibid.*, I, 347 (1757).
214*Ibid.*, I, 196.
215*Ibid.*, I, 4 (1736).

men among whom I have passed so many easy, and I may say, happy hours of my life."[216] I take a special interest in Cambridge, Erasmus said in 1518, "on account of the hospitality I have enjoyed there."[217]

Gray had a touch of Erasmus, too, in his reliance upon "ever amiable" friends:

> I return to your letter. It proves at least, that in the midst of your new gaieties, I still hold some place in your memory, and, what pleases me above all, it has an air of undissembled sincerity. Go on, my best and amiable friend, to show me your heart simply and without the shadow of disguise.[218]

That was Gray. A kindred touch of Bloomsbury helps to make attractive the English humanists of early Tudor London. One thinks of Thomas More's tribute to Peter Gilles at the beginning of *Utopia*:

> . . . he is both of wonderful virtuous conditions, and also singularly well learned, and towards all sorts of people exceeding gentle; but towards his friends so kind-hearted, so loving, so faithful, so trusty, and of so earnest affection, that it were very hard in any place to find a man that with him in all points of friendship may be compared. No man useth less simulation or dissimulation; in no man is more prudent simplicity.[219]

Or again, of Erasmus on More: "This disposition of yours I commend most highly, that nothing gives you greater pleasure than to become rich in faithful and sincere friends; in this you find the chief pleasure of this life."[220]

"I wish him all success," Erasmus wrote of a friend of Ammonio, "for I think he has a warm and friendly heart" (*videtur amici candidique animi*).[221] The friends he most valued were *candidi*: having the quality of "undissembled sincerity." In his Cambridge days, two friends seemed to Erasmus especially to have that gift: Ammonio and Bullock. They were both younger than he, Ammonio by ten years, Bullock by twenty. In both of them Erasmus could confide without reservation. They were fitted for that inner circle bound by what Ammonio called the *hilaritas Erasmi*.[222]

[216]*Ibid.*, III, 94 (1765).

[217]Letter 58.

[218]*Letters*, III, 272 (1770).

[219]*Utopia*, 14.

[220]*E.E.*, no. 1220 (July 5, 1521). Quoted in Miss Routh's *Thomas More and His Friends*, 117.

[221]Letter 37.

[222]Letter 22.

Erasmus wrote of himself: "Among friends his language was free, sometimes too much so; and, as often as he was deceived, he could not learn to distrust his friends."[223] He had moods which call to mind Marcel Proust: "I am growing weary of insincerity and friendship, two things which are practically identical."[224] Erasmus in 1501: "I find so much hypocrisy, so much perfidy in friendships, not only those of an ordinary kind, but those that are called Pyladean, that I am not inclined now to try any new ones."[225] Fortunately for his friends, such moods were fleeting. The pride of human affection, as Lionel Trilling has observed, is one of the few prides that have any true dignity.

Because he made new and good friends in Cambridge, he felt for the place a certain affection. He liked London more—because he had more friends there. Also, Cambridge did not give him his just deserts. To most of his Cambridge colleagues he was, at best, "un étranger d'esprit aventureux."[226] The Cambridge letters, as is well known, hardly suggest that the market town in the fens bore much resemblance to the land of lost content! Indeed, one thing the Cambridge climate did for him was raise his Italian days (in depressed moments) to the level of a sort of prelapsarian perfection.

> That is the land of lost content,
> I see it shining plain,
> The happy highways where I went
> And cannot come again.

His first letter from Cambridge, predicting poverty "looming ahead," sets the tone of "Was my coming here a mistake?" That was on a Sunday; by Monday he was complaining about the wines and the beer.[227] By November he was feeling the winter chill[228]—and talking of returning to London.[229] At the end of that first November—*hic, O Academiam*! What a University![230] What a "treadmill"[231]—by then he was deep in Jerome. Two years later he was still at Cambridge, "looking every day for a convenient

[223]Quoted Nichols, I, 12. The *Compendium Vitae*: *E.E.*, no. II.
[224]Quoted in George Painter, *Proust*, I, 298.
[225]*E.E.*, no. 159; tr. Nichols, I, 332.
[226]Renaudet, *Erasme et l'Italie*, 114.
[227]Letter 2.
[228]Letter 12.
[229]Letter 14.
[230]Letter 19.
[231]Letter 21.

moment to take wing"[232]—just as Thomas Gray was continually talking of going up to town. Later in the year (another November): "Everything is very deserted here, most people being away for fear of the plague; though even when all of them *are* present, it's a lonely place for me."[233] (Compare Thomas Gray, writing from Pembroke on August 12, 1760: "Cambridge is a delight of a place, now there is nobody in it. I do believe you would like it, if you knew what it was without inhabitants. It is they, I assure you, that get it an ill name and spoil all."[234]) "Immediately after Christmas, I'll rush to join you in London":[235] that is, Christmas 1513. By February 1514 he had done so—and he never went to Cambridge again. "There is absolutely no reason," he had written to Ammonio in November 1511, "why you should congratulate me on account of my Cambridge retreat; shame alone curbs my complaints."[236]

The *Praise of Folly* was thrice reprinted in 1512. The leading wit of Europe, in a provincial backwater! But Cambridge did provide him (for one of the few times in his life) with a settled income, however unsatisfactory; it gave him leisure to study, manuscripts to work on, and sympathetic companions to help him. "I'm also doing some service to learning, to the best of my ability; and," he wrote in October 1511, "have been 'beguiling' a few months."[237] At one point (perhaps in a fit of absence of mind) he even committed to paper the compromising statement that "Cambridge really suits me fairly well."[238] After leaving England in 1514, he was soon praising the Cambridge colleges with their "religion and . . . sobriety in living."[239] By 1517 he was feeling nostalgic about his friendship with John Watson of Peterhouse: "wherever on earth I go, I shall remember those most pleasant days when we were bosom companions."[240] In 1516, indeed, he had intended to revisit Cambridge, when he was in London for a brief period; but at the last moment, when he was already on his horse, he found himself obliged to wait on Fisher,

[232]Letter 28.
[233]Letter 37.
[234]Gray, *Letters*, II, 166.
[235]Letter 38.
[236]Letter 14.
[237]Letter 8.
[238]Letter 12.
[239]Letter 43.
[240]Letter 49.

in London and Rochester.[241] He wrote always, from that time, of Cambridge as a flourishing and distinguished university.

In spite of the cold and the damp and the disappointments, Erasmus could surely not help being a little captivated by "the Cambridge that has been the experience of centuries of youth, 'ever ancient and ever new' "; where "the beauty of stone and leaf and flower, the *genius loci*, the fair field of innumerable harvests of mind and heart, the nursery of poets many and great, lie far beyond the barking and fighting of dons."[242]

He specifically remembered, in later days, about a dozen Cambridge friends. Residents of the town such as the stationers Garrett Godfrey and Nicholas Spering; Fellows of Queens' such as Bullock, Humphrey Walkden, John Vaughan, and John Fawne (Vice-President of the College, and Vice-Chancellor from November 1512 until 1514); Thomas Green, Master of St. Catharine's and commissary to the Vice Chancellor; John Watson of Peterhouse (Master of Christ's from 1517); Richard Sampson, Fellow of Trinity Hall. Among the students he knew (and employed) he was especially fond of Robert Aldrich and John Bryan from King's, and Thomas Lupset of Pembroke. These Cambridge men, in his correspondence, have their memorial.

Who else might have seen Erasmus plain, in the Schools, on the Market Hill? Hugh Latimer, who had gone up to Peterhouse as a sizar, with John Watson as his tutor, in 1507, took his B.A. from Clare Hall in 1511 and continued there as Fellow. Thomas Cranmer was a Fellow of Jesus, having become M.A. in 1510 when he was about twenty-two; he had been in Cambridge, it seems, since 1503. (Edmund Cranmer, his younger brother, future Marian exile, was now an undergraduate.) Edward Crome—later to present to his college, Gonville Hall, a copy of Erasmus' New Testament—had been since 1509 President of Physwick Hostel, looking after the eighty or so "Fishwickians" with an efficiency later to be praised by Cranmer. Then—at a time when William Tyndale was hating the arts course at Oxford—there were the undergraduates: Thomas Bilney, later the first of the Cambridge Protestant martyrs, having first "heard Jesus speak" in Erasmus' Latin, was probably in his second year when Erasmus came to

[241]Letter 49. [242]David Knowles, *Listener* (March 12, 1959).

Cambridge; Thomas Arthur, to be one of Erasmus' translators and one of the Cambridge "Lutherans" of the 1520's, was at Trinity Hall; George Joye came to Cambridge (probably to Christ's) in 1510, and was to receive a Fellowship at Peterhouse in 1517, which he held till he fled abroad in 1528, there to publish the first printed versions in English of five books of the Old Testament, and to write *The Supper of the Lord* (1533);[243] George Stafford went up to Peterhouse in 1511, and was to be Fellow of Pembroke from 1515, dying in 1529 after some years of lectures on St. Paul, the effect of which invited comparison with Colet's impact on Oxford in the late 1490's.[244] It might also be noted that in 1514, just after Erasmus left the university, two friars, aged nineteen, came to Cambridge: the Augustinian Robert Barnes and the Carmelite John Bale.

In his letter to John Watson in 1517 Erasmus recalled the Cambridge "evenings we spent in perfectly delightful talk—not a single boring word."[245] Erasmus was an accomplished talker, "polite and charming in society, without any air of superiority" (said Beat Bild),[246] and speaking very freely—"sometimes," Erasmus himself felt, "too much so."[247] In view of the amount of work he had assigned himself, how did he find time to fold his legs and have out his talk? The answer: a regular routine, never without variety. His monastic training surely gave him wisdom here. Some observations of Erasmus on the arranging of a life of study are found in a letter he wrote to a Paris pupil in 1497:

avoid nocturnal lucubrations, and studies at unseasonable times. They exhaust the mind and seriously affect the health. The dawn, beloved of the Muses, is the fit time for study. After dinner either play, or walk, or take part in cheerful conversation. Possibly even among these amusements some room may be found for improvement. Take as much food as is required, not for your pleasure, but for your health. Before supper take a short walk, and after supper do the same. Before going to bed read something exquisite and worth remembering, of which you will be thinking when overcome by sleep, and for which you ask yourself again when you

[243] Sometimes attributed to Tyndale; but see W. D. J. Cargill Thompson in *Harvard Theological Review* (January 1960).

[244] Latimer, in 1552, for instance, was to quote some of what he remembered of Stafford's exposition of Romans, chapter XII; and to mention Colet in the same paragraph (*Sermons*, 440).

[245] Letter 49.

[246] Nichols, I, 37.

[247] *Ibid.*, 12.

wake. Let this maxim of Pliny rest always in your mind: All your time is lost which you do not impart to study. Remember that nothing is more fugitive than youth, which, once it has flown away, never returns.[248]

Stephen Leacock, Professor of Economic and Political Science at McGill, got through a deal of work largely by rising at 5 A.M.; but, said his brother, "you never caught him at it." Also, Leacock wrote that he would sooner have written *Alice in Wonderland* than the whole *Encyclopædia Britannica*—to which he was an important contributor. How many of Erasmus' Cambridge colleagues would have sacrificed their lectures in the Schools to have written *The Praise of Folly*? How much of Erasmus' comic artistry, correcting vice by means of ridicule, did he employ in his battles with the Cambridge Scotists, his lectures to his pupils, his meetings with his colleagues, or his talk with his friends? Did he, like Lucian, give recitals of his Dialogues? We do not know. For us, the curtain lifts only once—when Erasmus wrote to Colet a description of a discussion with his colleagues:[249]

When I put forth a suggestion about a master for your school, in the presence of several Masters, a person of some reputation smiled and said: "Who would endure to spend his life in yon school, among children, if he was fit to choose where and how to spend his life?" I replied with a good deal of modesty that this function of bringing up youth in good manners and good literature seemed to me one of the most honourable; that Christ did not despise the very young, and that no age of man was more deserving of generous help, and nowhere could a richer harvest be anticipated, since the young are the growing crop and growing timber of the commonwealth; I added that all who are truly religious hold the view that no service is more likely to gain merit in God's eyes than the leading of children to Christ. He grimaced and sneered: "If anyone wished to serve Christ properly, he should enter a monastery and live as a religious"—

a hit, perhaps, below the fifth rib! (Erasmus being a refugee from the religious life.)

I replied that St. Paul defines true religion in terms of works of love; and love, says he, consists in helping our neighbours as best we may. He spurned this as a foolish remark. "Lo," he said, "*we* give up all; *there* perfection lieth." "That man has not forsaken everything," said I, "who, when he could help very many by his labours, refuses to undertake a duty because it is regarded as humble." And with this I took my leave of the fellow.

Scene, a Cambridge common room. Time, October 1511.

[248]*E.E.*, no. 56; tr. Nichols, I, 110. [249]Letter 11.

By 1514 Erasmus had become very conscious of "old age, sickness, and toil," of "the weakness of my flesh."[250] His picture of the rewards of the scholar, written before he went to Cambridge, is not very comfortable humour: "so many watchings, so much sweat, so much vexation and loss of sleep, the most precious of all things. Add to this the waste of health, spoil of complexion, weakness of eyes or rather blindness, poverty, envy, abstinence from pleasure, over-hasty old age, untimely death."[251] Much of this—sometimes all of it—has often been dismissed as the old-maidish meanderings of a fussy hypochondriac. That is not fair. Beat Bild, in his obituary notice of Erasmus, bore witness that "his constitution was extremely delicate, and easily affected by trifling changes, as of wine or food or climate."[252] And throughout his time at Cambridge Erasmus was a sick man. Indeed, in December 1511 Paola Bombace wrote to Queens' from Bologna mentioning that in Italy there had been rumours of his death;[253] in the summer of 1513 it was "officially" stated in Basle that he was dead—a rumour scotched in general by autumn 1513, but still believed in Vienna at the beginning of 1514. He is not dead, the rebuttal presumably ran; he is attached to some institution in East Anglia. It was the opinion of Allen that the gaps in his correspondence during 1512 and 1513 may be explained by illness.[254]

He arrived at Cambridge in August 1511 still not quite recovered from an attack of the sweating-sickness, which had struck him in London, probably in late July. "My health is still a little shaky," he wrote to Ammonio from Queens' in August, "as a result of that sweating-sickness."[255]

This curious epidemic—usually known as the English sweat (*Sudor anglicus*) because its first appearance was in England in 1485, causing the postponement of the coronation of Henry VII —was described later in the century by the French physician, Ambroise Paré:[256]

> The people strucken with it languishing, fell down in a swoon, and lying in their beds, sweat continually, having a fever, a frequent, quick, and unequal

---

[250] Letter 43. [251] *Praise of Folly*, 86.
[252] 1540; tr. Nichols, I, 36. [253] *E.E.*, no. 251.
[254] *E.E.*, I, 526. [255] Letter 2. [256] *Works*, 821.

pulse; neither did they leave sweating till the disease left them, which was in one or two days at the most; yet freed of it, they languished long after, they all had a beating or palpitation of the heart, which held some for two or three years, and others all their life after.

John Caius wrote a book on the Sweat in 1552.[257] He described it as a fever of "one natural day," which "for the sudden sharpness and unwonted cruelness passed the pestilence." The first symptoms were pains in the joints and general palpitations; with this, went wind and stomach upset, a disagreeable taste in the mouth, and severe headache. The danger point began with a "marvellous heaviness," an uncontrollable wish to sleep. Then came the fetid perspiration, of "ungentle savour," pouring from the whole body in streams. Caius recommended that the patient be put to bed as soon as possible and be very well covered—sometimes, apparently, people were sewn into their sheets, and the sheets sown to the bed, so that no air could reach them. For twenty-four hours the patient should never be left unattended. No heavy food should be given; at the fifth hour the patient might drink some hot white wine, or milk and vinegar, and be gently massaged under the bed coverings. According to Caius, the fourteenth hour was "the last of trial and danger." But "many die after by too much boldness, when they think themselves most in surety, or negligence in attendance, when they think no necessity." The main thing was to prevent the patient's going to sleep—beat him with a rosemary branch, said Caius, or pull his ears and nose. If all went well there would be a "continual sweating the whole day and out of all parts," with a "lightness and cheerfulness of the body and lankness in all parts." But there might, if bad luck prevailed, be a bad sweat, discoloured and irritating. After the twenty-four hours, the patient might leave his bed, and begin convalescence, staying indoors for at least three days. Relapses were frequent, and the "sweat" could be caught many times.

This was a killing fever. Its last recorded appearance was in 1551, when during one July week 750 Londoners died of it, some in one or two hours. (By mid-August, contemporaries said, two thousand had died of the sweat in London and two hundred in

[257]This treatise was included in Hecker's *Epidemics of the Middle Ages.* I have incorporated details from Hecker's own essay, written in 1834.

Cambridge.[258]) More directly relevant to our story, Andrea Ammonio was killed by it, after eight hours, in 1517.

Erasmus was lucky, then, not to have died in the summer of 1511.

The Cambridge climate was notoriously bad for the health. Christopher Hales wrote to Bullinger from London in 1550: "the University of Oxford is not to be compared with that of Paris, or the schools of Italy; but still it is one in which a studious youth may be occupied with great advantage. The same is to be said of Cambridge, but I rather recommend Oxford on account of the greater salubrity of the air. Cambridge, by reason of the neighbouring Fen, is much exposed to fever, as I have experienced more frequently than I could wish."[259] William Harrison, educated at both Oxford and Cambridge, was to write, in the 1570's, that Cambridge "is somewhat near unto the fens, whereby the wholesomeness of the air is not a little corrupted." He mentioned that wood and coal tended to be scarce, as they had to be brought up the Cam.[260] After Erasmus had been at the university for two months, the fenland winter came on. At the beginning of November—after days of pouring rain—he was so hoarse that he had to "speak by nods and gestures."[261] Throughout November, illness prevented his dealing adequately with his correspondence or his work.

Then, in December, there was a worse blow. Ever since his visit to Venice in 1508,[262] when he was about forty, Erasmus had suffered from the stone. In 1514 he sent to the prior of Steyn some reasons why he did not wish to return to Holland. Among them was this consideration: "For several years now I have been a prey to the stone, a most troublesome and dangerous ailment; . . . I can't stand every kind of food, or even any and every climate; for this sickness of mine recurs so readily that I have to be extremely temperate in my habits, and I know the Dutch climate."[263] On December 8, 1511, Erasmus wrote from Cambridge: "I was brought painfully to bed, whereupon I was delivered of several large rocks."[264] Bladder stones, probably,

[258] *Original Letters: English Reformation*, II, 727.
[259] *Ibid.*, I, 190.
[260] *Description of England* (1577), Bk. II, chap. VI.
[261] Letter 12.
[262] Nichols, I, 438.
[263] Letter 43.
[264] Letter 23.

passed naturally—without surgery; by means of external bathing or massage, or, if that proved insufficient, by the injection of olive oil or some sort of lubricating syrup into the urethra. Such stones could be the width of a match stick, and up to a quarter of an inch long. The symptoms, needless to say, were agonizing. Paré wrote: "a most grievous pain torments the patient in making water, which he is forced to show by stamping with his feet, bending of his whole body, and the grinding of his teeth."[265]

Just over two years later, in his last Cambridge letter (January 1514), a further and more serious attack was mentioned: "A dangerous grapple with the stone, the worst he has ever suffered, has befallen your friend Erasmus. He has got into the hands of surgeons and apothecaries (*medicorum et pharmacopolarum*), alias butchers and harpies. I'm still in the throes of labour: the pest is still lodged inside my ribs, and when or what the issue will be is unknown."[266] If this was urinary lithiasis, a bladder stone, it is just possible that Erasmus was operated on. Cutting operations for stones in the kidney or the gall bladder, however, are relatively modern. Such an operation could not in theory be performed by an ordinary medical graduate: the Hippocratic Oath includes the undertaking "I will not use the knife, not even on sufferers from stone, but I will place to such as are craftsmen therein."[267] Would there have been such a "craftsman" in Cam-

[265]*Works* (English version, 1634), 664–80, deal with the stone. Paré's works appeared in French in 1575. For a list of pharmaceutical remedies prescribed for the stone in the sixteenth century—barley water, syrup of vinegar, alum, conserved cherries, and so on—see Emmison, *Tudor Secretary*, 252–3, 320–1.

[266]Letter 39. Erasmus was a difficult patient. In 1527 in Basle he came under the care of the German physician Theophrastus Bombast (1493–1541), who gave himself the name Paracelsus. Erasmus wrote to him in that year: "I have no time these days to take a course of treatment, to be an invalid, even to die, I am so overwhelmed with the toil of study. If however there is anything this side of a bodily dissolution which can moderate the illness, pray tell it to me" (*E.E.*, no. 1,809); he had been suffering from pain in the liver and from a diseased kidney—the signs of which he said he had detected in his urine several years ago. (See W. A. Murray, "Erasmus and Paracelsus," *Bibliothèque d'Humanisme et Renaissance*, XX [Geneva, 1958], 560–4.)

[267]"Even if the oath is admitted to be genuinely Hippocratic, which is far from certain, the difficulty remains that the authors of the Hippocratic collection appear to have no scruples about performing operations. It has been suggested that the mention of the stone hides a reference to castration, abhorrent to the Greeks but more acceptable to earlier Christians, who, with their admiration of celibacy, omitted the provision from their version of the oath" (F. R. Jevons, in the *Guardian*, April 8, 1961).

bridge in 1514?—a decent barber-surgeon, as distinct from the roaming stone-cutters who were among the mountebanks of the period? One wishes (as so often) that Erasmus had gone into more detail. It would seem rather unlikely that Erasmus was cut for the stone, if only because the operation was so dangerous and unpleasant (and expensive) that he would surely have mentioned it. It is also uncertain, from his words in the letter, whether the stone was in the bladder or elsewhere. However, if there were such an operation in Queens' it would have been almost precisely the same as that described by the Roman medical expert Celsus in the first century A.D.:[268] the so-called Apparatus Minor, requiring only a knife and a hook; the description is almost intolerable to read, so painful and uncertain must the operation have been—the fingers into the anus, the cut into the neck of the bladder, the stone extracted by the scoop, the sudden plunge into a bath of vinegar and salt. New methods of lithotomy did not begin to be experimented with until after 1520.

William Turner of Pembroke, "the true pioneer of natural science in England,"[269] thought that the stone was especially bred by "those meats and drinks that are of grosser substance and hotter than others be."[270] Wine under five years old he considered,

> very ill for them that are disposed to the stone, for it, having so much thick earthliness in it, giveth matter whereof the stone may be made in hot kidneys, that the heat of the kidneys may so bake it into stones as the heat of the brick kiln turneth the clay into brick or tile stones. Wherefore I must needs dispraise the manner of our delicate Englishmen and women that drink the Rhenish wine only for pleasure, whilst it is as yet as thick as puddle or horsepiss.[271]

---

[268]Celsus, *De Medicina*, tr. W. G. Spencer (Loeb Classical Library, III, 1938), 427–47. This work was first printed in Florence in 1478. Drawings of the operation may be found in Laurence Heister, *A General System of Surgery* (London, 1743), plates 28 and 29. Ambroise Paré dealt with the stone, in a section of his *Works* translated into English in 1634 by Thomas Johnson (664–80). Modern historical accounts include H. S. Shelley, "Cutting for the Stone," *Journal of the History of Medicine*, XIII (New Haven, 1958), 50–67; and H. W. Badenoch, "Cutting for the Stone," *St. Bartholomew's Hospital Journal*, LIX (April 1955), 90–95. I am indebted to Professor W. I. C. Morris and Dr. William Brockbank, both of Manchester, for drawing my attention to these works.

[269]C. E. Raven, *English Naturalists from Neckham to Ray*, 127.

[270]*A Book of Wines*, 18–19.

[271]*Ibid.*, 13.

Turner himself suffered from the stone; and he thought that well-matured white Rhine wine, not too alcoholic, was the best thing to drink: "small and waterish white wines." To illustrate this point he introduced a Cambridge touch. Such white wines, he said, drive "humours" into the "kidneys, water vessels and bladder . . . yet do they not leave them sticking fast in those places, but they drive them quite through all the water vessels into the chamber pot or urinal." That is to say, they do not

> bring many humours whereof the stone is made, to the kidneys and bladder, and let them lie there, as it were rotting in a dung hill: but as a fair and thin water cast into a canal of a street if it have one to drive it forward, not only carries itself away forth from the town into the common sink that is without the town, but also the filthiness that hath been in the canal long before.

He was thinking probably, of the King's Ditch, which ran hard by his own college. He went on to talk about Butchery Row (now Guildhall Street) and Slaughterhouse Lane (the present Corn Exchange St.), in the late 1520's:

> when I was a scholar at Cambridge, there was there a stinking butchery, and very noisome to them that went by it or through it. What if a man should have been hired for forty shillings in the year to keep the butchery and the rest of the town sweet by carrying out the puddings, guts, and stinking blood.

Well, that employee would not be considered very efficient if all he did was to "carry out all the filthiness out of the butchery once in the week unto the Market Hill and let it lie there." Nor would it be a good idea if this "master of the pudding-cart before named would let the filthiness of the butchery tarry so long there, until it stank so sore" that "both they of the butchery and all the neighbours about, were grievously vexed with the foul stink of that filth that tarried so long there." What he must do is "every second day to carry out all the uncleanness of the town."[272] And such was the purging effect of mature white German wine!

Erasmus, one imagines, on his rides round Cambridge, would have avoided Butchery Row or Slaughterhouse Lane. "How fragrant your slaughter-houses smell is very plainly seen, by people stopping their noses when they pass by them, and that they had

[272] *Ibid.*, 33–5.

rather have ten bawds for their neighbours than one butcher"—so says the Fishmonger to the Butcher in Erasmus' dialogue "Of the Eating of Fish." (The Butcher retaliates: "It may be some nice beau or other may stop his nose as he passes by a butcher's shop: but nobody can bear to be in the boat where your salt-fish is.")[273] There had been laid down certain regulations for slaughtering and the cleaning of ditches in Cambridge in 1503. John Foxe, who thought "clemency the gentlest affection of our nature" wrote of himself to Elizabeth I in 1575: "such is my disposition (I will say this of myself, foolishly perhaps, but truly) that I can scarce pass the shambles where beasts are slaughtered, but that my mind secretly recoils with a feeling of pain."[274] Erasmus would have sympathized.

The Turner thesis about the relation of wine and stone serves to introduce the much misunderstood question of Erasmus' aversion to the Cambridge beer. After being at Queens' for about a week he wrote: "The beer in this place doesn't suit me at all, and the wines aren't quite satisfactory either."[275] Some have countered with the opposite opinion of Samuel Pepys in 1668: "I walked to Magdalene College and there into the buttery, as a stranger, and there drank my bellyfull of their beer, which pleased me as the best I ever drank."[276] How absurd of Erasmus not to think so! The whim, the argument runs, of a finicky foreigner. (Dr. John Caius, however, thought that the immoderate beer-drinking of the English was a principal cause of the English Sweat.) The myth was dutifully kept up by Erasmus' friends. In November 1513 Ammonio wrote that he had been told "that you had indeed left Cambridge because of the plague and withdrawn somewhere or other"—to the Gonnell household at Landbeach, in fact—"but that since you were in difficulties, he said, because of the shortage of wine, and you thought the want of that was worse than the plague, you had gone back to Cambridge and were now there. Ah, what a mighty champion of Bacchus thou art."[277] That was amusing enough, and Erasmus would have appreciated it. But

[273] *Colloquies*, II, 41–2.
[274] Quoted by Gordon Rupp, *Six Makers of English Religion*, 62.
[275] Letter 2.
[276] Pepys, *Diary*, May 25, 1668.
[277] Letter 35.

that was also six weeks before his second serious attack of pain from the stone. And he himself commented: "I suspect that this sickness of mine is due to the beer which, for lack of wine, I've been drinking for some time."[278] He repeated the point in a letter of July 1514: "For several years now I have been a prey to the stone, a most troublesome and dangerous ailment; and for several years I have drunk nothing but wine, and only selected wine–unavoidably, because of my infirmity."[279]

In all things, look to the Greek. And in his first letter to Ammonio from Queens' Erasmus asked for "a cask of Greek wine, the best obtainable," to be sent up from London. "The best obtainable"–that was a hit at the Cambridge vintners. As it happens, Queens' was noted for its careful taste in wines. The accounts survive for July 1511 of the local vintner Thomas Marshall, a friend of Garrett Godfrey:[280] Queens' was his best customer, and the Fellows drank not white claret at 1*d.* a pint (the choice of Pembroke) but malmsey–or what passed for malmsey at 2*d.* a pint. (Rhine wine, if Marshall stocked it, would have been 1½*d.* a pint). It is probable that the wine Erasmus wanted from London was a malmsey, but of higher quality than Marshall's. Malmsey was one of the "high and yellowish wines" to be recommended by an Elizabethan authority as "wonderful wholesome in the winter time" for "aged persons,"[281] a wine from the sweet and juicy white Malvasia grape of Greece, transplanted to Crete, and the product shipped thence by the Venetians; Erasmus had acquired the taste in Venice. (Modern

[278]Letter 39.

[279]Letter 43.

[280]Printed by Ellis Minns in *Proceedings of the Cambridge Antiquarian Society*, XXXIV (1934), 50–8. For comparative wine prices in England at this time, see the table at the end of volume II of Simon's *History of the Wine Trade in England*, 272. A butt of malmsey such as that in which the Duke of Clarence met his end cost from £4. 6*s.* 8*d.* to £6. 12*s.* 0*d.*; a butt was supposed to hold 140 gallons. Marshall was in order in charging 1*s.* 4*d.* a gallon for malmsey. The wine was probably decanted into such a bottle as Holbein painted in his 1523 portrait of Erasmus.

[281]William Vaughan, *Directions for health, natural and artificial* (1600); quoted by Simon, *Drink*, 53. Vaughan also said that such Cretan wines are "only for married folks, because they strengthen the back." It is instructive to note in passing that in the Toronto University Library books about wine are classified under "Agriculture: Crops"; in the Cambridge University Library, under "Useful Arts."

malmsey comes from Cyprus and the Canaries; madeira is also from the malvasia grape, but is now fortified.) Erasmus asked for "quite dry wine." Relatively dry, that is to say—like the modern malvasia of Sardinia or the *malvasia bianca* of the Napa Valley, California. It was an expensive taste—like, say, asking for Kentucky bourbon in Toronto.

The Greek wine was accordingly sent up to Cambridge from London, in wooden casks holding, perhaps, three gallons. And this is perhaps the most famous theme in the story of Erasmus' stay in Cambridge. The first cask arrived in the middle of September 1511 and was "very welcome," though rather smaller than Erasmus had expected. He drank the contents in three weeks and sent the empty cask back to London on October 20. Ammonio had it refilled and returned it on October 27—but it did not arrive until November 10: unsealed, discoloured, and half consumed. The cask was back in London by the beginning of December. When Erasmus returned to Cambridge from a visit to London in February 1512, a third consignment of wine awaited him; but again the malmsey was spoilt—vinegary, one assumes. The fourth cask we know of was sent by Ammonio at the end of November 1513: "a gift of Cretan wine; small is the vessel, yet it containeth that which Jupiter, in the days of his childish nurture in that very Isle, piss'd from his own little penis."[282]

That was the sort of joke Erasmus rather enjoyed.

VII

IN THE AUTUMN OF 1517, three and a half years after Erasmus had left Cambridge, the university acquired a new lecturer in Greek: Richard Croke, aged twenty-eight.

Croke is the most important of Erasmus' Cambridge friends, although they never met there. He had gone to Eton in 1501, and up to King's, when he was seventeen, in April 1506, three weeks before the royal visit to Cambridge. At King's Croke was taught

[282]Letter 35.

by Robert Hacomblen, who, though he was not a man of the New Learning like Provost Doggett (who died in 1499), or John Argentine, who was Provost when Croke was an undergraduate, had attempted a translation from Aristotle, with a commentary. Croke commenced B.A. in 1509, the year when Hacomblen was elected Provost. And Croke then returned to London, to study with William Grocin in the rectory of St. Lawrence Jewry; he could have met Erasmus here, as early as the winter of 1509.

Next, Croke went to Paris. He continued to study Greek, under Erasmus' Venetian friend Girolamo Aleandro, who had been teaching Greek at the university since April 1509. When Erasmus crossed to Paris in the spring of 1511 to see to the publication of *The Praise of Folly* his main helper with the proofs was Richard Croke. And after Erasmus arrived in Cambridge, he wrote to Colet in September to ask him to send some money to Croke, "a young man of good promise."[283] Colet refused; perhaps he was tired of Erasmus' "dear boys."

From Paris Croke went on to Louvain and Cologne; and then, in 1515, when he was twenty-six, he was appointed by the University of Leipzig as its first lecturer in Greek. Sir John Sheppard, in a short study of Croke,[284] quoted some tributes to the lectures at Leipzig, including one by the Dutchman Conrad Muth (an alumnus of Deventer):

> Croke, the Briton—for that is how he describes himself, thought his facility of language and his Greek behaviour make him appear a very Greek—because he reads Theocritus most charmingly, and has a tripping, graceful tongue—has been taking holiday with me, praising Grocin, Aleandro, and I know not what other masters.

At the end of his period at Leipzig, in 1516 and 1517, Croke published two books there: an edition of Book IV of the Greek grammar of Gaza, and his own *Tabulae Graecas Literas Compendio*. Then Cambridge called him home.

In September 1517 he took the degree of M.A. in Cambridge; and in April 1518 Erasmus wrote to congratulate him on his appointment as lecturer in Greek.[285] Croke's first Cambridge lec-

[283]Letter 3.
[284]*Richard Croke*. See also Fairbank and Dickin, *Italic Hand*.
[285]Letter 58.

tures showed that his Master's voice was to echo once more, by proxy, round the lecture halls of the Schools Quadrangle:

I approve of John the Canonist; I admire Thomas; with a kiss I greet the subtlety of Scotus, which has resolved so many ambiguities of argument, concerning horns and crocodiles, with no less certainty and credit, and indeed utility, than he who, in the presence of great Alexander, threw grains of chick-pea onto a needle's point and never missed his throw.

A careful application to such niceties, Croke continued,

if pushed to the extreme, diminishes and narrows the intelligence, and generally draws the mind away from things more useful—I mean, from the Epistles of St. Paul, from the Gospels, and the Scriptures, which by all means a theologian ought thoroughly to learn, because it is his task to form men's minds, to summon them away from earthly things and raise them to the heavenly. And this will better be effected by Christ's precepts than by such ingenuities.

That inaugural lecture on the advantages of Greek literature was printed, with a second Cambridge oration, at Paris in 1520.[286] The second lecture was in the same vein:

Those persons who have never read Augustine or Jerome, no, nor the Epistles of St. Paul! They think they have shown themselves sufficiently fine preachers if they can fill up their allotted time—or stretch it—so that they themselves grow hoarse with shouting and we exhausted with the listening to folly.

Croke was concerned that the "gentlemen of Cambridge" should bring their whole minds to bear on the study of Greek. "The Oxford men, whom up to the present time you have outstripped in every department of knowledge, are betaking themselves to Greek in good earnest": they number among their leaders Grocin, Linacre, Tunstall, More, Pace—all "commended by Erasmus himself, unsurpassed as a judge of learning,—Erasmus! once, would he were still, your own Greek professor!" Therefore, "gentlemen of Cambridge, you must keep your vigils and breathe the smoke of the lamp."[287]

At the beginning of 1520, there came to Cambridge the German printer and bookseller John Laer, known as John Siberch, from Siegburg, near Bonn. Siberch had obtained from the university a loan of £20—quite a large sum; and the man most responsible

[286] *Orationes Ricardi Croci Duae*. Translations by Sir John Sheppard.

[287] From the inaugural oration, reported in full in Mullinger, *University of Cambridge*, I, 529–37; quotations from pp. 534–5.

for his coming was Richard Croke, "the principal initiator of Siberch's press."[288] During 1520 Siberch issued at Cambridge a book which had been printed for him in Cologne, and the sheets shipped over: Richard Croke's *Introductiones ad Rudimenta Graeca.*[289] Siberch printed at least ten books at Cambridge.[290] The first was the oration delivered by Henry Bullock on the occasion of Wolsey's visit to the university in 1520. The second, a Latin translation of a work of Lucian; the translation was by Henry Bullock, and Siberch included in the book a few lines set in Greek type—he used Greek type, in a small way, in six of his Cambridge books, the first printer so to do in England. Next came a work by Erasmus: the *De Conscribendis Epistolis,* printed from the manuscript belonging to Bullock.[291]

So the first Cambridge Press was a manifestation of the influence of the Croke-Bullock group in Cambridge—the Erasmians. Siberch, *typographus universitatis,* lived in The King's Arms, a house belonging to Michaelhouse, on the present site of the Waterhouse Court of Gonville and Caius; Dr. Caius bought the property in 1564.[292] It seems, from a letter of Robert Aldrich,[293] that Siberch was still in Cambridge at the end of 1526.

In 1522 Croke was appointed the first Public Orator. And in 1523 he became lecturer in Greek at St. John's, an appointment which confirmed the classical emphasis in that house. One of his colleagues, elected to a Fellowship in 1522, was George Day (1501–56), later Public Orator (1528–37), Master of the College (1537–8) and Provost of King's (1538–49). In 1524 Robert Pem-

288Goldschmidt, *First Cambridge Press,* 44.

289A fragment of the manuscript of this work, belonging to Siberch, is illustrated in Gray, *Earlier Cambridge Stationers,* plate XXV.

290Until 1949 the number was thought to be nine. Then, in an article in the *Transactions of the Cambridge Bibliographical Society,* F. S. Ferguson printed a report on a fragment of a tenth book Siberch printed at Cambridge. In December 1952, in the *Bodleian Library Record,* IV (3), D. M. Rogers discussed an Indulgence printed by the Siberch Press about 1523, and discovered as a waste sheet in a binding of the late 1520's—a binding by Nicholas Spering—"An Indulgence printed by John Siberch." Thus Siberch's output as a printer at Cambridge may now be put at eleven known pieces.

291The copy of the Siberch edition of this work in the library of Corpus has a binding by Nicholas Spering of Cambridge. Another copy was bought in 1951 by the Bodleian, which has the largest Siberch collection.

292Caius, *Annals,* 125.

293Letter 63.

ber, another future Greek scholar, was elected to a Fellowship at St. John's; and in that year also came up to the college John Redman, later to be the last Master of King's Hall (1542–46) and the first Master of Trinity (1546–51).

In 1526 there matriculated from St. John's a Cambridge boy who was to be the most distinguished of the Johnian Greeks—John Cheke. Cheke was born in 1514, the year when Erasmus left Cambridge, in a house (so tradition has it) on the corner of Market Hill and Petty Cury. His father, Peter Cheke, had been an Esquire Bedell of the university; his mother, Agnes Dufford (or Duffield) belonged to a well-known Cambridge family from the parish of St. Botolph's; her father, William, a Cambridge graduate, had a house and garden near Queens', which Peter and Agnes sold in 1524.[294] John's tutor at St. John's was George Day. He was elected Fellow in 1530; and he remained at the college until 1544, when he became tutor to Prince Edward.

In 1530 then, the Fellows of St. John's included Richard Croke, John Cheke, John Redman, Robert Pember, and George Day. And among the freshmen of that year were Thomas Watson (1513–84), later Fellow (1535), Master (1553–4), and Bishop of Lincoln (1556–9); and a Yorkshire boy, Roger Ascham (1515–68), who was elected to a Fellowship in 1534, and to a Greek lectureship at the college in 1538. Ascham remained in Cambridge until 1548, when he became tutor to the Princess Elizabeth. Cheke was in Cambridge till 1544; Thomas Smith until 1547; Watson till 1554; and Ascham's King's friend Walter Haddon (who had gone up to the college from Eton in 1533) until the 1550's. Cheke, in fact, returned to Cambridge in April 1549 as Provost of King's, to which office he had been nominated by Edward in October 1548; he remained there until October 1553. Thus to Roger Ascham the "good old days" in Cambridge were between, say, 1534 and 1548; he wrote in the 1560's:

> These men of worthy memory, M. Redman, M. Cheke, M. Smith, M. Haddon, M. Watson, put so to their helping hands, as that university and all students there, as long as learning shall last, shall be bound unto them if that trade in study be truly followed, which these men left behind them there.[295]

[294] Queens' College Muniment Room MS.

[295] *English Works*, 278.

Ascham, as he tells us in his *Toxophilus* (1544), had been told tales of Erasmus' Cambridge days by Garrett Godfrey. His own work pays frequent tribute to "Erasmus, the honour of learning of all our time."[296] And by Ascham's day the ideals of Erasmus had made their point in Cambridge. The Royal Injunctions of 1535 ordered each college to provide daily a lecture in both Greek and Latin. In the same year it was also officially laid down that the university as a whole should definitely maintain a public lecture in either Greek or Hebrew—which, the permanent residents in the university (gremials) could decide.[297] In 1540 came the founding of the five Regius Professorships: John Cheke was appointed Regius Professor of Greek.

Bullock had written to Erasmus in 1516 that "at Cambridge, men are devoting themselves ardently to Greek literature."[298] They were also falling under the spell of Erasmus. In 1530 John Caius, an undergraduate at Gonville Hall, translated some short works of Erasmus into English, for his own pleasure, including the six-page Paraphrase on the Epistle of Jude, and some of the *Ratio Verae Theologiae* (1519).[299] Caius also studied Greek in Cambridge, for when he went to Padua in 1539, when he was just under thirty, he lectured on the Greek text of Aristotle; and while in Italy he searched for accurate manuscripts of Hippocrates and Galen, just as Erasmus, in his day, had ransacked the libraries for uncorrupted texts: *fontes purissimi.*

The enthusiasm of some of that group of Cambridge scholars in the 1530's and the 1540's is conveyed in the pages of Roger Ascham. By the late 1530's there was (he wrote in the 1560's)[300]

> such a company of fellows and scholars in St. John's College as can scarce be found now in some whole university: which either for divinity on the one side or other, or for civil service to their prince and country, have been and are yet to this day, notable ornaments to this whole realm.

---

[296]*Ibid.*, 215.

[297]Dr. Legh's Injunctions, Heywood, *Statutes*, 198.

[298]Letter 51.

[299]Caius said this in his *Counsel Against the Sweat* (1552); printed in Hecker, *Epidemics of the Middle Ages.*

[300]Ascham, *English Works*, 280. R. R. Bolgar warns us that Ascham was writing about a small group of his friends, and that his account is probably exaggerated (*Classical Heritage*, 370).

There was, indeed, an interlude in Cambridge, the reign of Mary, when

> Old sophistry (I say not well: not old, but that new rotten sophistry) began to beard and shoulder logic in her own tongue; yea, I know, that heads were cast together and counsel devised that Duns, with all the rabble of barbarous questionists, should have dispossessed of their place and rooms Aristotle, Plato, Tully and Demosthenes, when good M. Redman, and those two worthy stars of that University, M. Cheke and M. Smith, with their scholars, had brought to flourish as notable in Cambridge, as ever they did in Greece and Italy.[301]

"All which miseries, at length, by God's providence, had their end 16 November 1558."[302] For Ascham John Cheke was *il maestro di color che sanno*: "my dearest friend and best master that ever I had or heard in learning."[303]

A later Tudor Johnian, Thomas Nashe, who went up to the college in the early 1580's, named among his "models of learning" John Cheke, Thomas Watson, John Redman, and Roger Ascham.[304] All except Watson were by then dead. But they were for Nashe, as they had been for Ascham, scholars "given to New Learning."

Nashe was in the tradition of those Cambridge men who, as young students, had heard from Garrett Godfrey stories of Erasmus, riding his horse on the Market Hill when he was "sore at his book."

VIII

"BY EMENDING THE New Testament, and by your notes on it, you have shed marvellous light on Christ:" thus John Watson of Peterhouse, writing to Erasmus from Cambridge in the summer of 1516.[305] In the same summer Erasmus reminded Henry Bullock that theology was being "recalled to the true sources"[306]—a benefit

[301] *Ibid.*, 281.
[302] *Ibid.*, 282.
[303] *Ibid.*, 297.
[304] Preface to Robert Greene's "Menaphon," 1589; *Works of Nashe*, III, 318.
[305] Letter 48.
[306] Letter 52.

not unappreciated in Cambridge, where Fisher and the Lady Margaret had furthered the training of divines "equipped for the sober preaching of the word of God";[307] divines such as Bullock himself, who began in the autumn of 1516 to lecture on St. Matthew with Erasmus' notes as guide,[308] having been also successfully preaching "Christ in purity" with "no boast or show of merely human subtleties."[309] The hopes of that exciting summer —that "we should see verily within a few years a true and godly kind of Christian spring up in every place, which would not only in ceremonies disputations and titles profess the name of Christ, but in their very heart and true conversation of living"[310]—were soon to be dispelled. Within five years the chill had descended, and the mists. Luther's works were burnt in Cambridge in the spring of 1521; even then he had over seventy titles to his credit. But for a brief moment in time, without controversy, the Cam had reflected the mellow light of the Dutch School, of the Brethren of the Common Life and the *Devotio Moderna.*

Robert Barnes, Prior of the Cambridge Augustinian Friars, was to convert Erasmus' tilts at the Christian Pharisees into a savage indignation—for example, in his sermon in St. Edward's Church on Christmas Eve 1525: "Judas sold our Master but once; you sell him as oft as he cometh into your hands"[311]—marring his almost Miltonic zest by a dwelling upon personalities (he could not resist a thrust at Dr. Robert Ridley, prebendary of St. Paul's, who was in the congregation, his nephew Nicholas having recently been elected to a Fellowship at Pembroke). And Barnes' interpretation of "the truth" and "the very gospel of God" was not that of Henry Bullock, who wrote against Luther in the Cambridge of the 1520's, or of Richard Croke, who was to be a witness against Cranmer in the Oxford of the 1550's.

"Remember ye not," asked William Tyndale of Thomas More in 1531, "how in our time, of all that taught grammar in England not one understood the Latin tongue? How came we then by that Latin tongue again?" The answer was simple: "out of the old

[307] Letter 46.
[308] Letter 53.
[309] Letter 52.
[310] *Exhortation* (English Translation 1529). No paging.
[311] *Works,* 211.

authors." And in the same way, the argument ran, we are again coming to the true faith. This was the imperative which appealed to some (maybe most) of the Cambridge intellectuals of the 1520's; and it was, in the event, irresistible (in spite of More's point that the faith is "perpetually taught unto His Church," and is not to be interpreted in terms of Latin grammar "like as master Lily late master of Paul's School brought up in London the right order in teaching of grammar and learning of the Latin tongue"[312]). The scriptures, wrote Hugh Latimer in 1531,[313] shortly after leaving Cambridge, are the "new learning": as the fathers are "new doctors," the text of Aristotle "new philosophy," and Cicero "new Latin."

William Whitaker, Master of St. John's and Regius Professor of Divinity, lecturing in Cambridge in the late 1580's, gave two reasons for honouring the influence of Erasmus on the Biblical theology of the English Reformation. First, Erasmus taught the Reformers to go beyond the "Latin streamlet" of the Vulgate to the "ancient well-spring" of Greek.[314] Second, he pressed for a vernacular Bible to be "read by the people":[315] most movingly, we must add, in the preface to the 1516 New Testament, expanded in later editions, and published in English in 1529. "The scripture of Christ should be translated into all tongues that it may be read diligently of the private and secular men and women." The hungry sheep must be fed. "I would to God the ploughman (*agricola*) would sing a text of the scripture at his ploughbeam, and that the weaver at his loom with this would drive away the tediousness of time. I would the wayfaring man with this pastime would expel the weariness of his journey. And to be short I would that all the communication (*colloquia*) of the Christian should be of the scripture":[316] "the unlearned and rude multitude which Christ died for ought to be provided for."[317] Bishop Jewel's memorable variations in the 1560's on the theme of the "poor simple people,"[318] the "ignorant and unlearned sort of people, that offend of simplicity, and have a zeal of God, although it be not according to knowledge,"[319] the "common sort of the lay

[312] More, *Confutation*, Part II, ccccci–ii.
[313] *Remains*, 319.
[314] *Disputation*, 157, 207.
[315] *Ibid.*, 249.
[316] *Exhortation.*
[317] *Enchiridion* (1518 Preface), 5.
[318] *Works*, II, 675.
[319] *Ibid.*, 997.

people,"[320] "children, and women, and servants, and men of the country"[321]— that was a strand of Anglicanism, often unacknowledged, which owed much to Erasmus.

But the influence of Erasmus on the Tudor Englishman's understanding of the scriptures goes further. William Tyndale translated into English in the early 1520's Erasmus' *Enchiridion Militis Christiani*,[322] written in 1502, with its emphasis on the "spiritual sense" of scripture—the "mystery," "full of pleasure and sweet juice," behind the "literal sense": the literal sense being the "cod," the "outer rind," "hard and unsavoury" (p. 60). The letter killeth: "Neither I think any other thing to be the cause why we see the charitable living of our monks and cloisterers to fail everywhere, to be so cold, so slacked, so faint and so to vanish away, but that they continue all their life and wax old in the letter and never enforce to come to the spiritual knowledge of scripture, neither hear they Christ crying in the gospel: the flesh, that is to say the letter, or that ye see outward, profiteth not at all. It is the spirit within that quickeneth or giveth life" (p. 68). And so, "of the interpreters of scripture, choose them above all other that go furtherest from the letter, which chiefly next after Paul be Origen, Ambrose, Jerome and Augustine. For I see the divines of latter time stick very much in the letter" (p. 66).

Thus Erasmus. Tyndale, as he developed his opinions in the 1520's, drew away in some respects from the *Enchiridion*. Under the Oxford influence of Colet, Erasmus had included the pseudo-Dionysius among his guides to scripture (p. 147), and paid tribute to "the followers of Plato" (p. 145); also, Tyndale was suspicious of the Origen tradition of scripture interpretation, which went against "the order and process of the text,"[323] and brought in an abundance of allegories and the mists of a "mystical sense."[324] But they continued to have much in common: a conviction that "the scripture corrupt with glosses is no more

[320] *Ibid.*, 676.
[321] *Works*, IV, 1187.
[322] Published 1533, with "a new and marvellous profitable preface"—of August 1518 (*E.E.*, no. 858).
[323] *Doctrinal Treatises*, 307.
[324] *Answer to More*, 111.

God's word";[325] a desire "to bring the scripture unto the right sense and to dig again the wells of Abraham and to purge and cleanse them of the earth of worldly wisdom";[326] a suspicion of "the literal sense which killeth"[327]—the words are Tyndale: they could be Erasmus. We must look, said Tyndale, for the "right" sense of the scripture: the "plain,"[328] "simple"[329] sense, found by critical comparison, by "the process of the text or by a like text of another place."[330] What William Fulke, Master of Pembroke, was to call in 1580 the "true and natural sense," the "most plain meaning of the speaker."[331] (Confusingly, Tyndale called this "right" sense the "literal sense": the literal sense of "look ere thou leap" being "do nothing suddenly or without advisement."[332]) And there is a "spiritual understanding of the text"[333] understanding by the Spirit, in the heart, in love and faith; without this, all scriptural study is barren dispute about words. "God is a spirit and all his works are spiritual. His literal sense is spiritual and all his words are spiritual."[334] And so, throughout the writings of the English Reformers, there is present an awareness of the dangers of a literal, "carnal" understanding of "spiritual words": what George Joye called in 1533 the "strange Thomistical sense from the flat letter."[335]

Again, here is Erasmus on the use of secular learning in Christian scholarship: "pick and choose out of the books of the Gentiles of everything the best: and also if thou by the example of the bee, flying round about by the gardens of old authors shall suck out only the wholesome and sweet juice (the poison refused and left behind) thy mind shall be better apparelled."[336] And here is Tyndale in 1528: "if they go abroad and walk by the fields and meadows of all manner doctors and philosophers, they could catch no harm: they should discern the poison from the honey and bring home nothing but that which is wholesome."[337]

325*Expositions*, 72.
326*Doctrinal Treatises*, 46.
327*Expositions*, 72.
328*Doctrinal Treatises*, 399.
329*Ibid.*, 393.
330*Ibid.*, 305.
331*Answers*, 281, 272.
332*Doctrinal Treatises*, 304–5.
333*Ibid.*, 312.
334*Ibid.*, 309.
335In Tyndale, *Answer to More*, 244.
336*Enchiridion*, 70.
337*Obedience of a Christian Man, Doctrinal Treatises*, 156. In the preface Tyndale advised the reader to consult Erasmus' *Paraclesis* and his Paraphrase of Matthew (161–2).

The early Cambridge Lutherans and Zwinglians, then, often caught and held the Erasmian note. We hear it in a 1532 description of the Day of Judgement by the Etonian John Frith, who became a B.A. of King's in 1525: "He shall ask you, whether you have fed the hungry and given drink to the thirsty, and not whether you have builded abbeys and chantries. He shall ask you whether you have harboured the harbourless and clothed the naked, and not whether you have gilded images or given copes to churches. He shall ask you whether you have visited the sick, and gone to the prisoners, and not whether you have gone a pilgrimage to Walsingham or Canturbury."[338] It is only a short step from Frith's trenchant tale of the abbot who rebuked the inordinately contemplative monk—"You must needs work, for Mary hath need of Martha"[339]—to Tyndale's dislike of a fugitive and cloistered virtue. "He that bideth in the world, as monks call it, hath more faith than the cloisterer; for he hangeth on God in all things. He must trust God to send him good speed, good luck, favour, help, a good master, a good neighbour, a good servant, a good wife, a good chapman-merchant, to send his merchandise safe to land, and a thousand like. He also loveth more: which appeareth in that he doth service always unto his neighbour."[340]

In 1547 the Injunction of 1538 was confirmed—that the Bible in English should be set up in every church within a year of the next visitation; and it was further ordered that within twelve months there should also be in each church a copy of the English version, begun about 1544, of Erasmus' Paraphrases on the Gospels.[341] This volume, containing also a Paraphrase of the Acts of the Apostles (a massive tome of over 1200 pages—there were two pages, for instance, on the first verse of St. John's Gospel) was printed in 1548. Clergy below the rank of B.D. were to own, in addition, the Paraphrases on the Epistles, eventually printed in 1549.[342] Thus the literary furniture of the English

338*A Mirror to Know Thyself*, *Works*, 278.
339*Ibid.*, 275–6.
340*Doctrinal Treatises*, 280.
341Cardwell, *Documentary Annals*, I, 9.
342*Ibid.*, 13. By the Elizabethan Injunctions of 1559, clergy under the degree of M.A. were to own the second volume (*ibid.*, 218).

parish church from the middle of the sixteenth century consisted of the Bible, the Book of Common Prayer, the Book of Homilies, and the Paraphrases of Erasmus. (The churchwardens of Great St. Mary's, Cambridge, bought in 1550 two Prayer Books, at 4*s.* each, a Book of Homilies, at 1*s.* 8*d.*, and the Paraphrases, at 5*s.* 6*d.*[343]) In his preface to the volume of Gospel Paraphrases, Nicholas Udall, sometime of Corpus Christi College, Oxford, wrote that Erasmus

> briefly compriseth the pith of all the minds and meanings of all the good doctors of the church that ever wrote. In justification of faith, in honouring God only, in repentance and purity of a Christian man's life, in detesting of imagery, and corrupt honouring of saints, in opening and defacing the tyranny, the blasphemy, hypocrisy, the ambition, the usurpation of the see of Rome, in noting the abuses of all the abominable sects and rabbles of counterfeit religions and idle cloisters, in bewraying the juggling sleights and fine practice of popery, in choice of meats, in esteeming the difference of days, in manifesting of vain ceremonies under the colour and pretence of holiness crept into Christ's Church, in reprehending pilgrimages with all circumstances of idolatry and superstition, in describing of a Prince's office, in teaching obedience of the people towards their rulers and governors, in declaring of a pastor's duty, in showing the part of an evangelical preacher, and what or how his doctrine ought to be out of the scriptures, in blasing the antichristian decrees of popery under the name of traditions and constitutions of our mother church, in decising the right difference between the spirit and the letter, and finally in all other points or articles of our religion, having now of late years been in controversy, Erasmus like as he is nowhere vehement, so is he everywhere both sincere and full.

This is the high-water mark in the story of the "myth" of the Protestant Erasmus. And it is interesting to note that in Cranmer's manuscript notes on justification[344] there is a list of the opinions of twenty-four theologians, only one of whom belonged to the sixteenth century—and that was Erasmus. (Whitgift, too, was to be quite at home with Erasmus' New Testament notes.[345])

In Cambridge too the "myth" continued. John Milton was to make a variation on one theme, in *Paradise Lost*, with his descrip-

[343]Foster, *Churchwardens' Accounts*, 120.

[344]Printed from Cranmer's MS. in *Remains*, 203–11. A note of Erasmus on Romans IV: "His qui pure simpliciterque Christo fidunt, hoc praestat fides, ut pro justis habeantur, nulla legis observatae commendatione, sed solius fidei" (207).

[345]For instance, *Works*, I, 163; III, 515.

tion of the violent wind dispelling the monks and friars at the gate of heaven:

> then might ye see
> Cowls, hoods and habits with their wearers tost
> And fluttered into rags, then relics, beads,
> Indulgences, dispenses, pardons, bulls,
> The sport of winds: all these upwhirled aloft
> Fly o're the backside of the world far off
> Into a limbo large and broad, since called
> The Paradise of Fools.

And we are told by Milton—age nineteen, in a summer oration at Christ's in 1628—that "there is in the hands of everyone that most clever *Praise of Folly*, a work not by a writer of the lowest rank."[346] *Hilaritas Erasmi.*

And in the 1640's, with the development of the school of "Cambridge Platonists"—very different from the Oxford Platonism of Colet!—the accent of Erasmus breaks through once more. Truth, wrote Benjamin Whichcote, "lies in a little compass and narrow room": "vitals in religion are few."[347] Not unlike a dominant theme of Erasmus: that the *universa philosophia Christi* should be gathered "out of the pure fountain of the gospel and the epistles and most approved interpreters, and so plainly that yet it might be clerkly and erudite, and so briefly that it might also be plain. Those things which concern faith or belief, let them be contained in a few articles."[348] *Regula charitatis christianae.*

IX

TO END AT the beginning. In the summer of 1509, shortly after the accession of Henry VIII, Erasmus returned to England, after spending two and a half years in Italy. Unfortunately, at this time, there are great gaps in his preserved correspondence. From December 1508, when he wrote to Aldo Manuzio from Padua,

[346] *Prolusion* VI.
[347] Quoted in Campagnac, *Cambridge Platonists*, 72.
[348] *Enchiridion* (1518 Preface), 10. See Thompson's edition of Erasmus' 1524 *Dialogue Concerning Faith.*

until April 1511, when he sent a letter to Andrea Ammonio from Dover just before crossing the Channel, there is silence. He came back to England in 1509 because he was led to expect that the most lucrative patronage would be his; and at first he intended settling in England for life.[349] The "highest advantages"[350] had been promised—or half promised. And the key to the irritation of many of his Cambridge letters is this feeling of hope cheated, expectation betrayed.

The twenty or so months between his return to England and his trip to Paris were spent in London. Erasmus was given a room at the House of Thomas More, in Bucklersbury. Another permanent house guest there was Andrea Ammonio. *The Praise of Folly* was written during this period, pobably in the second part of 1509. "As I was coming awhile since out of Italy for England," runs the prefatory letter to More, "that I might not waste all that time I was sit to on horseback in foolish and illiterate trifles, I chose rather one while to revolve with myself something of our common studies, and another while to enjoy the remembrance of my friends, of whom I left here some no less learned than pleasant." And the similarity of "More" and "Moria" led him to resolve "to make some sport with the praise of folly."[351] In England the resolution was fulfilled:

> I was staying with More after my return from Italy, when I was kept several days in the house by lumbago. My library had not yet arrived; and if it had, my illness forbade exertion in more serious studies. So, for want of employment, I began to amuse myself with the praise of folly, not with any intention of publishing the result, but to relieve the discomfort of sickness by this sort of distraction. I showed a specimen of the unfinished work to some friends in order to heighten the enjoyment of the ridiculous by sharing it. They were mightily pleased, and insisted on my going on. I complied, and spent some seven days on the work.[352]

When Erasmus went to Paris in April 1511 to see the printers, the manuscript of *The Praise of Folly* went with him. He also carried a set of Latin verses by Ammonio. The letter to Ammonio

[349]From the *Compendium Vitae*, Erasmus' autobiographical sketch; quoted Nichols, I, 11. For the period 1509–11 see J. K. Sowards, "The Two Lost Years of Erasmus," *Studies in the Renaissance*, IX, 1962, 161–86.

[350]*Ibid.*

[351]Preface, 1–2.

[352]From a letter to Martin Dorp, May 1515; *E.E.*, no. 337 (II, 94); tr. Nichols, II, 5.

from Dover on April 10, instructed the Italian to make sure that More returned to Colet the books which Erasmus had borrowed and left in More's house.[353]

Erasmus stayed in Paris until June, lodging with an Englishman called Eden in a house in the Rue Saint-Jean-de-Beauvais (off what is now the Boulevard Saint Germain)—the left bank, the printing quarter. One of the friends of Mr. Eden was a clothier of Bury St. Edmunds called Gardiner. And at this time his son, Stephen Gardiner, a boy of about fourteen, was also lodging in the Rue Saint Jean. In 1526 Stephen was to remind Erasmus of the "little boy to whom each day you gave instructions to prepare for you lettuces cooked with butter and olive oil . . . you used to declare that dish was garnished by him for you more skilfully than ever was done before."[354] Gardiner was also impressed by Erasmus' buying "a great number of books, both Greek and Latin."

The printer Erasmus picked for *The Praise of Folly* was Gilles de Gourmont, who had been working in Paris since 1506 and was the first printer outside Italy to set entire books in Greek type. Not that he made a very good job of the Latin *Moriae Encomium.* Erasmus said later that this first edition, which appeared in June, was badly botched. (There was to be another edition in August, printed at Strasburg.) Ammonio's verses were also printed in May or June.

In May Ammonio wrote to Erasmus from London: "You are marvellously missed. As people know that we lodge together, I am deafened with the cries, What of Erasmus? When will he return?"[355] It seems that Erasmus had intended to be away from England for some months; to stay with Lord Mountjoy, who since November 1509 had been Lieutenant of the castle at Hamme, an English garrison in the Marches of Calais, fifteen miles south-west of Antwerp, and near Saint Omer, where Erasmus was always a welcome guest at the monastery. But for some reason Erasmus elected to return to London in June.

He did not stay for long in Bucklersbury. More's wife, Jane

[353]*E.E.*, no. 218.
[354]*E.E.*, no. 1,669. See Biographical Register, Gardiner.
[355]*E.E.*, no. 221; tr. Nichols, II, 14.

Colt, died in this summer of 1511. We do not know the exact date; she was alive in the later part of May, and More had married again by the end of October. Perhaps Jane died of the sweating-sickness which swept through London in July or early August. Erasmus, at any rate, moved during the summer to a room in the rectory of William Grocin, at St. Lawrence Jewry, next to the Guildhall—only a short walk from Bucklersbury. Ammonio stayed on *chez* More until October. Then he moved out, probably because he did not get along with the new Mrs. More, Dame Alice Middleton, whom More had married in September (probably). However, Erasmus still had a room reserved for him in Bucklersbury, and, so far as More went, was still a welcome guest after his remarriage; he was to stay there for a few days at the end of September, on a short trip from Cambridge.

Some time in July Fisher persuaded Erasmus to accept a position at Cambridge as lecturer in Greek. The post would be specially created for him; no one had professed Greek in Cambridge before. Erasmus had taught Greek for a time in Paris in 1505; and the prospect of a regular and highly paid university lectureship was not unattractive to him, conscious of the fact that for two years he had been dependent on the hospitality of his London friends. This point he was to make clear later:

> I can't see how I could live in London, except with Grocin; and certainly there's no one in the world I'd sooner live with, but I'm ashamed to cause him the expense, particularly when I don't possess the means of returning the favour, and he won't allow me to contribute anything to meet the cost, so kind is he. I wasn't particularly anxious to leave London, but it was this consideration of pride, above all, that moved me to do it.[356]

Fisher was insistent—it would be quite a coup for Cambridge to have Erasmus as a Visiting Professor. Erasmus had refused offers from universities before: from Oxford in 1499, from Louvain in 1502. But this time he accepted.

At the beginning of August Erasmus was struck down by the sweating-sickness. Even by the middle of the month he was hardly fit enough to travel. But arrangements went forward. A Cambridge carrier had been hired to take his books from

[356]Letter 15.

London to Cambridge—the chests arrived much later, badly battered.[357] Erasmus made sure that his borrowed horse could survive the journey to Cambridge, seventy miles or so! (Later, in 1513, he was to have the use of another horse in Cambridge, lent him by the Gonnells.) Henry Bullock, at Queens', sent a carrier down to London with a horse for Erasmus' servant (though the horse the servant was given in London was not, in fact, the same one which had left Cambridge). And, on or about Monday August 18, 1511, Erasmus and his servant left the City of London and rode north.

The journey, like all Erasmus' travelling was very uncomfortable. He was a nervous horseman himself, and the servant's horse was in bad condition. The first day they had nothing to eat *en route*. They broke the journey and stayed somewhere overnight. The next day there was a bad storm, rain, thunder, and lightning, and Erasmus' horse began to stumble. (Presumably he did not have the opportunity on this horseback expedition to read very much, or to plan another *Praise of Folly*!) One is reminded of his description of another bad journey: "What do you suppose was your Erasmus' state of mind? If the horse was alarmed, his rider was no less so: as often as he pricked up his ears, my courage went down; when he lost his footing, my heart jumped into my mouth."[358] The pair arrived in Cambridge on the evening of the second day. Or perhaps it was a trio—Bullock may have gone down to London to escort Erasmus and the servant up to the university. Erasmus settled into his rooms at Queens'. Almost the first thing he did was to put himself into the hands of a Cambridge doctor, for his uncertain health had hardly been improved by the drenching. Fortunately there was a Dutch physician in the town, Dr. Bont, whose patent medicines seem to have given him some reputation as an alchemist.

Erasmus' first surviving Cambridge letter was written from Queens' on Sunday August 24, 1511.

[357]Letter 14, November 11, 1511.
[358]Erasmus to Mountjoy, February 1499. *E.E.*, no. 88; tr. Nichols, I, 184.

LETTERS FROM
CAMBRIDGE

LETTER 1 • ERASMUS TO COLET

Queens' College Cambridge, August 24, 1511

My dear Colet, if my bad luck can make you laugh, there's plenty of material at hand for your amusement. Apart from the earlier happenings in London, my servant's horse was fearfully lame, since the carrier changed the horse Bullock had sent down. Point number two—there was nothing to eat the whole journey through! The following day, unending rain, right up to dinner-time; after dinner, thunder and lightning and showers; three times my horse fell headlong to the ground. Bullock has studied the stars like an astrologer, and announced his findings: "Great Jove is rather annoyed with us," said he.

Already, I think he's right. What I see looming ahead are the sure signs of "Christian poverty"; and I entertain so very little hope of any gain that I'm sure I shall have to spend, here and now, every penny I can squeeze from my patrons.

There is a physician here, a fellow-countryman of mine[1] who relies on the fifth essence[2] to promise amazing feats—he makes old men young and brings the dead to life! This gives me hope that I'll grow young again, if only I can get a taste of this fifth essence. If *this* comes my way, I shan't be altogether sorry I came! On the subject of gain, I see nothing in prospect. What can I filch from people who haven't a rag to their backs?—I who am not utterly shameless, and yet am quite definitely born minus a silver spoon.

Farewell, my kind counsellor and teacher. When I begin to lecture, I'll report how it goes, to give you even more occasion for laughter. P.S. I may even begin to tackle your own St Paul: you see how brazen yours truly is becoming!

LETTER 2 • ERASMUS TO AMMONIO

Queens' College Cambridge, August 25, 1511

I am sending you a letter I have addressed to Bombace.[3] So far there is nothing new to tell you about my own affairs, except that the

[1]*Medicus nostras.* This was probably the *medicus Bont* who was to die of the plague near Cambridge in October 1513 (see Letter 29). Allen noted that Bont was a common Netherlands name (*E.E.*, I, 533).

[2]Dr. Bont appears to have been a Cambridge alchemist! The fifth element, or essence, according to Aristotelian and scholastic physics, was the substance of which the heavenly bodies (and heaven) were made, and of which (some said) the human soul was composed: Aether.

[3]Paolo Bombace was a Greek Professor at the University of Bologna, whom

journey was very uncomfortable, and that my health is still a little shaky as a result of that sweating-sickness I told you of. I expect I shall stay at this college for several days anyway. Being anxious to devote my chief attention to getting well, I haven't as yet provided myself with a lecture-audience. The beer in this place doesn't suit me at all and the wines aren't quite satisfactory either. If you are in a position to arrange for a cask of Greek wine, the best obtainable, to be shipped to me here, you will have done what will make your friend perfectly happy. (But I'd like it to be quite *dry* wine). Don't worry at all about the payment; I'll even have this sent in advance, if you wish. I'm already beginning to enjoy the first of the advantages we derive from the Holy Pontiff's bulls;[4] how?—by dying of thirst! You can guess the rest. And I haven't even made the crossing yet.

LETTER 3 • ERASMUS TO COLET

Cambridge, September 13 (1511)

I am enclosing, at your request, the Office of Chrysostom,[5] and also a letter in which, unless I'm mistaken, there will be things you won't like;[6] because you despise systems and books of rules,[7] whereas I allow them some importance, especially in a teacher. Don't be in a hurry to believe anyone about Linacre. I have solid grounds for my

---

Erasmus had met in 1507 and thought very delightful and friendly. He later became secretary to Pope Clement VII and died in 1532. This letter from Cambridge to Bologna has not survived; Bombace wrote from Bologna to Cambridge in December 1511 with reference to the rumours of Erasmus' death, and giving some accounts of events in Bologna. (Italian paraphrase: *E.E.*, no. 251.)

[4]*Ex bullis sanctissimis.* An enigmatic reference. Nichols thought it was an allusion to Julius' plans to organize a League against the French: this raised the price of wine (II, 21). Allen considered it more probable that Erasmus was referring to the expenses of his efforts to press forward (with the aid of Ammonio, a papal representative in London) his suit for a papal dispensation (*E.E.*, I, 466).

[5]*Missa Sancti Joannis Chrysostomi* (Paris, 1537).

[6]*De Ratione Studii.*

[7]A reference to the sentiments expressed in Colet's Accidence, written about 1509: "Latin speech was before the rules, not the rules before the Latin speech"; so the master should "leave the rules," after the parts of speech have been mastered, and concentrate on good authors, "desiring none other rules but their examples" and speaking with his pupils the "clean" "pure" Latin: "reading of good books, diligent information of taught masters, studious advertence and taking heed of learners, hearing eloquent men speak, and finally easy imitation with tongue and pen, more availeth shortly to get the true eloquent speech than all the traditions, rules and precepts of masters." (Lupton, *Colet*, 291–2). In fact

conviction that he holds you in the highest regard, and is not greatly upset by your rejection of his grammar—though it's human nature to be passionately attached to one's own writings, just as parents are to their children. But if in fact this *is* rather a sore point with him, then you'll have to play a skilful part, as you know how, so as to conceal your feelings and avoid reopening that particular wound; and make your apologies by your looks and your obliging behaviour rather than by making excuses—especially excuses at second-hand. In this way, any injury that rankles in him will gradually pass away as time elapses. But how excessively impertinent I am to say these things to you, like the proverbial sow teaching Minerva!

So far I haven't come across anyone I consider suitable to be a master in your school,[8] but I'll continue to make enquiries, and as soon as I find one I'll let you know.

Sometimes I have to do battle on your behalf against the Thomists and Scotists; but more about them when we meet. I'm beginning a translation of Basil's commentary on Isaiah;[9] a work which delights me personally. I'll give a sample of it to the Bishop of Rochester[10] and find out whether he's willing to give me a little something by way of emolument for the toil it causes me. I know very well you're smiling at that and saying, what a beggar! Yes, and I hate myself too. I've quite made up my mind that I must either get hold of some fortune or other to relieve me of this beggarly role or else imitate Diogenes in a thoroughgoing fashion.[11]

P.S. If you have at your disposal any fund earmarked for granting

---

these opinions of Colet are quite in tune with the *De Ratione*. Erasmus was teasing. But Colet didn't always quite respond to Erasmus' sense of humour (see Letter 26). Colet was ultimately more frivolous than Erasmus: in placing primary emphasis on things of secondary importance—in being, in other words, a "puritan."

[8]See Introduction, p. 57.

[9]*Basilii in Esaiam Commentariolus* (Basle, 1518).

[10]John Fisher.

[11]Erasmus was rather fond of the example of Diogenes; cf. a letter of his from Freiburg, August 1531: "What strange thing has happened, you will ask; have I married a wife? Indeed I am engaged in a matter, which is no less troublesome, and equally remote from my character and genius. I have bought a house here, of respectable name, but of exorbitant price. So that Erasmus, who used at any cost to redeem his leisure for literature, is now familiar with contracts of purchase, opinions of counsel, conveyances, covenants, and conditions; he is pulling down and building up, he is engaged with masons, smiths, carpenters, and glaziers—you know the sort of people—with so much repugnance, that I would rather spend three years in any literary work, however exacting, than be troubled for a single month with this kind of business. I have never understood before, as I do now, the supreme wisdom of Diogenes, who took refuge in a tub, rather than be worried with such matters." (Translated by Nichols, I, lxxxvi.)

a subsidy, I request you to send a few nobles[12] to Richard Croke, a former servant-pupil of Grocin's, who is at present a student in arts at Paris. Unless I'm quite mistaken, he is a young man of good promise, one on whom you'd be justified in bestowing assistance.

LETTER 4 • COLET TO ERASMUS

(London, end of September, 1511)

You write to ask "what I'm going to disapprove of" (these are your words). Is there anything about Erasmus I could fail to approve of? I have read your piece "On Studies," hurriedly at the time, since I haven't yet had a chance to go through it carefully because of my distractions; and not only do I agree with all of it as I read, but I'm full of admiration for your own mental gifts, plus masterly technique, erudition, fluency, and power of expression. Often have I wished the boys at my school could be trained on your method, i.e., that which you have prescribed as correct; also I have often wished that they could be taught by just such men as you in your great wisdom have depicted. When I came to the passage at the end of your epistle where you claim the ability to bring youths to a reasonable command of expression, in both Latin and Greek, in fewer years than the conventional pedagogue requires for giving them baby-talk, then how I longed to have you, Erasmus, as a teacher in my school! But I'm hopeful that you'll lend me some assistance, if only in training my teachers when you have taken leave of your Cambridge men. I shall keep your draft-copies intact, as you request. About our friend Linacre I shall do as you so kindly and so shrewdly advise. Please don't give up your efforts to find a master for me, if there should be anyone at Cambridge who has the qualities of lack of conceit coupled with willingness to be subordinate to the High Master.

About that remark in your letter concerning your occasional skirmishes on my behalf with the Scotist militia; I rejoice to have such a stout a fighter and loyal champion to defend me! But from your point of view this is a thoroughly unequal contest, and one that brings no kudos; for what lustre do *you* gain when you have repulsed a swarm

[12]The noble was a gold coin, first minted under Edward III, and was worth 10 shillings by the reign of Edward IV. It was worth less now.

of flies and stabbed them to death? And what a credit will you earn in my eyes by felling reeds? It's an unavoidable rather than a glorious or doughty fray, but at least it shows the concern and loving care you have at heart for myself.

Do go on, Erasmus, to give us Basil, for in doing so you'll be giving us Isaiah. I think you will do well, and best look after your own interest, if you do "imitate Diogenes" and, rejoicing in your poverty, reckon yourself as king of kings. In the lives of Christian heroes, the world's gain follows those who flee from it. From whence came so many powers and such wealth in the Church but from her shunning of these things?[13] But I know such paradoxes as this are not to your taste.

I am surprised by what you write about Richard Croke: for what have I to do with others' money, or what cause have you to suspect I have supervision of moneys entrusted to me in any way whatsoever? It is not my practice to stand by the bedsides of dying men or wheedle rich widows or meddle in the wills and testaments of the wealthy; I do not seek to become the confidant of rich persons, or praise their vices and infirmities, or bid them redeem their wickednesses by applying money as *I* think fit. I tell you, in this country anyone not of that kidney will find it hard to come by money for charitable purposes. I have the handling of my own money and no other; and you yourself know the ends for which I disburse that.[14] Still, I was somewhat amused and at the same time charmed, Erasmus, to see the innate uprightness of character that caused you, in that grinding poverty of yours, to prefer to plead others' causes rather than your own. Well, to cap the matter, though I have nothing of others' money to offer other men, yet if you play the beggar in this disarming manner, I have some of my own private money for yourself; and if you ask for it without blushing for shame, then poverty will (albeit poorly) come to poverty's aid. Farewell, and I beg you be sure to write often to me, your friend.

[13]For a sustained exposition of this theme see Colet's lectures on Romans (tr. Lupton, 118–21): "money, possessions, tithes, oblations, and whatever else is of an earthly nature . . . are not of the kingdom of God. . . . You will find nothing that has befallen the church to have done more mischief than possessions and titles of *meum* and *tuum* and power of claiming property." One of the points at issue between the Dean and Bishop Fitzjames in 1513 was to be Colet's typically extreme opinion about the temporal revenues of the church.

[14]Colet's annual income was about £200: £144 from the Deanery, the rest from other preferments. The money inherited from his father he was using for the new school. (Lupton, *Colet*, 122.)

LETTER 5 • ERASMUS TO AMMONIO

Queens' College Cambridge, September 16, 1511

My dear and delightful Andrea, you have raised my spirits twice over by not only sending the very welcome consignment of wine but adding to it something far more welcome—a letter,[15] which absolutely tastes of your mind and character; and there never was, and never will be, anything more delicious (in my opinion) than that. Then I have a double reason for thanking you as I do. You're angry at the mention of payment; now, for my part, I wasn't unaware that you had a heart generous enough to grace a royal fortune! But I calculated that you would probably send me a rather large cask; one that would last several months—and even the one you did send was larger than any decent man could accept as a free gift.

I had a hearty laugh over the Greek note. It would be hard-hearted indeed of me not to forgive More, plunged as he is in such important business.

I'm most surprised that you are sitting on your nest unendingly as you do, and that you never fly away. If you should ever be disposed to pay another visit to this university, you'll be warmly welcomed here by many people—myself especially. As for your invitation to me to come back to your neighbourhood if my illness continues, I can't see anything to attract me in London, except the company of two or three of my friends. But we'll speak about this another time. I hear the mighty Julius is dead.[16]

Goodbye, and please write to me often; you can't do anything that would please me more.

At the end of September or the beginning of October Erasmus made a short trip to London, probably to see Josse Bade (1462–1535), the Netherlander who since 1507 had been printer to the University of Paris. He had published Erasmus' edition of Valla's notes on the New Testament (1505), his Latin translations from

[15]This letter of Ammonio has not survived.

[16]The Pope had been taken ill in Rome on 17 August. By the twentieth his life was in danger. He recovered consciousness on the twenty-second: "If you do not give me wine," he said to the captain of the guard, "I will have you shut up in the Castel S. Angelo" (Creighton, *History of the Papacy*, V, 155). He had a relapse on Monday the twenty-fifth—the day after Erasmus wrote his first Cambridge letter. On the twenty-seventh he was given up for dead. But in fact he began to convalesce on the twenty-eighth. (Pastor, *History of the Popes*, VI, 368–72.) He survived until 20 February 1513.

Euripides (1506), and the Erasmus-More translations from Lucian (1506).

Erasmus stayed at More's house in Bucklersbury, where Ammonio also had a room. So little ceremony was there *chez* More that Erasmus did not meet Ammonio on this hurried visit, being under the impression that he had already moved out to St Thomas's, down the street. More's recent second marriage made Bucklersbury less attractive for his old friends. Erasmus tactfully described Dame Alice Middleton as "a woman on the verge of old age," "by no means a docile character," "not precisely beautiful . . . but a keen and watchful housewife."[17]

LETTER 6 • ERASMUS TO COLET

Cambridge, October 5, 1511

(Erasmus had not yet received Colet's letter, Number 4.)

I think I am at this moment on the scent of the kind of man you mentioned: more of this when we meet. Last time I was in London, I did not call on you, to avoid being a nuisance; for I had to ride off straight away after dinner. One-eyed Peter,[18] whom chance set in my way, told me you had sent a reply to my last letter, but this I haven't yet received. I should be planning to come back to see you about the beginning of December, if the plague didn't frighten me off; especially should Mountjoy return, so that I can use his house, which at present is impossible because of Mr. Watchdog.[19]

LETTER 7 • ERASMUS TO AMMONIO

Cambridge, October 5, 1511

A kind of attendant imp of misfortune prevented me from seeing you although I was extremely close at hand. For, at my first arrival in

[17] *E.E.*, no. 999. Translated by Barbara Flower in Huizinga, *Erasmus*, 236.

[18] Peter Meghen, born at Hertogenbosch (where Erasmus had spent two or three years at school, 1484–7). Meghen was a general copier and messenger for the More-Colet-Erasmus circle. In 1517 he was to carry over to More from Antwerp the portrait of Erasmus by Quentin Matsys, now in Rome National Gallery.

[19] Lord Mountjoy at the moment was at Hamme, the English outpost in East

London nothing would have seemed less likely than that you should still be staying at More's house, especially as Josse the bookseller had informed me you were now at St. Thomas's.[20] Early next morning I knocked at the door of your room, but you were not at home. After I came back from church,[21] I heard a noise of horsemen. I requested Linacre to look outside, since I was busy writing something or other; he said it was—you, taking your departure. But after you had already gone I was full of longing to have a talk with you; however, there will be a chance to do this at some other time.

Please tell me what news you have in London about Lord Mountjoy's arrival, and in the second place, whether the plague is as bad as the common report has it; and lastly, give me any news about Italian and French affairs that may safely be entrusted to a letter.

LETTER 8 • ERASMUS TO AMMONIO

Cambridge, October 16, 1511

I have no pretext for writing (since there's no news), except that I've made up my mind to send away no reliable messenger who comes to hand, without a letter to you from me. I wrote just a few days ago; I long to hear how you are, and whether my friend Mountjoy is back yet; and next, how things are in Italy and what Julius the Most

---

Flanders. He did not in fact return to Knightrider Street until November 5. Mr. Watchdog (*Cerberus*) has never been identified; Allen suggested that some porter might be meant.

[20] *In Collegio divi Thomae*: St. Thomas' School, "the Hospital of S. Thomas of Acons in west Cheap" (Stow, *Survey of London*, I, 73). One of the two big schools in the City of London (if we do not include the new St. Paul's, which was just starting); the other was St. Anthony's, Threadneedle St., where More had gone to school and of which Roger Wentford was Headmaster. The school was just across the road from where Bucklersbury joined Cheapside, hardly more than three or four minutes from More's house. In fact Ammonio did not make the move until the last week of October.

[21] This is a rare reference to churchgoing. David Knowles writes of Erasmus: "the extent of his daily conformity to normal Catholic practice is, like so much else about him, obscure. Thus, for example, he undoubtedly approached the Sacrament of Penance at times, but whether he frequented it is another matter; he never abandoned belief in the Real Presence and undoubtedly attended Mass, but whether he habitually offered the Holy Sacrifice as a priest, or communicated, seems unascertainable" (*Religious Orders in England*, III, 145). The papal dispensation of 1517 absolved him from offences relating to his "defect of birth" (a bastard priest) and enjoined "salutary penances" if any such had been incurred by his "celebrating mass or other divine offices" (*E.E.*, no. 517; tr. Nichols, II, 462).

Invincible is up to. About the beginning of winter I'll move back to London if the gods allow, provided the winter's cold can put a stop to the plague which I hear is spreading there. For that matter, it isn't very far from Cambridge either.

Up to this moment[22] I've been lecturing on Chrysoloras' Grammar, but the audience is small; perhaps more people will attend when I start Theodore's Grammar.[23] Perhaps also I will undertake lecturing in theology, for that's under discussion at present. The stipend is too small to tempt me, but in the meantime I'm also doing some service to learning, to the best of my ability; and, to use Ovid's expression, have been "beguiling" a few months. Look after yourself, my dear Andrea, dearest to me of all mankind, and be sure to write to me often.

LETTER 9 • ERASMUS TO AMMONIO

(Cambridge, c. October 20, 1511)

I am sending back your wine-cask. I kept it lingering over-long in my living-quarters, just so as to enjoy the very smell of its Greek wine! And now, as a reward for wine of the finest quality, you are to receive verses of the worst—precisely (in Homer's famous phrase) "brass, in return for gold." Yes, and I'm original in teaching *iambic* verses on this occasion to sing songs of *praise*! My Ode shall be appended here:

Whoe'er reflects, Ammonio, on thy dower—
The great and total beauty of thy face
(Reward of close beholders); thy tall stature,
Fit for the kings of old; grace mixed o'er all
With majesty in countenance and in frame;
Eyes that shine forth in gentle manhood's fire,
A tongue that sounds alluring melodies;
Character, too, that's never out of season
(Being friendly, kind, sweeter than honeycombs);
Love, laughter, wit, enjoyment, fun; the three
Graces, in short: a mild, forgiving nature;
Fresh innocence of heart and, strange to tell,
A wise astuteness lacking policy:
Also a temper free from love of gain,
Prone to be generous far beyond the scale
Of thy possessions; and a mind how full
(Ready to pour forth too!) and burnished bright
(Can one small head contain so many books?);

[22]Lectures started at the beginning of October.
[23]Theodore Gaza.

—All these, no less of eloquence adorns
And kindness, precious as rare, doth season all.
The glare and glittering eye of cruel spite
By that agreeable and modest mien
Thou dost repel: spite of so lordly gifts
Naught of high-mindedness that nature mars.
Whoe'er (then) weighs such riches, in one man
Composed, will he not justly swear, to *thee*
Alone was nature truly mother-kind,
Others but stepsons? even though thyself
These goods to thine own self dost chiefly owe.
—Fortune, thou'st still thy duty, such great gifts
To match with thine assistance; otherwise,
Surely shalt thou seem envious, or quite blind.

I request you will convey to the bishops to whom they are addressed[24] the letters I've added to yours—either when you visit Court yourself or when you can find a reliable carrier. Bullock sends you his greetings; he's an honest friend,[25] and rather like yourself. I'm looking out for a letter from you, since I've only had one so far.[26] If there is a chance to gain audience with your friends the bishops, conduct yourself as you've always done towards your friend Erasmus. If your poems are on sale in London,[27] please send a single copy to me here.

LETTER 10 • AMMONIO TO ERASMUS

London, October 27, 1511

(This is the first surviving letter of Ammonio to Erasmus at Cambridge—not the first he actually sent. It was very delayed in transit; Erasmus was not to receive it until November 24.)

My cherished Erasmus, your letter went far beyond anything I hoped for, though it fell short of what I longed for. To tell the truth, you have written to me more often than I thought you would, yet much less often than I dreamt of; and this supremely affectionate act of kindness on your part is so much valued in my eyes that *had* it been possible for the bonds between us to be drawn any tighter, you'd have linked me

[24]Richard Foxe, Bishop of Winchester, and Thomas Ruthall, Bishop of Durham.
[25]*Amicus candidus.*
[26]That is, the letter which arrived with the wine cask on September 16 and which we do not have.
[27]The volume of verse which had been published at Paris in the spring, Erasmus having taken the manuscript from London with him.

indissolubly in the bond of debt to yourself by performing it. Nothing I receive gives me more pleasure than a letter from you; and I think I have had solid evidence for discerning that I stand higher than most men in *your* affections (indeed I thought so before; but now I believe it's possible to be sure of it); but I haven't had an opportunity to be equally serviceable to yourself, partly because of His Majesty's business[28] (see what a pompous excuse I'm making!) and the highly intricate affairs of certain friends, and partly through the fault of those to whom I entrusted my second letter to you, for I understand this was not delivered to you in spite of the substantial fee I gave for its conveyance.

On my part, I've had three letters from you; two of them were full of sugar; but the third was full of honey![29] And although at first, from the address and the mention of Greek wine, I did not doubt it was destined for myself, yet presently when I came to the poetry I suddenly began to suspect that you were writing to somebody else, since I failed to recognize as my own the qualities you praise there. However, as soon as I realized that you were in fact speaking of me, I said to myself: "Why do you hesitate to believe what Erasmus says about you? After all, you'd trust *him* even with your life." In short, I should have deceived myself had I not come to the opinion that your affection for me had deceived your otherwise superlatively keen judgement. In any case I will freely confess to you my somewhat enlarged self-satisfaction as a result of reading your poetic effusion—simply for the reason that I have had Erasmus to sing my praises. In this I consider myself luckier than Alexander the Great, and not one scrap do I envy Achilles. But it is I rather than you who can say with truth "brass for gold," since in exchange for brazen wine I have gained verses of gold, nay emerald, or (rather) more costly than gold or jewels or any kind of precious ore. But I'm vastly greedy, and not content even with this enormous profit: for if I can recover the cask you are sending back empty, I shall command it to make a return voyage to you, recharged with its vital fluid, so as to see if I can coax you to the production of further verses; since even if your lines are full of fibs, still they sing a most charming tune.

I hope in a few days to be able to deliver your letters personally

[28]Ammonio, in succession to Pietro Carmiliano, had recently been appointed secretary "of the Latin tongue" to Henry VIII: that is, for the writing of letters in Latin; there were also a French secretary and the principal secretary (later to be called secretary of state).

[29]Erasmus had actually written five letters to Ammonio; the "honeyed" one was the last, of October 20 (Letter 9).

to my lords of Winchester and Durham; and if my words can do anything to recommend you further to them, I will orate better than Cicero himself. For is there anyone, however inarticulate, whom the possession of such an excellent case would fail to render fluent, nay (I say) a master of oratory?

This is the report of events in Italy: the Spanish king[30] is now on the verge of open war with France and the English will not (it is guessed) stay idly looking on. Pope Julius has gone to the shrine of the Mother of God at Loretto to give thanks to Our Lady for his recovery. The Venetians have, it is said, ambushed and destroyed more than five hundred French horse. The Emperor[31] feels the chill so badly that he dares not come out of his heated apartments. The men of Florence and Pisa have been pursued with dreadful curses because they are lending a council-site to those Cardinals who are guilty of schism.[32] The Cardinal Archbishop of Reggio[33] has passed away.

Here in London we have not yet come to terms with the plague. I myself have at last moved into St. Thomas's where I am no more willing to stay than at More's house. It's true that I no longer see "the harpy's crooked beak"[34] but there are plenty of other things to annoy

[30]*Hispanus.* Ferdinand, who was technically King of Aragon, and regent of Castile. "Although some writers occasionally referred to the 'King of Spain', constitutionally the title did not exist. The monarch used the various titles corresponding to each of his estates" (J. M. Batista i Roca in *New Cambridge Modern History*, I, 323).

[31]Maximilian of Habsburg, Emperor in fact since 1493 and technically Emperor-elect since 1508.

[32]Louis XII had "attempted to bring about a singular victory for the conciliar theory" (R. Aubenas in *New Cambridge Modern History*, I, 83). He had obtained from the French clergy a pronouncement that a General Council was necessary; and in May 1511 five cardinals, led by the Spanish Bernardo Carvajal, issued at Milan an invitation to a Council, requesting Julius to attend. The Council was called into existence at Pisa (by three proctors in an empty church) in September 1511. Meetings actually began on November 1, a week after the schismatic cardinals had been deprived by Julius. There were present the "cardinals" Carvajal, William Briçonnet, René de Brie, and Aimon d'Albret; commissioners representing three other cardinals (including Francesco Borgia); fifteen prelates, five abbots, and representatives of Louis XII and of the Universities of Paris, Toulouse, and Poitou. Machiavelli came to Pisa, to see Carvajal, on the sixth. The Council, unpopular in Pisa, left on November 15, and translated itself to Milan; here the first session was held in January 1512 and the last in June. The members then moved first to Asti, and then to Lyon; here, very quickly, the whole thing ended with a whimper. (Creighton, V, 159–64; Pastor, VI, 415.) See Letter 20.

[33]Cardinal Peter Isuaglies, a Sicilian, had died on September 29 (*E.E.*, I, 476).

[34]A Greek phrase, being "an ungallant allusion to the nose of Dame Alice" (Chambers, *More*, 111, following *E.E.*, I, 476).

me; so much so that I swear I don't know how I can contrive to live in England any more. In the first place, they tell me it would be unsuitable to my condition to reside with our Italian merchants, which would be congenial to me; secondly I am quite out of sympathy with this nation's dirty habits, habits with which I am already well enough acquainted, and yet my poverty will not permit me to take a lease of a house and live as I should like to live. But to drive away these distasteful reflexions, I too will turn poet!

> Thy potency in verse, Erasmus mine,
> Myself hath urged to move this stock-dull wit
> And, Museless, match *thee* in th' Iambick line.
> But, straight, Apollo scolds me: Art thou fit,
> Poor frog, to Master Bull's girth to aspire?
> Can swans be rivalled when a crow's beak opes?
> Down fell incontinent my leaden lyre
> From a fool's grasp, to break a fool's fond hopes;
> My seething brain, short-vexed, grew cold again;
> Scarce could I send thee one short painful page!
> Yet this I'll add, tho' Muses curst remain:
> Farewell Erasmus, glory of our age.

Tomorrow I'll proceed to Court and will carry out your business there with zeal and attention; and I shall arrange with someone that, when the Cambridge carriers in due course come to London, a second cask of wine shall be delivered to you along with this letter.[35] Please return Bullock's greeting a thousandfold for me.

LETTER 11 • ERASMUS TO COLET

Cambridge, October 29 (1511)

(The reply to Colet's letter of September: Number 4.)

At the moment I'm completely absorbed in finishing off my *Copia* ("Writer's Resources"); so much so that it could appear I was—to make a riddle of it—at once wallowing in "resources" and also minus any resources at all. And how I wish I could put an end to my "Resources" and my poverty both at once!—for presently I'll be writing finis to the *Copia*, provided only that the Muses give better fortune to my studies than Fortune has hitherto given to my purse.

[35] Erasmus received the cask (but not the letter) two weeks later—November 10.

This has been the reason why my replies to your letters were short and inadequate.

As for the Scotists, I'm not seriously campaigning against them, for if I do I'll only waste "my oil and my trouble" and in addition "stir up a hornet's nest"—they're a hopelessly stubborn tribe, unrivalled in their complacent self-esteem. I have virtually lost interest in translating Basil, not only because certain conjectures hint that the work isn't genuine, but also since the Bishop of Rochester seemed rather unenthusiastic after I sent him a sample of my projected translation, explaining in a letter that I intended Basil should be presented to readers of Latin under the Bishop's auspices and from his own University: also, as I have learnt from a friend, he suspects I am polishing up a previous version and not translating from the Greek! What won't men think of?

As for your joke about Diogenes, I'm glad I can give you pleasure, however I do it. But if my present luck continues, I'll be playing Diogenes in earnest—not as thinking myself mightiest of all kings, but as utterly despising life itself. How otherwise *could* one act Diogenes, at my age and in my state of health? For, surely, a man who neglects his life will spurn all else thereafter. But this he can do anywhere, even among the remotest savages; yet this, too, would (I believe) have a better outcome than my present choice of an ambition which, even if it were not discreditable, is still the most unfortunate by far.

I wrote you about Croke, not because I thought you held funds in trust (for I know you have cast from you even money that was forced upon you unasked), but because I thought you would be more willing to bestow on a fellow-Englishman anything you might chance to have; and, in addition, a favour is better bestowed on a *young* man, provided he's promising, and this young man is being let down, as it is, by some people who had promised to help him.

As for your offer of money to myself, there I recognize your old kindly attitude towards me and am full of the deepest gratitude. But my feelings were a little piqued by that remark (tho' made in fun) "if you beg humbly." Perhaps you mean—and you're right—that my impatience with my lot comes entirely from sinful human pride; since a truly gentle and Christian spirit takes everything in good part. I'm all the more suprised to see how you've linked humility and immodesty, since you write at once "if you beg humbly" and "if you ask without shame." For if you follow ordinary usage in defining humility as the very opposite of arrogance, what traffic can "shamelessness" hold with "modesty"? But if by "humbly" you mean "in a servile and abject manner," then, my dear Colet, you're quite at odds with Seneca, who thinks nothing so dear as what is bought by begging—for, says Seneca, he who waits for that *humble* word "I beseech" from a friend, is no friend in deed at all. Once when Socrates was conversing with his friends he said "I should have bought a cloak today, if I had not run short of cash." Seneca says that a man who gives only after hearing a remark like this, gives too late. Someone else placed money under the pillow of a sleeping friend who was needy and sick but who concealed both these conditions because of a certain sense of honour; when I read this story as a young man, I was as deeply impressed by the modesty of the one as touched by the other's openheartedness.

But I ask you, what could be more shameless or abject than I, who have been long a-begging publicly in England? I have received so much from the Archbishop[36] that it would be worse than the purest blackguardly conduct to take anything more from him, even if he were to offer it. From "X"[37] I have asked alms with some boldness, but he has outdone the shamelessness of my requests by the shamelessness of his way of refusing. Now I am even appearing too immodest to our friend Linacre; though he knew I was leaving London[38] furnished with barely six nobles (and he well knows my health, and also that winter's coming on), yet he solicitously advises me to spare the Archbishop and Lord Mountjoy and rather to draw in my horns, tighten my belt, and steel myself to bear poverty like a hero; what friendly advice! Yet it's for precisely this reason most of all that I hate my luck, viz. that it won't allow me to be modest. When my strength was adequate, it was a pleasure to conceal how poor I was; but it's impossible now, unless I were to take pleasure in neglecting my life itself. However, I haven't put on a brazen mask to such an extent that I ask just anyone for anything at all. As for other people, I fear I may ask them in vain. But how am I to beg from you, pray?—especially when you yourself aren't particularly well situated for giving *this* kind of help.

However, if you approve of immodesty, I'll end this letter with as shameless a conclusion as is possible for me. I can't be so brazen as

[36]William Warham, Archbishop of Canterbury.

[37]Both Nichols and Allen assume that Erasmus is here referring to Mountjoy, which would seem likely in view of the linking of Warham and Mountjoy a few lines further on.

[38]That is, after his short trip to London at the beginning of the month. Six nobles were worth about fifty shillings.

not, under any conditions, to beg from you at all; yet I'm not so proud as to reject a gift, if any friend as good as yourself should freely offer it, especially in the prevailing circumstances. Goodbye. (I've forgotten the brevity I'd mentioned at the start!)

P.S.—Something occurs to me I know you'll laugh at.[39] When I put forth a suggestion about a master for your school, in the presence of several Masters, a person of some reputation smiled and said: "Who would endure to spend his life in yon school, among children, if he was fit to choose where and how to spend his life?" I replied with a good deal of modesty that this function of bringing up youth in good manners and good literature seemed to me one of the most honourable; that Christ did not despise the very young, and that no age of man was more deserving of generous help, and nowhere could a richer harvest be anticipated, since the young are the growing crop and growing timber of the commonwealth; I added that all who are truly religious hold the view that no service is more likely to gain merit in God's eyes than the leading of children to Christ. He grimaced, and sneered: "If anyone wished to serve Christ properly, he should enter a monastery and live as a religious." I replied that St. Paul defines true religion in terms of works of love; and love, says he, consists in helping our neighbours as best we may. He spurned this as a foolish remark. "Lo," said he, "*we* give up all; *there* perfection lieth." "That man has not forsaken everything," said I, "who, when he could help very many by his labours, refuses to undertake a duty because it is regarded as humble." And with this I took my leave of the fellow, to avoid starting a quarrel. Here you see a sample of the Scotists' wisdom and the way in which they talk!

[39]The story reminds one of Erasmus' own comment on Colet, who "took a delight in the purity and simplicity of nature that is in children; a nature that Christ bids his disciples imitate" (*E.E.*, IV, 520; tr. Lupton, *Vitrier and Colet*, 32). St. Paul's School was dedicated to the Child Jesus. Erasmus' and Colet's prayers "to the boy Jesus" are still used at the school. Erasmus' prayer is as follows: "We pray unto thee, Jesus Christ, who as a boy twelve years old, seated in the temple, taught the teachers themselves, to whom the voice of the Father, sent from heaven, granted authority to teach all men, saying: This is my beloved son in whom I am well pleased: hear him; who art the perfection of all the eternal wisdom of the Father, deign to illuminate our minds so that we learn thoroughly the lessons of virtuous literature, and that we may use them to thy glory, who liveth and reigneth, with the Father and the Holy Ghost, ever one God, world without end" (translation in Clark, *John Milton at St Paul's School*, 45–6). A picture of the boy Jesus was placed above the chair of the High Master, and over it a representation of God the Father; at Erasmus' suggestion the words "Hear Ye Him" were added to the latter (*E.E.*, IV, 518; *Vitrier and Colet*, 27–8).

LETTER 12 • ERASMUS TO AMMONIO

Cambridge, November 2, 1511

At long last I've sent back your wine-cask, together with some misgotten verses.[40] The carrier says he delivered this to More since you were absent at the time. I'll return to London about the first of January —so at least we'll be less chilled, even if we have to keep each other warm! For I'd rather summer than winter, here at Cambridge. One last point: it isn't good to be, for too long, at such a distance from my personal Jupiter.[41] (All the same, Cambridge really suits me fairly well.[42]) Also I see some prospect of financial gain, if a man has it in him to act the busybody. I'd dearly like to know what effect my letters had on the bishops of Winchester and Durham, and also anything else that's new. If you will kindly have the letter I've attached to yours forwarded to Italy, I shall be much obliged. At present we have exactly what Homer called "unquenchable rain." I suppose Jove has heard the prayers of the author whose little book I gave you, where he calls on springs, rivers, lakes, and pools to lend their tears in lamenting Italy's tragedy. "A wolf saw me first":[43] so I have to speak by nods and gestures, my hoarseness is so bad. Write to me often.

LETTER 13 • AMMONIO TO ERASMUS

London, November 8, 1511

Either my servant is exceptionally unlucky, so that all he does turns out badly, or else the Cambridge rabble surpasses even the rest of the disobliging British nation in incivility, so unaware is it of life's obligations and of absolutely every kind of civilized behaviour. I long to see a few of this sort measure their length on a gallows! Why, they

[40]The cask and the letter had been sent to London on October 20 (see Letter 9) and Ammonio had acknowledged them in his letter of October 27 (Letter 10); but Erasmus hadn't yet received this.

[41]Mountjoy, probably.

[42]*hic locus non omnino mihi displicet.*

[43]*Folly* referred to someone who became tongue-tied and "could say never a word, as if he had seen a wolf at unaware" (Chaloner translation, 1549; in Nugent, *Thought of the English Renaissance*, 63). *Lupus in sermone* meant a sudden, embarrassed silence: "talk of the devil" (note by Hoyt Hudson, quoted *ibid.*, 668).

practically have no idea what it means to be responsible for a letter, and what it entails to fail to deliver it afterwards; to put in the mildest way possible, they don't *know* how many people they are cheating, just to humour themselves, or how many men's good names for conscientiousness they may be ruining; and moreover they are unaware that more than one person's well-being depends often on a single letter.

As soon as I got your letter I tried to answer it as quickly as I could,[44] in order to please you, if not by my literary style, at least by conscientiousness in dispatch. I gave the trifle they demanded for the carriage of the letter. Finally I sent back, along with the letter, a second cask of Greek wine; however, I see that only a single letter reached you,[45] and along with the good turn I tried to do, the care I devoted to writing has been lost. Oh, these savages! I swear I'd gladly see them torn to pieces any day! However, I'm consoled by one thing—the reflection that you've so fully grasped my feelings towards yourself that, even though I never wrote, you'd still regard me as an admirer and friend. My servant Thomas[46] says that on the last occasion he entrusted the letter and (as I said) a second cask of Greek wine to the man who carried your books to Cambridge; but I don't know to whom he gave other letters. If the wine has been drunk up, try and see you get back at least the cask. But enough of this bad temper—I'm just seething with it at the moment.

I gave your letters personally to my lords of Winchester and Durham; both received them with looks of utmost delight and praised to the skies your rare talents. Winchester seems to blame you for negotiating with him at a distance and never coming to see him; I replied, as it occurred to me to put it on the spur of the moment, "that it was a rather awkwardly shy modesty that made you do this, but that you were quite devoted (as I knew) to his lordship"; together with some other remarks appropriate to the occasion. But all this was before they had a chance to read your letters. Afterwards they were so busied with public affairs that I decided not to interrupt them on the subject of yourself—but shall not omit to do this at the proper season. Your Patron,[47] as I've heard (for I haven't yet seen him) has

[44]That is, Erasmus' letter of about October 20 (Letter 9) and Ammonio's reply of October 27 (Letter 10).

[45]The letter which Erasmus referred to on September 16 (Letter 5) and which has not survived.

[46]Erasmus was to describe Thomas as "such a sensible and wide-awake servant" (December 1513, Letter 38).

[47]*Tuus Maecenas*. Mountjoy had arrived back in London on November 5.

been in London for three days. Jupiter is very angry with us here; it rains by day and by night, and seldom stops. The plague has almost ceased to rage; but, unless the government takes some effective measures of relief, a famine is going to follow, and this will be every bit as terrible as the plague. I'm not surprised that the price of firewood has gone up: every day there are a great number of heretics to make bonfires for us, and still their number continues to grow. Why, even my servant Thomas's own brother, who's more like lump of wood than a human being, has instituted a sect on his own, if you please, and has followers too.

But to pass to Italian affairs. At Rome a League has been agreed upon between the Pope, the Spanish King, and the Venetians. Its terms, which have been announced, are as follows: the Spanish king shall provide for the aid of the Pope 1,200 heavy-armed horse, known as "lance," also 1,000 light horse and 10,000 foot-soldiers; while the Pope is to keep up 500 heavy horse and 8,000 infantry, and in addition he is to give a monthly allowance of 40,000 gold pieces to pay the auxiliaries; and the Venetians are to muster the largest army they shall be able to field. The Council at Pisa is falling apart. The Cardinal of Santa Croce, who began the schism, is said to have won a pardon from the Pope by the Spanish king's help and fled south for refuge to the district of Campania.—I had forgotten to say that it is permissible for any Christian prince to enter the said league if he elects to do so within forty days; after which time the Pope's sanction shall be requisite for admission thereto.[18] What *my* fellow-citizens are going to do they have so far failed to discuss—with (it is guessed) a great saving in oarsmen! The Emperor will be merely an onlooker at this business. It's rumoured that the Florentines are preparing to desert the French.

Now you know all that has been reported on Italian affairs to this date.

About your hoarseness: if you'd been here, I'd have dealt with it at once by administering one little draught. I'm grieved that the hope of your return to London is put off as far as the first of January. However, I'm happy that your Cambridge territory has suited you fairly well; we'll console our yearning for you with the thought of the great advantages you have there. Your other letters shall be diligently for-

[48]The Holy League, an alliance between the papacy, Spain, and Venice, had been signed on October 4 and announced on the fifth. Henry VIII joined it thirty-nine days later, on November 13; four days later he agreed with Ferdinand to attack France in the spring of 1512. Maximilian joined the Holy League in November 1512.

warded to Italy tomorrow, for they have arrived just in time, almost at the moment when the courier was leaving. Give many greetings for me to our friend Bullock.

LETTER 14 • ERASMUS TO AMMONIO

Cambridge, November 11 (1511)

On the tenth of November your letter was delivered to me—to be specific, your angry one; together with a half-full cask of Greek wine.[49] The fellow who brought it demanded two groats:[50] I gave him sixpence. Then after a close look at your letter, I noticed that the cask had not been sent with your last letter, which you wrote on eighth November, but with a previous letter (this was evident even from the colour of the wine). Indeed when first you sent it I was surprised that you were dispatching it unsealed by the hands of men to whom nothing is sealed. Obviously we have here to deal, my dear Andrea, with men who combine extreme boorishness with the extremity of evil cunning; and there is absolutely no reason why you should congratulate me on account of my Cambridge retreat; shame alone curbs my complaints. However, we'll speak of this privately when we meet.

I wasn't looking for a second cask, except that you, in that remarkable way of yours, took my praise of the wine for a fresh order. As far as I'm concerned I am more anxious about recovering your letter than about either the wine or the casks; for if you have sent *only* casks nos. 1 and 2, neither of them is lost. I sent back no. 1 and (unless I'm mistaken) received it back again with your last letter. Talk of my carrier! What if you'd seen my book-chests, battered on all sides? What would you have said if you'd heard his trumped-up story about the horse?—and that bald-headed rascal never hove in sight here. I declare it's folly to expect a single act of human decency from these monsters. But I couldn't restrain my laughter on seeing even Andrea (born to the Graces, to friendship and to gentleness) capable of

[49]That is, the letter of November 8 (Letter 13); and the cask sent on October 27 (with Letter 10).

[50]The groat, a silver coin dating in England from the middle of the fourteenth century, was worth 4*d*. But, because of later debasement, an "old groat" would be worth 5*d*. or 6*d*. by now. Erasmus gave the man not much more than half what he asked.

bilious rage, while *I'm* now practising the role of Mr. Mildman, after I've practically

> learnt at mine own fortune's hand
> To mourn for my defeat,

and am beginning to approve of Virgil's motto

> The conquered's one hope of deliverance is—
> To hope for no deliverance.

In a word, it seems to me I deserve every kind of misfortune, whenever I reflect what Italy was, which I've left behind, and how Rome was smiling on me when I left her: "alas for the exchange, but one's duty is to arrange the present situation well."

What you tell me of Italian affairs is anything but happy news to me, not because I love the French but because I hate war.[51] For when every day we see the most trivial of raids taking several years to end (and not easily, at that), what will be the prospect if such an extensive war once breaks out? Yet I've nobody to vent my annoyance upon, except that circumcised physician of the Pontiff's[52] who either is surely a poor workman, or else the sources of hellebore are quite exhausted. But "the fates themselves will find a way." I have less sympathy with those heretics you mention, just because it's when winter is upon us that they have sent up the price of fuel. I am not so troubled as you are about the question of famine, so long as it's possible to exist. Thank you for delivering my letters to the Bishops of Winchester and Durham, and also for your most kind support, and for the wine you sent to me even though I wasn't looking for it, and for your great assiduity in forwarding my letters to Italy. But why do I draw up a *short* list of your various services to me, when you play the part of Ammonio, i.e., of a shining light of friendship, in *everything*?

Before I withdraw to London I must get ready some warm hive in which to hide myself during the coming winter[53]—I'd like to be not

[51]The jingle *non studio Galli, sed odio belli* is hard to render: perhaps "not philo-Gallic but belli-phobic" or "not as a friend to the French but as one who abhors wars" (D.F.S.T.).

[52]Julius II, during his illness in August, was said to have a Jewish doctor (Rabbi Samuel Zarfati).

[53]Compare the complaints of Martin Bucer, who was to come to Cambridge as Regius Professor of Divinity at the end of 1549: "think what it must be for this frail body of mine which has been from my childhood utterly unable to bear the cold, to be without a stove during the winter, which is occasionally most severe, and at all times injurious; and also to be without my usual wine and diet" —this from Cambridge on December 26, 1550. Paul Fagius had died in Cam-

too far away from St. Paul's: for I've made up my mind to avoid Mountjoy's house as long as yon Cerberus[54] sits in wait! Yet even in London I can't see a place that would really do for the winter unless I was prepared to evict the owner! Perhaps there's something with the Austin Friars.[55] I'm invited by private letter to the house of Francis of Padua, who promises me an Italian sort of life; please pass on to me any advice you have to give on this subject. I congratulate Lord Mountjoy on his safe and happy return, and I request you to see that he receives my letter. I wrote also to the Bishop of Rochester,[56] by the same carrier who brought you my last; if a suitable opportunity offers, please find whether it reached him. As for the other two Bishops, please go on with them as you've begun; I'll await your reply before I leave Cambridge. Bullock returns your greetings, and is enormously pleased at having them. If you ever meet More, ask whether he has delivered my letter to the Archbishop and whether he himself has sent me any communication either from himself or from others.

LETTER 15 • ERASMUS TO ROGER WENTFORD

(Cambridge, November 1511?)

You advise against publication of my *Copia*;[57] in which—unless it was the thought of my own fame that influenced you!—I personally recognize your goodwill to me, of which I see two proofs: (1) being a little blinded by extreme affection for me, you esteem your friend Erasmus' trifling work so highly that you treat it as a rare treasure, not (in

---

bridge on November 13: "at first he was in a room without a fire, where he was severely affected by the cold" (*Original Letters: English Reformation*, ed. Robinson, II, 549–51). Tiled stoves of the German sort only became common in England (and then among the well-to-do) in the reign of Elizabeth. Edward VI gave Bucer a stove at the beginning of 1551; but he died in March.

[54]The "Mr. Watchdog" of Letter 6.

[55]The Augustinian Friary was off Old Broad Street; on the way, nowadays, from the Stock Exchange to Liverpool Street Station—not much more than a quarter of a mile from Bucklersbury, and about half a mile from St. Paul's. The Friary Church was to be given by Edward VI to the Protestant Dutch in London; it was destroyed by a land-mine in 1940 and a new church was built on the site in the early 1950's.

[56]This letter to Fisher, of about November 2, has not survived. Fisher's reply (Letter 16) shows that it was a request for money.

[57]The *De Copia* was in fact to be published in July 1512.

your opinion) to be shared with the *profanum vulgus*; (2) you are so devoted to keeping up my reputation that you have overshot your friendship with still more friendship, driving out (as it were) a nail with a nail. Still, I myself think it will do my reputation more good if those writings you mention are not published (or even copied) by anyone without most careful revision; and care like this is what I dislike more than a dog or a serpent, especially as I see no profit come of it but impairment of the eyes, premature old age and starvation, and a mere scrap of fame coupled with a wagon-load of unpopularity.[58] For (to answer your question about my situation) I am—so far as *promises* of gold are concerned—unmistakably wealthy; apart from which, I live in stark hunger! You express a great deal of sorrow at the emptiness of my purse; you'll express still more of it if you ever find out that I brought it to London[59] well-stuffed with more than seventy-two nobles, of which not a jot remains. From this you'll be able to guess how money slips away, here at Cambridge, where I have to spend out of my own pocket for every single purpose, and must deal with two ravening monsters, each of them a Charybdis!

When you so generously and (as I feel sure) so sincerely offer me money of your own, I cherish and I heartily salute that same old spirit in my bosom friend Roger which I long since tested and proved true. If only Fortune had given him means that equalled his kindness! And so she will, some day, unless she is an open foe to kind-natured men. —I can't see how I could live in London, except with Grocin; and certainly there's nobody in the world I'd sooner live with, but I'm ashamed to cause him the expense, particularly when I don't possess

[58]This echoes the passage devoted to the grammarian in *The Praise of Folly*: "adding, changing, putting in, blotting out, revising, reprinting, showing it to friends, and nine years in correcting, yet never fully satisfied; at so great a rate do they purchase this vain reward, to wit, praise, and that too of a very few, with so many watchings, so much sweat, so much vexation and loss of sleep, the most precious of all things. Add to this the waste of health, spoil of complexion, weakness of eyes or rather blindness, poverty, envy, abstinence from pleasure, over-hasty old age, untimely death, and the like; so highly does this wise man value the approbation of one or two blear-eyed fellows." (Tr. by John Wilson, Ann Arbor edition, 86–7.)

[59]There is a confusion in the Latin texts here. Allen has it that the full purse was brought *istuc*: thither—that is, presumably, to London, on his return from Paris in June. Nichols suggested that the reading should be *istinc*: from there—that is, from London to Cambridge. (London is implicit: it is not in the Latin text.) However, it is clear that Erasmus had 72 nobles (worth almost £30) in the summer of 1511, whether or not he took all that money to Cambridge in August. By the beginning of October, after his trip to London, he had 6 nobles (about 50 shillings). And now he has none.

the means of returning the favour, and he won't allow me to contribute anything to meet the cost, so kind is he. I wasn't particularly anxious to leave London, but it was this consideration of pride above all that moved me to do it. Meanwhile, to avoid being idle, I am finishing a book "On Letter-Writing";[60] also I intend to polish up my *Copia*, while at the same time I often curse these unfruitful, miserable literary pursuits of mine.

P.S. Please give my warmest greetings to Master Grocin, who was patron and teacher to us both. I have arranged about the boy with Mr. William[61] even though Linacre had previously made the same arrangement with him.

LETTER 16 • JOHN FISHER TO ERASMUS

London (c. November 18, 1511?)

Greetings, Erasmus, and my blessing. I beg you to take no offence from my failure to write a letter when last I sent a package to you: the bearer was in haste to be out of London, and I myself was on the point of leaving my house when I met him. So, though I had not had an opportunity to write, still I sent you the small present you had asked me for. To be sure, I did not give it out of yonder larger-than-average trust-fund you suppose to be in my hands! Believe me, Erasmus, whatever people may say, there is *no* money lodged with me which could be dispensed as I solely chose. The bestowal of the money you refer to is prescribed for me so strictly that I cannot alter it, however much I may wish to do so.

On my part, I will not see you in want, so long as there is anything left over from my slender resources; for I can see how indispensable you are to our own University. At the same time I will also take pains, as often as the chance comes my way, to beg for others' help when my own shall fail. Your friend—our friend—Mountjoy will, I am sure, remember you if ever he has pledged his help; and I shall be glad to urge him on to do it (he's at Court at present).

[60] *De Conscribendis Epistolis*. Pirated at Cambridge by John Siberch, 1521; authorized printed edition, Basle, 1522.

[61] This was almost certainly William Gonnell, the Cambridgeshire schoolmaster; the boy was John Smith, who became Erasmus' servant-pupil instead of going to the school of which Wentford was Headmaster—St. Anthony's, Threadneedle Street.

LETTER 17 • AMMONIO TO ERASMUS

London, November 18 (1511)

The Cambridge carriers had already left when John More brought me your letter[62] without any letter to Mountjoy; and so I must wait for those scoundrels' return, or else for some change that may bring me a bearer to whom to give this letter to you. I understand you have at long last received the cask with the seal broken, and half-empty—and not free, by any means; for I think you bought dear at sixpence that flat stuff, those butcher's offals; and moreover I know how yon bald-headed fellow[63] has got into the habit of playing tricks. But you are right to give me a warning that no act of human decency is to be expected of these monsters; I must say, if Socrates himself had had a brush with that kind of brute, even *he* would never have been able to keep unvarying patience or good countenance. However, I didn't send a further consignment of the wine because you'd praised it, but because I'd in fact done a good stroke of business! For I'd received gold where I had given brass, and so I was trying to see if you had other verses you'd be willing to exchange in the same way—not because I take delight in falsehood but because of their elegance and ease and that friendly myopia which makes you think me other than I am.

I have heard from Linacre that your friend the Archbishop has earmarked a source of funds for you[64] and is looking for a place to serve as a reliable base for your support. If this is so, it will cut down your complaints! But if there is any surplus, pour it into a friend's lap, and from me you will receive interest; for I think you're decidedly lucky in comparison with myself. You see, you have gained what you were after—consummate learning, and a name supremely famous wherever eloquence in the Roman tongue extends; thus to put the matter briefly, you have won your immortality, while I have chased after fortune even to "the most distant Britons" and never been able to attain to her; for she continually recedes further away from me, nay frightens me still more. I had two peerless friends, who yet were men for whom the predictions and speculations of all their fellows foretold lifelong poverty and humility; Fortune has promoted

[62]Letter 14. Letters to Ammonio were sometimes delivered to More's house, either by mistake (he had now been living in St. Thomas's for almost a month) or because he was out of town.

[63]The "bald-headed rascal" mentioned by Erasmus in Letter 14.

[64]Perhaps a reference to the rectory of Aldington, Kent, to which Erasmus was to be presented in four months' time.

them, quite marvellously and as if on special purpose to spite myself, both to the highest dignity: one she has made Vice-Chancellor of the Holy See, the other (just recently) Supreme Penitentiary.[65] Each of them is now reproaching me with folly for preferring Britain to himself and to the city of Rome, the home of Fortune; and by him I am in turn despised, and not altogether undeservedly. I may add that, whereas you send your reputation before you wherever you turn, and cannot fail to find powerful patrons everywhere, I'll be unable to scrape together any means to support my declining years, except among those whom I have given much hard work, many years, and no little expense to oblige. Where to flee I don't know, seeing that I've quite grown old in this "Cimmerian darkness of the North": premature grey hairs, which they call the standard-bearers of death, are rushing out in serried ranks all over my head. But it's a long dirge; and this is the interest I keep for you!

I haven't yet paid my respects to Lord Mountjoy; it's my misfortune to keep postponing my duty from day to day. The Bishop of Durham is promising you his aid and personal attachment, while the Bishop of Winchester expresses himself in a less public way but in a more friendly vein. He was under the impression that you already held a benefice; I replied that you'd been given the expectation of a benefice but that no benefice had yet been forthcoming. He smiled and asked: "Was that particular hope something you could use to buy food?" I smiled in turn, and said: "Rather Erasmus has purchased these expectations by spending money and time." Thereupon he bade me to speak to him about this on another occasion, at my greater convenience. I haven't yet seen fit to do this, but was extremely glad that the Bishop of Winchester spoke so affectionately about you. As to the future, I'll see to it that you don't lack any kindness at my hands.

About the "hive" for you to withdraw to, I don't know what definite news I could give. The Austin friars have nobody with whom you could share a dwelling. I don't know whether you'd like me to ask the blind poet.[66] I hear there are certain empty rooms there, which

[65]The Vice-Chancellor was Sisto della Rovere; the Supreme Penitentiary Leonardo Grosso della Rovere. They were of a Lucca family, like Ammonio (*E.E.*, I, 487); the same family as Julius II.

[66]That is, the French Augustinian Friar Bernard André (c. 1450–c. 1522). André was born at Toulouse (of a distinguished family, it seems) and came to England in 1485. He was blind by then and already compared himself to Homer. He was introduced to the new king, probably by Richard Foxe. Henry, who tended to be impressed by distinguished European intellectuals, was always generous to him. André taught at Oxford in the late 1480's and was also made one of the poets laureate. From 1498 he held various livings, or pensions therefrom—

could be leased, but they'd have to be furnished. As to the Hospital[67] where I myself am, they say every corner is filled; besides, the table they keep is worse than mediocre. There is, as you know, a college near St. Paul's, belonging to certain learned men, who, they say, live rather well;[68] but in my opinion it would be living in a sewer! Perhaps it wouldn't do any harm to have a try at Francis,[69] but he seems to me

---

an allowance of £24, for instance, from a living which he resigned in 1505. One of his poetical works, *Les Douze Triomphes de Henry VII*, a comparison of the deeds of Henry and Hercules, written about 1497, was printed in 1858 by James Gairdner in his *Memorials of King Henry the Seventh* (Rolls Series). Gairdner's preface to that volume is one of the two substantial accounts of André; the other being William Nelson's *John Skelton* (1939), chapter I, "The Scholars of Henry VII." André was an educationalist, the author of "a Latin vocabulary, several grammars, treatises on rhetoric and on elegant composition, an *Art of Letter Writing*, an *Orthography*, and an *Art of Memory*" (Nelson, 19–20; Nelson printed a list of his MS. works, 239–42). In 1496 André was appointed tutor to Prince Arthur, Henry's eldest son; another of the boy's tutors was Thomas Linacre. André resigned this position in 1500 to devote himself fully to history. He was the "royal historiographer," commissioned by Henry VII to write the official biography, so to speak. Gairdner printed his *Vita Henrici VII*, which takes the story to 1497, and also two excerpts from the *Annals*, which André kept from 1500 and showed to the king at the end of every year. Gairdner commented: "as a strictly contemporary record therefore, of the days of Henry VII, the historical writings of Bernard André may be said to stand alone" (viii). This is certainly true of the period before 1502 (when the Italian Polydore Vergil came to England); Vergil wrote his account of the reign of Henry VIII in 1513, though it was not published until 1534. See Denys Hay, *Polydore Vergil*, 1952. Professor Hay writes that André's history "remained largely unknown and consequently uninfluential" (155). Erasmus' relations with André were not in fact too good. Erasmus thought him a lightweight, with little talent; moreover, André had lent him about £8 which he was unable to pay back—eventually Mountjoy paid the debt.

[67]St. Thomas's.

[68]That is, the community house, something like a collegiate foundation, of the London Doctors of Civil Law: the College of Advocates, or, from the 1530's, "the College of Civilians called Doctors' Commons." Experts in the Roman Civil Law were in especial demand in diplomatic and international affairs, in the admiralty (that is, commercial and maritime) courts, and in the ecclesiastical courts. The records of Doctors' Commons go back to 1511; it was therefore a new "college" at the time Ammonio wrote—dating from the last years of the reign of Henry VII, probably. It was in Paternoster Row, just north of St. Paul's, in a house which later became the Queen's Head Tavern. The society admitted honorary members; More became a member in December 1514, and Colet, Grocin, and Tunstall belonged to it. The community moved in 1568 into Mountjoy House (the home in 1511 of William Blount) in Knightrider Street, three or four minutes south of St. Paul's, which was leased from the Dean and Chapter and the lease taken over in February 1568, on behalf of Trinity Hall, Cambridge. The house perished in the Great Fire, but was rebuilt. Doctors' Commons was abolished in 1857, and its jurisdiction taken over by the new Probate Court. See William Senior, *Doctors' Commons and the Old Court of Admiralty: A Short History of the Civilians in England* (London, 1922).

[69]Francis of Padua, mentioned by Erasmus in Letter 14.

a more pitiable object than the old beggar Irus himself. In a word, I've nothing yet to report about this business; if anything comes into my mind, you'll be informed about it. Why should I ask you about Griffo's friendliness,[70] especially at this particular time when Messer Giambattista Boncanti is away? Write back and tell me your wishes; meanwhile, if you should return to London you won't want for a room.

Up to the present I haven't seen More; I thought, too, that it wouldn't do to make a special point of asking him whether he has delivered that letter—he can hardly have helped delivering it, for never a day passes but he either sees the Archbishop or addresses him. I've no news from Italy; but then I haven't received so much as a line myself. I'd like you to give Bullock once more my warmest greetings, since he so much appreciates them. About the best turn you can do me is to take every possible care to stay in excellent health.

LETTER 18 • ERASMUS TO AMMONIO

Cambridge, November 26, 1511

(This letter is exceptionally full of phrases in Greek, for the amusement of Ammonio. They are given in italics here.)

At long last, on November 24, I received your letter written on October 27;[71] a letter, my dear Andrea, to give it the briefest possible praise, entirely worthy of you, which means that it was as learned as it was open-hearted.[72] If I reply to it rather briefly, you must put this

[70]Pietro Griffo (1471–1516) was born in Pisa. He first came to England in the papal service, in 1506, but then stayed for a short time only. He came again at the beginning of 1509 as the deputy collector of papal revenue (the collector was Adriano Castelli, his previous deputy being Polydore Vergil, who was reluctant to give up the office, and did so only in the middle of April). Henry VIII disliked Griffo, probably because of his position as a papal "spy" in England, and in the spring of 1511 he was arranging to return to Italy. In fact he left the country in June 1512; in November he was made Bishop of Forli (southwest of Ravenna). He was a friend of Colet, who on one occasion had shown him round the parish church of Stepney. He wrote an historical study of papal taxation in England, the manuscript of which is in the Vatican Library. (This note is based on an article by Denys Hay in *Italian Studies,* February 1939 [II, no. 7]: "Pietro Griffo, an Italian in England: 1506–12.")

[71]Erasmus says in this present letter that he heard three times from Ammonio: that is, in the letters of September (now missing), October 27 (just received, Letter 10), and November 8 (Letter 13).

[72]*candidas atque doctas.*

down to St. Jerome, whom I've undertaken to expound[73]—a much harder assignment (*by the Muses I swear it*) than one would think. And yet it isn't the effort that tortures me so much as the worry involved. In praising my verses as much as you do, I see you're merely *playing the rhetorician and, to show your skill with words, deliberately making an elephant out of a fly*. I personally think them (*a*) very clumsy, (*b*) entirely truthful—in this, if in nothing else, I sing *two octaves* apart from you! And I borrowed the idea of that song from nowhere but yourself (being your own), but not because of my artistic skill or the excellence of my brush. But tell me, what's this great discovery of yours you write about, viz., that Erasmus is fond of Ammonio? For, if I were capable of refusing to love a man of your character—one, too, to whom I'm so much indebted—then indeed I'd be Erasmus *not from Eros but just the opposite*, i.e., *the most unlovable*:[74] one who deserves to be called brute by wild brutes, and savage by the very tribes of Tartary.

What's this you tell me? *The Pope* gone to Loretto? *What piety*! As to the war that's been set afoot, I'm afraid now at last the Greek proverb the *singed moth's doom* may come to pass. For if anything happens to the Roman church, then who, I ask you, could more properly be blamed for it than the all-too-mighty *Julius*? But pray suppose the French driven out of Italy and then reflect, please, whether you prefer to have the Spaniards as your masters—or the Venetians, whose rule is intolerable even to their own countrymen. *Priests* are something princes will never put up with; and yet they won't ever be able to agree among themselves because of their worse-than-mortal faction-feuds. I fear Italy is to have a change of masters, and, because she can't endure the French, may have to endure French rule multiplied

[73]Allen commented: "This may be taken to mark Erasmus' tenure of the Lady Margaret Professorship of Divinity" (*E.E.*, I, 492).

[74]Erasmus (a not uncommon name) was so baptized after the Italian martyr St. Erasmus, Bishop of Formia (between Naples and Rome), who died in 303, the patron saint of sailors, and one of the fourteen "auxiliary saints"; others were St. George and St. Christopher, patron saint of wayfarers. *Folly* says that there is a sort of man that has "gotten a foolish but pleasant persuasion" that if he "make his application to Erasmus on certain days with some small wax candles and proper prayers, that he shall quickly be rich" (tr. Wilson, 66). In modern times Erasmus would have had the surname Rogers; he was so called by the Pope in 1517: Erasmus Rogers of Rotterdam—Erasmo Rogerii Roterodamensi (*E.E.*, no. 518). Rogers was probably his mother's family name. Beat Bild, writing in 1540, said that Erasmus wished he had changed his name to Erasmius, a Latinization of *erasmios*, meaning "amiable"; and his godson, the son of John Froben, was called Erasmius. For who on earth, said Erasmus, has heard of anyone called "Love" (*Amor*) "which is what *Erasmos* means in Greek" (*E.E.*, I, 70–1).

by two. But this is *Fate's* business; *we are only armchair strategists here*! I'm sorry your change of country hasn't suited you, but even so I'm rather happy that a *citizen and kindred spirit* has come my way. For although these English[75] are quite *Cyprian oxen and eaters of ordure*, they still believe that they alone *eat heavenly fare and feast on the brain of Zeus.* I'm most delighted that you are *Lucianizing*, and when I get back to London, that is, before December 13 if heaven so wills, *we'll pursue Greek studies together.* Meanwhile I'll await your letter, in which please tell me any news of my friend Mountjoy, for although I've written to him twice[76] I know his ways; he never utters *a syllable* in reply. Next, what hope your *bishops* hold out. Thirdly, whether the plague has subsided yet, and what nest you think I'd best withdraw to.

I've now received three letters from you. I wrote to Colet and to One-Eyed Peter, but suspect these letters have been stopped. I gave More a letter to deliver to the Bishop of Rochester; I don't know whether he has delivered it. Illness was the cause of my failure to reply to your poem; when my vigour returns I won't be completely silent. Good-bye, Andrea; you're a better friend to me than any Pylades.

LETTER 19 • ERASMUS TO AMMONIO

Cambridge, November 27 (1511)

Please observe how shameless I'm being: I'm sending you the *Icaromenippus* for you to copy out, if you can do this without boredom or inconvenience, or else ask More to give it to his brother for copying.[77] Reason: I'm preparing some morsels in readiness for January 1, though (unless I'm mistaken) it will be futile. And here in Cambridge —what a University![78] No one can be found who will write even moderately well at any price. But, my dear Andrea, I'd rather anything than that you should assume any tedious task for my sake. I request you to have my letters delivered to their addressees.

[75]*Isti*: those people. Did Erasmus mean the Cambridge dons?

[76]Neither of these letters to Mountjoy has survived.

[77]A dialogue by Lucian; printed with others in June 1514. More's brother: John More.

[78]*Et hic, O Academiam!*

LETTER 20 • AMMONIO TO ERASMUS[79]

London, November 28 (1511)

For one reason or another I have twice omitted to write to you by those scoundrels of yours; but three or four days ago I gave a letter for you to a priest, which I finished in haste, because he said he was himself hastening his departure.[80] I mentioned that the Bishop of Winchester showed a very friendly disposition towards you, though he is so occupied by this whirl of business that he can scarcely find time for anything else. Nevertheless, if you wish me to press him, I will do so; but consider whether you had not better be here yourself; in my opinion you might advance matters much. There is no reason for alarm as to your health; health prevails here; the very name of plague is never heard. Besides, if you are afraid of that Cerberus of Mountjoy's, we shall soon, if we go together, discover some chamber, which you will not altogether dislike; for if I were to seek by myself, I should not easily find anything good enough for Erasmus.

We have had a letter from Italy, by which we understand that the French party still prevails, while the Spanish appear in small numbers, and those half starved and barefoot; that the Council of Pisa is going on; that the Cardinals of Santa Croce, Cosenza, Bayeux, and Narbonne[81] have been degraded in a general Conclave and deprived of all their preferments; and finally that the Bolognese are fairly punished for their treason by famine, plague, slaughter, and rapine.[82] That is all

[79]This translation is by Nichols, II, 50–1.

[80]This letter has not survived.

[81]On October 24, at a Consistory in Rome (attended by eighteen cardinals) Julius had declared these four schismatic cardinals to be deprived of their dignities: Barnardo Carvajal, René de Brie, Francesco Borgia, and William Briçonnet. He also annulled the Council of Pisa, the official meetings of which nevertheless began on November 1. (Creighton, V, 157; Pastor, VI, 374.) See Letter 10, note 32.

[82]In November 1506 Julius II had entered Bologna in triumph, Giovanni Bentivoglio having fled at the end of October (the Bentivogli had ruled the city for a century). It was at that time that Michelangelo was summoned to meet the Pope at Bologna. Vasari tells us that Julius "commissioned him to begin at once a bronze figure of himself, ten feet high." The statue was unveiled in February 1508. In May 1511, however, the French captured Bologna, and the Bentivogli were restored. The statue, says Vasari, was "torn down by the Bentivogli, and the bronze was sold to the duke of Ferrara, who made it into a cannon called the Julia" (*Lives*, 266–7). Paolo Bombace was to write to Erasmus from Bologna on December 21, 1511, telling him of the citizens digging trenches and fortifications against the expected papal army (*E.E.*, no. 251). These civil defence measures were unsuccessful. Julius recaptured Bologna in June 1512, and the city was to remain under the sway of the papacy until 1860.

I hear from Italy. Farewell, my Erasmus. Give my greetings to our friend Bullock.

LETTER 21 • ERASMUS TO AMMONIO

Cambridge, December 2, 1511

Your letters, my dear Andrea, make me want to fly to London for an opportunity to enjoy closer communion with so pleasant a friend; *per contra* the same letters make it possible for me to endure staying here, just because they refresh me so often with your conversational nectar that it seems to me I'm not away from London at all.

But what's this, pray? Are you really comparing my fortune with yours—the anemone with the rose? I ask you, is there a single point of luck in which you aren't miles ahead of myself? Take my reputation—such as it is: I can't reckon anything on its credit side, except that it holds a candle to my distress and refuses to let my misery remain a secret. As a consequence, it's already more difficult to regard my luck with shame than with a shudder. But this is a wound I'd rather not reopen. Say that my fortune is worthy of Erasmus; I have a fancy to put this construction on it. As for your fortune, you'll be quite right to protest about it if anyone tries to assess your gifts: anyone who could measure *these* would surely assign you the Supreme Pontiff's place! But, my dear Andrea, you're familiar with the celebrated "blind sport of fortune." Cases where her irrational behaviour has swept men to the heights oughtn't to give you such acute pain. If, however, you become quite determined to better yourself, you must abandon some part of that which makes you attractive to all *nice people*—to wit, your modesty. I personally think that, as things are, even if nothing is added, you're the luckiest of men, considering your nationality, appearance, age, talents, character, and the approval you have from the best sort of people. And unless my predictions are hopelessly out, the day is not far distant when your splendid gifts will be matched with the fairest rewards that fortune has to offer.

You lament leaving Rome; but what good does it do to count the waves in one's wake? "One's duty is to arrange the *present* situation well." Furthermore, I think I can pretty well guess why the thought of grey hairs vexes you so much: you're afraid the girls will tease you! Oh, what a bitter blow, yes, a thing "to gnaw the heart!"

I'm grateful both to you and to the Bishop of Winchester, and with good reason, because you have furthered my interest in such a friendly way, while *he* gives me such warm support. But be sure to avoid insisting in any way.

About a room: all I'm after is an apartment well protected from draughts, with a good fire—I'll arrange my provisions in my usual fashion. I'd rather you didn't breathe a word about the following matter for a while; but if you can get wind of anything, I'd like to know whether my patron has paid those twenty nobles to Bernard;[83] this is what makes me tend to avoid London, as I hate nothing so much as being dunned! Still, you are free to negotiate with him about a house, if you happen to meet him.

Two days ago I sent off the cask with a very short letter.[84] I have received two letters from you and am answering them with this one. If, however, Jerome weren't torturing me so acutely, I'd take up the contest with you, not only in verses but in whole volumes. Still, within ten days my month will be up. Bullock has written to you. If you happen to see Colet and any mention of myself arises, offer your help in any project he entertains for me. If Sixtin[85] comes your way, please tell him that his letter gave me the utmost pleasure. I still have to work at this treadmill for seven or eight days; after that, we'll club together at our ease and pleasure.

PS. I have written also a second letter to you;[86] it was delivered, I think, by some bookseller or other called Garrett.[87]

[83]That is, the money which Bernard André had lent to Erasmus, and which Mountjoy had said he would pay back; in fact Mountjoy did settle the debt. Twenty nobles were worth about £8.

[84]This note of November 30 has not survived.

[85]John Sixtin was a Frisian, who had studied at Oxford in the 1490's and then was Registrar to Bishop John Arundell of Exeter from 1502 to 1504. He then went to Italy and took a law doctorate at Siena. In 1510 he returned to England and lived in London until his death in 1519, though he held livings in Devon and Durham. He was well known as a member of the Colet-More-Linacre-Grocin circle. Erasmus seems to have met him in Oxford in 1499 and to have valued his experience as an ecclesiastical lawyer in advising him about the confirmation of his dispensation from monastic vows—a perpetual worry with Erasmus until 1517. The letter from Sixtin to which Erasmus refers was written in London on November 19 (*E.E.*, no. 244).

[86]That of November 27, sent with the Lucian dialogue.

[87]Garrett Godfrey. *Gerardus quispiam bibliopola.* The use of *quispiam* here instead of *ille*, or *quidam*, is probably a whimsical pretence of Erasmus to know little of Garrett Godfrey when in fact he knew him well; compare Cicero's similar pretence with the Greek philosophers and poets. (D.F.S.T.)

LETTER 22 • AMMONIO TO ERASMUS[88]

London, December 5, 1511

Is it thus, Erasmus, that you make sport of your Ammonio? You ask in what respect I am not many miles ahead of Erasmus, when I know well that my place is hundreds of yards below him. If our conditions could be reversed, I might soon make you deny what you now say, for I would challenge you at once to change places with me. You think me worthy of the highest honours of the Church. Is this a sign of that love which I covet, or is it an Erasmic jest? But what a prophet you are, when you divine my reason for lamenting my grey hairs. As if those young women looked at one's hair, and not much more at one's purse. A gold piece shining between my finger and thumb can make me handsomer than Nireus himself. I grieve, not for that, but because I see myself grown old without use. Again you advise well: we must make the best of what we have. But I should like you to show me the way without absolutely playing the philosopher.

I reminded the Bishop of Winchester of you again; but the occasion was not fortunate. When you are here, we will find some excellent opportunity. As to the chamber, I understand pretty nearly what you want; but you do not answer whether you would like to lodge with Griffo. I shall meet Sixtin and will give him your message about the letter. I shall also speak with Mountjoy and smell out, as cleverly as I can, whether those nobles have been paid.

I do not know whether you have heard that Allen is here in person.[89] I have often intended to mention it to you, but it has escaped my memory. He has been recalled on some honourable pretext, but really because, as I hear, he was conducting the Archbishop of Canterbury's business at Rome imprudently.

I wish those eight days, that you say you will spend at Cambridge, to be shorter than these of winter, and the nights no longer than the days, so that we may the sooner be amusing ourselves in spite of Fortune, and I enjoying the gaiety of Erasmus.[90]

I received from the bookseller your two letters with the *Icaromenippus* and have answered them. Bullock's epistle, the cask, and those two short letters of yours have not yet been delivered to me.

[88]Translation by Nichols (slightly amended), II, 53–5.
[89]John Allen. See Letter 23, note 92.
[90]*Hilaritas Erasmi.*

LETTER 23 • ERASMUS TO AMMONIO

Cambridge, December 9 (1511)

May all the Muses hate me, my dear Andrea, if I am "putting it on" at all about your luck; no, it's all from the heart.

On Conception Day[91] I was brought painfully to bed, whereupon I was delivered of several large rocks. Please include this kind of stone among the pebbles you use for working out the calculus of my "happiness!"

Take care to avoid saying anything "out of turn" in your conversations with the Bishop of Winchester.

You want my advice about "arranging the present well." All right, I'll act "the sow teaching Minerva" without playing philosopher too much, which you won't allow. To begin with, make yourself quite brazen-faced, to avoid ever feeling shame. Next, intrude in all the affairs of everyone. Elbow people out of the way whenever possible. Don't love or hate anyone sincerely, but measure everything by your own advantage; let your whole course of behaviour be directed to this one goal. Give nothing, unless you look for a return, and agree with everyone about everything.

But—you say—there's nothing special about all this. Come then, here's a piece of advice just tailored for you, since you wish it, but (mind you) I whisper it confidentially. You are familiar with the "British jealousy" men speak of; use this for your own profit. Always ride two horses at once; bribe different suitors to cultivate you. Threaten to go away, and actually get ready to do so. Flourish letters in which you're tempted away by generous promises. Sometimes remove your presence deliberately in order that, by the denial of your help, your indispensability may be painfully accentuated.

I have no business to do with X.[92] If he'd done a single thing wisely, it would have seemed a marvel in my eyes, for he's "more foolish than folly itself;" but his successor isn't much wiser. Griffo is a man I like tremendously in every way, but still I like my freedom better. The carrier claims he delivered the letter and the cask.

[91]December 8.

[92]John Allen. (Ammonio had mentioned him in his letter of the fifth, Letter 22.) Allen (1476–1534) was among other things rector of Aldington, Kent—the living in which Erasmus was to succeed him in March (*E.E.*, I, 489). Was Erasmus referring to *himself* here as "his successor"? Probably; he was not technically given Aldington until March 22, 1512, but perhaps arrangements had already been made.

There is now a gap in the letters; the next certain date we have is February 6, 1512, two months after Letter 23. Erasmus was then in London.

One good thing had happened in London: Mountjoy had been persuaded to pay off Erasmus' debt to Bernard André.[93] But apart from that, Erasmus was feeling peeved. A scheme for his going to Rome had come to nothing.

In the summer of 1511 Julius II had made arrangements for a General Council—the Fifth Lateran Council—to meet early in 1512. On February 4, 1512, in London, four delegates from England to the forthcoming Council were named: Silvestro Gigli, Bishop of Worcester; Richard Kidderminster, Abbot of the Benedictine House at Winchcombe, Gloucestershire; Thomas Docwra, Prior in England of the knights of St John of Jerusalem and King's councillor; and John Fisher.[94] At that time the Council was due to begin on April 19.

Now, Fisher asked Erasmus to go with him to Rome. But, as Erasmus wrote on February 6, "I received notice of this too late to have time for arranging my own affairs."[95] Thus he had to refuse Fisher's invitation.

In the event, Fisher did not go to Italy. The plans for the Council were very uncertain; in the middle of February the Pope seemed anxious to put it off until the autumn. By March, the beginning of May was announced as the opening date. On April 1 Gigli and Sir Robert Wingfield were listed as the English ambassadors thereto; Fisher, Kidderminster, and Docwra had decided not to go.[96] The Fifth Lateran Council in fact first met on May 3; there was a second session on May 17; and then the meetings were prorogued until November. Wingfield does not seem to have attended the sessions. The only Englishman who probably did was Christopher Bainbridge, Cardinal and Archbishop of York, who was permanently in Rome as English ambassador.

"Had I been advised a little sooner," wrote Erasmus from London on February 8,[97] "I'd have accompanied him [Fisher] to

[93] *E.E.*, no. 254.
[94] *Letters and Papers Henry VIII*, I, no. 2085.
[95] *E.E.*, no. 252; tr. Thomson.
[96] *Letters and Papers*, I, no. 3109.
[97] *E.E.*, no. 253; tr. Thomson.

Rome." And he went on to be nostalgic about his visit to Rome three years before:

> To be able to forget the city I'd have to seek out a kind of River of Oblivion, in order not to be any more tortured by my longing for it: for it's impossible not to feel anguish whenever I remember what I left behind there so lightly—climate, countryside, libraries, walks, and delightful scholarly conversations: so many of the world's most brilliant men: such fortune and such hopes!

But there was nothing else for it: back to a fenland February! One is reminded of Rupert Brooke—"Go back to Cambridge and laugh and talk with those old dull people on that airless plain. The thought fills me with hideous *ennui.*"[98]

On February 6 John Colet, at the invitation of Warham, preached in St. Paul's his Sermon to Convocation, an address which, though it lasted well under an hour, "marks an epoch in the history of the English Church."[99] "Ye are come together today," the Dean began,

> to enter council; in the which, what you will do, and what matters ye will handle, yet we understand not. But we wish that once, remembering your name and profession, you would mind the reformation of the church's matter. For it was never more needed, and the state of the church did never desire more your endeavours.

(Such too were the wishes of some of the organizers of the Fifth Lateran Council; both in Rome and in London the wish was unfulfilled.) Colet continued:

> To exhort you, reverend fathers, to the endeavours of reformation of the church's estate, (because that nothing hath so disfigured the face of the church as hath the fashion of secular and worldly living in clerks and priests) I know not where more conveniently to take beginning of my tale than of the Apostle Paul, in whose temple you are gathered together.

He took, as his main text, "Be ye not conformable to this world, but be ye reformed." "Be ye not conformable": that is, preached Colet, avoid devilish pride, carnal concupiscence, worldly covetousness, and secular business. "But be ye reformed." "It is an old

[98]Quoted in Edward Marsh's Memoir of Brooke, xxvi.

[99]Lupton, *Colet*, 178. The following quotations from the sermon are from the text printed by Lupton (293–304), from a copy in Lambeth Library. Lupton thought it probable that this English version was by Colet himself. Dr. Gee (1928) thought it more likely that the translation was the work of Thomas Lupset (*Life and Work of Thomas Lupset*, 169–70).

proverb, Physician heal thyself": and "there are no trespasses, but that there be laws against them in the body of the canon law." "Wherefore in this your assembly let those laws that are made be called before you and rehearsed," especially those concerning admission to the priesthood:

It is not enough for a priest, after my judgement, to construe a collect, to put forward a question, or to answer to a sopheme; but much more a good, a pure and a holy life, approved manners, meetly learning of holy scripture, some knowledge of the sacraments; chiefly and above all things, the fear of God and love of the heavenly life.

And also those relating to ecclesiastical promotion; to "the personal residence of curates in their churches"; to the duties of "monks, canons and religious men"; to "the residence of bishops in their diocese"; to "the good bestowing of the patrimony of Christ"; and to the ecclesiastical courts.

Ye will have the church's liberty, and not to be drawn afore secular judges: and that also is right. For it is in the psalms, Touch ye not mine anointed. But if ye desire this liberty, first unloose yourself from the worldly bondage, and from the services of men; and lift up yourself into the true liberty, the spiritual liberty of Christ, into grace from sins; and serve you God, and reign in Him. And then, believe me, the people will not touch the anointed of their Lord God.

The sermon was in print very shortly after and copies were sent up to Cambridge.[100]

Meanwhile, at the very beginning of February, Ammonio had been appointed a Canon of the Collegiate Chapel of St. Stephen's, Westminster. Founded originally by King Stephen, and refounded in the fourteenth century for a Dean, twelve canons, and thirteen vicars, the Chapel was within the precincts of the palace of Westminster, east of the Abbey, nearer the river, on the present site of St. Stephen's Hall; the House of Commons sat there from about 1550 until 1834.[101] The Dean and Canons lived in Chanon, or Channell, Row, otherwise known as St. Stephen's Alley: the

[100]For Colet's earlier thoughts on the nature of priesthood and true spirituality, the abuses of ecclesiastical law and legal disputes (a pre-echo of Robert Barnes' sermon in St. Edward's Church, Cambridge, on Christmas Eve, 1525), the evils of contention over property and tithes, the liberty of the church, and the claims of the canon law, see the following passages in Lupton's editions of Colet's works: *Hierachies*, 123–4; *Romans*, 118–21, 128–9; *Corinthians*, 43–4; *Creation*, 59, 89–90, 110, 144.

[101]For St. Stephen's, see Stow, *Survey of London*, II, 102, 120.

modern Cannon Row, running from Bridge Street down towards Scotland Yard, parallel to Parliament Street and Whitehall.[102] Ammonio may have moved there from Cheapside during February—very convenient for him as one of the three royal secretaries, except that at the end of the month the residential quarters of the palace of Westminster were destroyed by fire, and Henry lived mainly at "our manor of Greenwich" until he moved into Wolsey's York House—Whitehall—in 1529.

Erasmus wrote to Ammonio from Cambridge on February 19.

LETTER 24 • ERASMUS TO AMMONIO[103]

Cambridge, February 19 (1512)

I specially request that, if anything fresh occurs, you will take care to let me know at once. For as I was leaving London, I heard that the envoy had been recalled from his journey by a letter from the King, the Pope having given notice that there would be no General Council until November. A new story! Your cask is, I hear, still remaining at Cambridge with the wine in it, but spoiled. The dolts! If there is anything of importance, in which you think me specially interested[104] do not hesitate to send a messenger on horseback, but first communicate with Colet. Farewell. I pray God John[105] may do well.

So Erasmus was in Cambridge for the second half of February 1512. His next letter from the university was nine weeks after Letter 24: for some of that time he was again in London, for at last, after six years of waiting,[106] he had been given an English living: Aldington.

The rectory of Aldington, Kent, was in the deanery of Lympne and the diocese of Canterbury, and was in Warham's gift. It was

[102]For Cannon Row, see *ibid.*, II, 102, 122, 375.

[103]This translation is by Nichols: II, 61–2.

[104]A reference to the now imminent presentation of Erasmus to a parish living —or perhaps to the matter of the dispensation?

[105]Probably John More, now aged three, who was ill.

[106]In April 1506 Erasmus was wondering whether he might be given an English benefice (Nichols, I, 399; *E.E.*, no. 189). When he came to England in 1509 he thought he had definitely been promised one.

one of the richest parochial livings in the diocese, and the second wealthiest in the deanery. The *Valor Ecclesiasticus* of 1535 was to value it at £45 3*s*. 4*d*.,[107] though its effective (and taxable) value was only about £38, as the rector had to pay a yearly salary of £6 13*s*. 4*d*. to a chapel priest. In 1514 Erasmus gave the value of the living as "about 100 nobles"[108] or £40.

Erasmus was formally presented to Aldington on March 22, 1512.

Within three months, however, he resigned as rector, and the living was taken over by John Thornton, suffragan bishop to Warham in the diocese of Canterbury; with the arrangement that the rector should pay Erasmus for life an annual pension—assessed in 1535 (just before Erasmus' death) as £15 1*s*. 2*d*.[109]

According to Beat Bild (Beatus Rhenanus), writing in 1540, Erasmus

> had some scruple at first in accepting, considering that the entire emoluments rather belonged to the pastor, whose business it undeniably was to be present night and day to instruct the people placed under his charge; but the Archbishop met his hesitation with the following question: "Who, said he, "has a fairer claim to live out of a church income than yourself, the one person who by your valuable writings instructs and educates the pastors themselves, and not them alone but all the churches of the world."[110]

(A passage pre-echoing some of the arguments in the debate between Cartwright and Whitgift in the 1570's.) The official reason given for Erasmus' resignation as rector was his ignorance of English. But perhaps a more pressing consideration was his doubt, in view of his illegitimate birth, about his priestly orders. Or did he develop scruples, spurred by Colet's words in the February Convocation Sermon about "personal residence of curates in their cures?" (But Colet had already attacked pensions.)

The pension, at any rate, was his. But how much of it attracted tax? The 1512 Convocation had voted a 10 per cent tax to the crown, due on July 7, 1512, and for the following five years. Was

[107] *Valor Ecclesiasticus*, I (1810), 46.

[108] Letter 43.

[109] *Valor Ecclesiasticus*, I, 46: "to be allowed for one yearly pension unto master Erasmus for term of his life."

[110] Nichols, I, 33; *E.E.*, I, 62.

Erasmus liable to pay the 1512 tenth—about £4—before the pension arrangements were completed? If so, perhaps the prospect of further rectorial taxation helped to decide him to resign! One thing is certain: by the summer of 1513 Erasmus and Thornton were quarrelling about "sharing the burden of the tenths."[111] In the 1535 *Valor Ecclesiasticus* it is clear that Erasmus' pension was not to be liable to tenths: the poor rector was himself to pay 10 per cent of the whole taxable value of the living, pension included. On the other hand, the five tenths due in the years 1524 to 1528 apparently *did* include Erasmus' pension. The arrangements were rather vague in 1513, or so Thornton thought. In addition to this worry, Erasmus probably paid a levy on stipendiaries, equal to a tenth, due from his pension on July 1, 1513.[112]

The tenths were royal taxes. What of fees to the papal tax collector? Here again the position is uncertain. Thornton presumably paid the first fruits (annates) following his institution to the rectory, assuming that they were paid at all—by now annates (unlike the first year charges on bishoprics and such higher livings) were "paid only on certain and comparatively rare occasions,"[113] and, if they were paid, did not amount to more than half the value of the living. However, Erasmus was probably liable to pay something to Rome in his brief period as rector; and he almost certainly would have had to pay an annate on his pension during the first year, maybe half its value.

So the financial blessings of Aldington were not unqualified. And it may be that the £12 Erasmus was to mention as due to him at the end of September 1513[114] in fact represents the only clear profit he made in the first year and a half of the arrangement.

Erasmus was certainly in London at the end of April.

[111]Letter 33.

[112]The information in this paragraph was very kindly supplied to me by Mr. Michael Kelly, of Princeton, and King's College Cambridge.

[113]J. Scarisbrick, "Clerical Taxation in England 1485–1547," *Journal of Ecclesiastical History*, April 1960. Mr. Scarisbrick's important article modifies and supersedes all previous accounts of papal and royal taxation of the early Tudor Church.

[114]Letter 28. For information about the Aldington affair, see Samuel Knight's *Life of Erasmus* (1726): 155–9, and Appendix, xl–xliii.

LETTER 25 • ERASMUS TO AMMONIO

Cambridge, May 9 (1512)

Please pass on to me any reliable rumours circulating at your end;[115] for I'm very anxious to hear whether it's true that Pope Julius is acting like Julius Caesar, and also whether our Lord Christ keeps His ancient way of testing most severely in misfortune's storms those whose discipleship he most desires to reveal. For my part, dear Andrea, I have taken a solemn vow for the good outcome of the Church's affairs (I see you approve my piety already!): I am going to pay a visit to Our Lady of Walsingham, and I will there hang up a votive offering of a Greek poem. Look for it, if ever you reach the place.

Bullock is applying himself busily to Greek. You're second to none in his affections. Be sure to give my greetings to Monsieur John,[116] who is the Grand Master of kindness in every respect. Will you pass on my thanks to Messer Carmiliano[117] for writing such eminently friendly falsehoods about me in that superbly accomplished letter he wrote to Bryan[118] in which he calls me "most learned of learned men." Of course I can't recognize myself in words of praise like these; but this fact itself makes me all the more indebted to his extraordinary goodwill and devotion towards me. For me it undoubtedly was both an honour and a pleasure to receive compliments at the hands of a much complimented person.

[115]Probably a reference to the dispensation proceedings.

[116]John of Lorraine, Ammonio's secretary; he of the "warm and friendly heart."

[117]Pietro Carmiliano of Brescia (d. 1527) was one of the group of learned Italian priests resident in London; like Ammonio, he was a Canon of St. Stephen's, Westminster, and had preceded Ammonio as Royal Secretary. He had come to England in the reign of Edward IV, who employed him in the Rolls Office. Henry VII made him royal chaplain and secretary; like Bernard André, he wrote poems in praise of the King; like André and John Skelton he was a poet laureate. Carmiliano was (again like André) interested in education, and his name is connected with various textbooks of grammar and rhetoric. Like Ammonio, he was to go to France with the English invasion force later in 1512. Erasmus and More apparently rather looked down on his versifying, because of his inelegancies in Latin. But Dr. Nelson has written of him as among those who represented the effective beginning of humanist scholarship in England (Nelson, *John Skelton*, 13, 21, 27, 37, 121). He published in 1508 *The solemnities and triumphs done at the spousals and marriage of the King's daughter, the Lady Mary, to the Prince of Castile* (ed. J. Gairdner, 1895 [Camden Miscellany IX]).

[118]John Bryan of King's.

Erasmus' Greek Prayer to Our Lady of Walsingham was printed in 1726 by Samuel Knight.[119]

Hail Mary, blessed mother of Jesus, the only woman to be the Virgin Mother of a God. Men bring you various gifts, some gold, some silver, while some like to offer precious stones. In return they may ask for health, or for riches, or for a life as long as Nestor's, or that their pregnant wives may make them proud fathers. This worshipper, however, comes with piety but in poverty; and just brings you some verses—for he has nothing else to offer in place of this meanest of gifts. But he asks for the greatest reward: a heart that honours God, and is free from all blemishes.

Erasmus went to Walsingham, in May 1512, with a group of Cambridge students, including Robert Aldrich, an undergraduate at King's. It was a ride of nearly seventy miles. In 1526 Erasmus was to publish an account of this visit, as part of his Dialogue "A Pilgrimage for Religion's Sake." The Dialogue was first translated into English in 1537, the year after the dissolution of the monasteries began. The translation in the following excerpts is by C. R. Thompson.[120] There are two speakers: Menedemus and Ogygius. The piquancy of the dialogue is enhanced by the fact that Walsingham was a house of Augustinian canons, Erasmus' own order.

OGYGIUS: The village has scarcely any means of support apart from the tourist trade. There's a college of canons, to whom, however, the Latins add the title of regulars: an order midway between monks and the canons called seculars.

MENEDEMUS: You're telling me of amphibians, such as the beaver.

OGYGIUS: Yes, and the crocodile. But details aside, I'll try to satisfy you in a few words. In unfavourable matters they're canons; in favourable ones, monks.

MENEDEMUS: So far you're telling me a riddle.

OGYGIUS: But I'll add a precise illustration. If the Roman pontiff assailed all monks with a thunderbolt, then they'd be canons, not monks. Yet if he permitted all monks to take wives, then they'd be monks.

MENEDEMUS: Strange favours! I wish they'd take mine too.

Ogygius at length turns his attention to the milk of the Virgin.

Next, through an interpreter who understands the language well (a smooth-tongued young man named Robert Aldrich, I believe) I tried as civilly as I could to find out what proof he had that this *was* the Virgin's milk. . . .

[119]Appendix, number xvi. Translation by Christopher Bacon.
[120]C. R. Thompson, *Ten Colloquies of Erasmus,* New York, 1957.

And Aldrich reads aloud the "authentic record"—written on a high board: "as Aldrich read, I followed along, not trusting him completely in so vital a matter."

Later, when the party was preparing to leave, one of the custodians approaches Ogygius with a question. Here, to make fun of the ignorance of Greek among the canons, Erasmus has Ogygius confess that this is his second visit to Walsingham; there is no reason to assume that Erasmus paid two visits—the time schedule is just literary licence.

OGYGIUS: He asks if I was the man who two years earlier had put up a votive tablet in Hebrew. I admit it.
MENEDEMUS: Do you write Hebrew?
OGYGIUS: Of course not, but anything they don't understand they call Hebrew.

The subprior is called.

OGYGIUS: This man greeted me decently enough. He tells me how hard many persons toil to read those lines, and how often they wipe their spectacles in vain. Whenever some aged Doctor of Divinity or Law came along he was marched off to the tablet. One would say the letters were Arabic; another, that they were fictitious characters. . . . Upon request, I gave the meaning of the verses, in Latin, translating word for word. I refused the small tip proffered for this bit of work.

The account ends with a piece of Erasmian moralizing:

OGYGIUS: We shall be pure if we worship the Virgin zealously.
MENEDEMUS: How does she like to be worshipped?
OGYGIUS: You will adore her most acceptably if you imitate her.
MENEDEMUS: Precisely—but that's very hard to do.
OGYGIUS: Yes, but most glorious.

That is very like a passage in *The Praise of Folly*, published just one year before Erasmus went to Walsingham:

How many are there that burn candles to the Virgin Mother, and that too at noonday when there's no need of them! But how few there are that study to imitate her in pureness of life, humility and love of heavenly things, which is the true worship and most acceptable to heaven.[121]

Erasmus went on, in the second part of this Dialogue, to describe his pilgrimage to Canterbury with John Colet. This must have

[121] Translation by John Wilson, Ann Arbor paperback edition, 79.

taken place during the summer of 1512 or the early summer of 1513.

After the letter to Ammonio in May 1512, there is another, and lengthy, gap in the Cambridge correspondence, a gap of fourteen months.

In the autumn of 1512 Erasmus was certainly living in London again. We have a letter[122] he wrote to Peter Gilles at that time, which may be printed here because it refers to the work he had been doing at Cambridge. Gilles lived at Antwerp.

Nothing more sweetly delightful than your letter ever happened to me. If I am answering it briefly, you at any rate would readily forgive me for this if you knew the volume and the rigours of the studies that have almost worn me out. As soon as I gain relief from *these*, I'll load my friend Gilles down, not just with letters but with proper books! Will you please see that the enclosures reach Josse Bade's hands as quickly as may be?

I have got ready my work on Adages; I've expanded it to such an extent that I've quite changed it into something new—but much better, unless I'm mistaken (though it wasn't particularly bad before). So, he needn't be afraid of other men's publications. There had been an agreement with the bookseller Francis [Berkman] that I should supply him with the copy, but he went off without even saying "Good morning" to me.[123] I am happy to accept the price he named in his letter, since I'm really not much concerned about the trifle of gain I'd make. He should arrange everything himself in person, to ensure that the work comes from his press in a style that it would be hard for anyone to rival.

Presently I shall have finished my revision of the New Testament; I shall also finish off St. Jerome's letters. I shall correct Seneca too, if I can find the time. Possibly I may come after Easter to see you all in person; but if this turns out to be impossible, I'll take especial care to send the Adages so soon as I can get a reliable man by whom to send them. I'm rather concerned in case the printer doesn't do justice to *this* work (it's half-Greek) with his Greek font of type. So he should take the greatest possible care to see to everything in advance, and should personally rehearse himself to some extent in the use of Greek letters; this will subsequently help him in the publication of further books. He is not to send either money or books here, until I write to inform him fully about my intentions. I don't yet see the Dialogues of Lucian (which I sent him) appearing. I notice that some of them have been printed at Louvain; and am anxious to hear more about this. I've translated a good many books of Plutarch, which I will send subsequently after revising the text. By the hand of a certain Englishman I have received Bade's last letter, in which he writes that he has put the "Praise of Folly" into print: but I haven't seen it here yet.

[122]*E.E.*, no. 264; tr. Thomson.

[123]For more about Francis Berkman, the literary agent, see Letter 38.

That letter is placed by Allen in the autumn of 1512. Erasmus was certainly in London in November 1512 (*E.E.*, 267) and in January 1513 (*E.E.*, 268 and 269, the latter being a preface to the revised edition of the *Adages*, dated by Erasmus from London, 5 January). The next surviving letter (*E.E.*, 270) was written from Cambridge to Colet on July 11, 1513, by which time Erasmus had been in Cambridge for at least ten days.

Hugh Latimer (at that time a Fellow of Clare) later referred to a season when "Doctor Colet was in trouble, and should have been burnt, if God had not turned the King's heart to the contrary."[124] What in fact happened was that at the beginning of July, after Henry had left the country, Colet was brought before Warham on a charge of irregularity by the Bishop of London, Richard Fitzjames (c. 1445–1522), sometime Warden of Merton (1483–1507) and Fisher's predecessor as Bishop of Rochester (1497–1504). The charges appear to have concerned his criticism of the place of images in worship, his unorthodoxy in certain points of scriptural interpretation, his opinions about the temporal revenues of the church, and (most decisive) his inordinate criticisms of the bishop. Warham acquitted Colet of the charges.[125] But Fitzjames suspended Colet from preaching for a period (probably from July to October 1513); and Warham "allowed the suspension to stand for the sake of ecclesiastical order, till it expired, thereby saving the bishop from an awkward position."[126]

The final paragraph of the next letter "may mark the beginning of Colet's troubles with the bishop."[127]

[124]Latimer, Seventh Sermon on the Lord's Prayer, 1552 (Everyman edition), 374.

[125]This episode entered into the "myth" of the later Reformers. Tyndale in 1531 said that Fitzjames "would have made the old Dean of Paul's a heretic, for translating the Paternoster in English, had not the Bishop of Canterbury holp the Dean" (*Answer to More*, Parker Society, 168). In the 1540's John Bale wrote that Colet's offence was "for reading of Paul's Epistles by his life" *Bale*, Parker Society, 395). For Bale, Colet was *alter Paulus*, a prophet in line with Wycliffe. To Matthew Parker he was the Oxford divine who imposed "the rule of sacred scripture" (*De Antiquitate*, 1572, 353). And in *The Lives of Thirty-two English Divines*, edited by Samuel Clarke and published in 1677, Colet was placed first, Coverdale being second. Erasmus' 1521 account of the 1513 case is in *E.E.*, IV, 524; tr. Lupton, *Vitrier and Colet*.

[126]P. S. Allen, "Dean Colet and Archbishop Warham," *E.H.R.* (April 1902), 306.

[127]*Ibid.*, 305.

LETTER 26 • ERASMUS TO COLET

Cambridge, July 11 (1513)

You actually reply in earnest to a letter I wrote in fun; perhaps it was a breach of decorum to jest with such a powerful patron! All the same, I had a fancy at the time to be witty and frivolous in company with a friend as peerless as you; I wasn't thinking of your rank so much as of your kindness. Your good nature will enable you to take my foolish sally in good part.

You write that I am in your debt even against my will. Generally speaking, my dear Colet, it's unpleasant, as Seneca says, to be in debt to a man one doesn't wish to owe anything to. Still, I know nobody on earth whose debtor I'd rather be than yours. And your attitude towards me has always been such that, if no good works had been thrown into the scale, I was bound all the same to pile up an enormous load of obligation to you. In fact, however, such a quantity of kindnesses, and material benefits too, has come to swell the balance that I'd be the most thankless of men if I failed to acknowledge it. You say you are far from well off. I fully believe this and fully sympathize. However, unusual pressure from my own poverty made me trouble you in yours. How reluctantly I did so you may guess from just one fact—my extreme lateness in asking for the fulfilment of an old promise of yours. (I'm not surprised that your promise has slipped your memory, immersed as you are in a great variety of affairs.) Once in your own garden, when there happened to be some talk about my *Copia*, and I'd expressed an intention of inscribing it—as a book for youth—to our youthful Prince,[128] you proceeded to request that I should dedicate it—as a new book—to your new school. I replied with a smile that your school was rather modestly endowed: that what I needed was somebody in a position to furnish a little ready money; and you began to smile in agreement. Next, when I had mentioned my many categories of expenses, you put some questions to me, and then proceeded to say that while you were unable to provide what my circumstances demanded, still you would be happy to give me fifteen angels.[129] And when you cheerfully repeated this offer, I asked if it

[128]Henry VIII, who came to the throne in April 1509 at the age of seventeen.

[129]About £5 in value. The angel was a gold coin, bearing the stamp of an angel, first issued under Edward IV as a substitute for the gold noble—the angel was smaller and more practical, but they were interchangeable. It was last issued by Charles I in 1642. "The angel was recognised abroad as the characteristic coin of England, similar in this respect to the fiorino d'oro or florin of Florence and the

seemed sufficient. You replied even more cheerfully, that you'd certainly be glad to pay this. Upon this I said: "I, too, shall be glad to accept it."

Perhaps you will recall the episode, now that I've mentioned it. I could add further proofs, if you did not freely believe me already. There are of course a few people, friends too (for I have nothing to do with any enemies of yours, nor do I care a straw for their remarks), who are apt to describe you as a somewhat hard man, and as being over-careful in disbursing money; and they said (so I interpreted it, with their approval) that this was not through any fault of meanness, but that, since your decent shyness of character prevented you from saying "no" to people who were shamelessly importunate in pressing you, therefore you were on the sparing side vis-à-vis your friends, who caused you no embarrassment—since you couldn't fully satisfy both! However none of this applies in my case; for though I don't exactly make a nuisance of myself with annoying demands I always have found you most generous. I didn't, then, hear this from your detractors but from men who sincerely wish you well. However, I am not in the habit of either agreeing with their opinion or violently combating it, except by acknowledging your unsurpassed kindness to myself. If you find it not displeasing to grant the balance of what you have promised, I shall accept it (my circumstances being what they are) not as a debt but as a good turn, which I shall repay in any way I ever can, and at least shall hold in grateful remembrance.

I was distressed to read what you wrote at the end of your letter: that the burden of business was oppressing you more vexatiously than usual. I'd like to see you withdrawn to as great a distance as possible from the world's affairs: not because I fear this world may entangle you in her allurements and claim possession of you as her own, but because I'd rather see your distinguished talents, eloquence, and learning wholly devoted to Christ. But if you can't completely get clear, still beware of sinking daily deeper in that bog. Perhaps defeat would be better than victory at such a cost; for the greatest of all blessings is peace of mind. These are the thorns which always accompany riches; meanwhile, confront the vain babblings of ill-

---

ducat of Venice" (Donald C. Baker, "The *Angel* of English Literature," *Studies in the Renaissance*, VI. [New York, 1959], 87). At this time it was worth about 6*s.* 8*d.* A little later in the reign the angel was considered worth between 7*s.* and 8*s.*; by 1600 it was worth 10*s.* See also J. D. Mackie, *The Earlier Tudors*, appendix: "Tudor Coinage."

disposed people with an upright and pure conscience; present yourself whole to our one unchanging Lord Christ, and the world's windings will not vex you so much. But why do I as "the sow, teach Minerva," or, being sick myself, attempt to cure the physician? Farewell, best of teachers.

P.S. I have finished the collation of the New Testament and am now starting on St. Jerome. After this is done, back I fly to you and yours. Your protegé—yes, he is yours indeed—Thomas Lupset[130] is helping me and delighting me greatly with his company every day, and with the assistance he's giving me in the revision of these texts. And I return aid for aid: which is something I'd do more liberally if his studies allowed the time, for I shouldn't like to take a young man away from those. Believe me, nothing on earth outdoes him in affection for yourself.

LETTER 27 • ERASMUS TO THOMAS MORE

Cambridge (July 1513)

Lupset thinks that with our help he has been reborn and quite returned from Hell. But the Masters are trying every trick to drag the youth back to their treadmill; for that very day he tore up his books of (scholastic) sophistry and bought Greek ones instead! Please see you play *your* part well when the right time comes along. Nothing is more attractive or affectionate than this youth's disposition.

I'm translating a book by Plutarch, "On How To Tell a Flatterer from a Friend"[131]—*rather* long, but I like it the best of them all. I'll finish it, God willing, within a week. Taking a broad view, this seems to me more to the point than combatting *à outrance* with Vigilantius[132] under the banner of Jerome.

If you see our friend Lazarus[133] (a man just born for the Muses and the Graces) please be sure to greet him, and encourage him to finish making a fair copy of those things of mine he has in his

[130]Thomas Lupset was eighteen and probably at the end of his second year in Cambridge. He left Cambridge, without graduating, in the autumn of 1513.

[131]Plutarch, *de Discrimine Adulatoris et Amici*; to be published (with other translations) by Froben, Basle, August 1514.

[132]The work mentioned is Jerome's *Contra Vigilantium* (written about 406).

[133]No one seems able to identify the man behind this allusion.

possession; for I have a few brand-new things I'm sure he'll like very much.

At the end of June Henry VIII had crossed the Channel to his town of Calais with 11,000 men; 14,000 had gone over in May. Lord Mountjoy (under the general direction of Wolsey) had been one of the overseers for the shipment of the army from the Cinque Ports,[134] and the royal party (the "middle ward") included Ammonio, Pietro Carmiliano—who took his lute[135]—and Bishops Ruthall and Foxe, each Bishop in charge of 100 men.[136] The campaign was to have its hazards. On August 11, Foxe (who was 65) was to be "much hurt by the kick of his mule; for some days he could neither sit nor stand."[137]

The allied English and German troops (the latter under Maximilian) defeated the French in the "battle of the spurs," fought on August 16 at Guinegate, near Thérouanne (thirty miles from Calais and eight from Saint Omer, with its Benedictine house where Erasmus had written, eleven years before, the *Enchiridion Militis Christiani*).

On September 19, the allied forces captured Tournai, fifty miles from Thérouanne, in the province of Hainault. A "magnificent city," wrote a campaigner of 1513, "with its river Scheldt, which Caesar mentions by the same name; its bridges, water mills, and splendid buildings; no one can conceive its beauty who has not seen it."[138] Mountjoy—based at Hamme, fifty miles away—was for a time the effective administrator; in January 1514 he took the title of Bailiff of Tournai.[139] (The city was to be restored to France in October 1518, having been more expensive than useful.)

The force returned to England in October 1513. Ruthall brought back some French money, which he gave to Erasmus.

134*Letters and Papers Henry VIII*, I, nos. 4082, 4083, 4126.

135Carmiliano was in favour as royal lutanist until 1517, when the king heard a boy player who appeared to please him more (John Stevens, *Music and Poetry in the Early Tudor Court* [London, 1961], 266).

136*Letters and Papers*, nos. 4306, 4314.

137*Ibid.*, 624. Diary of John Taylor.

138*Ibid.*, 626.

139*Ibid.*, no. 4660.

LETTER 28 • ERASMUS TO AMMONIO

(Cambridge) September 1 (1513)

I have already written you a letter,[140] which has probably by now been delivered. But I was highly gratified that you mentioned your friend Erasmus—and so affectionately too!—in your letter to John.[141] The "*precepts of good health,*" which I previously inscribed to the Master of the Rolls, have recently been set up in type, quite nicely too, in London.[142] Your John has promised that he will send you one or two copies of this. If the recipient of my little book's dedication is present in camp, and if you happen to have a chance, please give him my greetings and present him with a copy. (I've revised it so thoroughly that he'll hardly believe it's the same book!)

The plague is raging as fiercely in London as the war is with you; so I'm staying at Cambridge, looking every day for a convenient moment to take wing—but I don't get the chance. Another thing that holds me back is the thirty nobles I expect to receive at Michaelmas.[143] Sixtin has already flown off to Brabant. My mind is so excited at the thought of emending Jerome's text, with notes, that I seem to myself as if inspired by some god or other. I've already almost finished emending him by collating a large number of ancient manuscripts, and this I am doing at enormous personal expense.

I was heartily amused by the picture of life in camp, so vividly sketched in your letter to John: so well did you bring before one's eyes the neighing, shouting, stampeding, braying of trumpets, roar and flash of cannon, vomiting of the sick, and groans of the dying! You'll be lucky indeed if (may God of his goodness vouchsafe this issue) you return to us unscathed! And what enthralling tales you'll be able to tell for the rest of your life about the hardships you're suffering now!

[140] This letter of Erasmus to Ammonio, August 1513, has not survived.

[141] John of Lorraine, Ammonio's secretary, who was still living in London.

[142] Plutarch, *De Tuenda Bona Valetudine Precepta*, had been printed in London by Richard Pynson in July 1513 and dedicated to John Young, Master of the Rolls. The Master of the Rolls was second-in-command of the Chancery, the Lord Chancellor's deputy; he was the head of the administrative secretariat, was responsible for the Chancery records, and appointed the keeper of the records in the Tower; his official residence was "at the Rolls"—the Rolls House in Chancery Lane, where the Public Record Office now stands.

[143] Thirty nobles: about £12 in value. This probably refers to the half-yearly pension from Aldington. Michaelmas is September 29.

But I beseech you urgently by the Muses and Graces, my dear Ammonio, to see to it, as I warned you in my last letter, that you don't fight unprotected. Be as fierce as you like with your pen; with *it*, you are free to slay a hundred thousand foes in a single day. I rejoice in the success of our cause, to a degree that it would not be permissible to express, either verbally or in a letter.

If ever you visit Saint Omer, and a suitable occasion arises, please give my greeting to the Abbot of St. Bertin, my most esteemed patron; also to his bursar, Antony of Luxemburg, Canon at Saint Omer, and to Master Guisbert, the Abbey physician and town physician (they are two of my best friends); and, in addition, to the Dean of the said church,[144] who is a man of exemplary character, and a great lover of literature too: if you should get a chance to speak to him, I beg you to ask him what's become of my former servant Maurice, whom I shall assuredly be glad to help in any way I can. I'd not dare to ask you (harassed as you are by numerous hardships and at the same time, as my guess is, by many distractions also) to write at some time to me too; however, if ever you find it no imposition to do so, it will give me as much pleasure as anything could.

I know it's unnecessary for anyone, much less myself, to ask you to support your own John's scheme and help him to advance it as successfully as possible; I am well acquainted with the high esteem in which you hold him. On his side, he's completely devoted to you; and it isn't Ammonio's way to play second fiddle in affection. It is in you that he has reposed his principal hopes of success in the business.

I beg you most particularly to be sure to give my greetings to Baptista;[145] the letter I'm looking for from him must be written in Greek, or not at all! I pray that some benevolent deity will send more favourable breezes; for "this wind allows one neither to stay nor sail."

It may be mentioned here that on September 9, at the battle of Flodden, James IV of Scotland was killed, and maybe 10,000 others, including his natural son Alexander Stuart, who had been a favourite pupil of Erasmus in Italy; they had first met in Padua, and then toured Siena, Rome, and the south. At that time Alexander was about fifteen—and Archbishop of St. Andrews. He was about twenty when he was killed. He had given Erasmus a seal-

[144]The Dean of the Abbey was Sidrach de Lalaing, who had been appointed in March (*E.E.*, I, 531).

[145]Probably the Italian John Baptista Boerio, physician to Henry VII and Henry VIII, whose sons Erasmus had tutored in Italy (dull boys, it seems).

ring in 1509: *cum onyche Terminum exprimente*. Erasmus still had it when he died.[146]

In the middle of September Erasmus moved out of Cambridge for a time, to stay at Landbeach (five miles to the north) with William Gonnell, the young school-master, and his father and mother. This move was dictated by the danger of plague in Cambridge itself. The next letter was written on his return. It shows that Erasmus had made previous trips to the Gonnell household at Landbeach—the Gonnells lent him a horse and took care of it for him.

LETTER 29 • ERASMUS TO WILLIAM GONNELL

Cambridge, September 26 (1513)

My horse, dear Gonnell, always comes back to me in better condition, and fresher, too; in which regard he shows well how carefully and wisely he's been fed. Therefore, I heartily beseech you to continue to look after "our" nag as you have begun to do. (Why shouldn't I call him "our?" After all, friends have everything in common!) I'll take care that you don't appear to have spent your efforts on a person who forgets, or is lacking in gratitude.

A day or two after receiving the horse from Landbeach, Erasmus made a short visit to London; Colet wrote to him, in Cambridge, on the seventh, wondering why Erasmus hadn't been to see him.[147] Back in Cambridge, the plague was worse, and lectures, which should have begun at the beginning of October, were cancelled until the first week of November.

Another house guest of the Gonnells in September had been Robert Smith, a man of some authority in the town of Cambridge, whose son John had been Erasmus' servant-pupil, on and off, for two years since November 1511. At Landbeach Mr. Smith had been very tiresome—as was apparently his wont.

[146]P. S. Allen, "Erasmus' Money and Rings in 1534," *Bodleian Quarterly Record*, II (18, 1948), 142–4.

[147]This letter is lost; Erasmus refers to it in Letter 33, in which he gives some details of this trip.

LETTER 30 • ERASMUS TO ROGER WENTFORD

(mid-October, 1513?)

When John's father was staying with us, he told me he wished to entrust his son to another man, and I didn't utter a word against the proposal. He gave me notice till All-Hallows' Day,[148] and I accepted. I added that if he wished to take him away that very moment I'd view the idea favourably. I can't be angry at him, knowing as I do that whatever he does about the boy is done at the suggestion of another person.[149] A good while ago, when he had taken him away, he subsequently returned him to me on your initiative, though I wasn't really very eager, having by this time turned my attention elsewhere. Another time when he'd withdrawn him for a fortnight he brought him back himself and was willing to allow him to accompany me even on my crossing the sea. He has been brought up in my household as a gentleman and at my own personal expense; and though he has not made such good progress as I desired, still I will confidently maintain that he knows more Latin that he'd have been likely to get in any school, even Lily's,[150] in the space of three years (and you're aware that the first steps are hardly visible); so far from true is it that he has quite thrown away his time. But since I see the numbskull of a father driven hither and thither by the suggestions he receives, the mother foolishly fond, I'm not disposed to waste my good services. Now, nothing is so completely lost as what is bestowed upon ungrateful persons; I don't think they are ungrateful, but even more does one lose what is bestowed on uncomprehending ones! For even if the ungrateful pretend to be otherwise, they still feel inwardly a sense of obligation, and will eventually at some time repay for mere shame; but he who doesn't *understand* a benefit goes so far as to think *he* is the creditor! Thus, just as it is foolish to lay under obligation people who are devoid of understanding, so it is the height of madness to do good turns to unwilling recipients. The fellow remarked to a close friend of mine that my ignorance of English was a hindrance to the boy's learning, whereas on the contrary this is the very thing that makes him, willy-nilly, learn Latin all the better!

"Where do these remarks lead?" you ask. Why, to this: when the

[148]November 2.
[149]Mrs. Smith.
[150]St. Paul's, of which William Lily was High Master.

father was negotiating with me about the point, I was almost sure of acquiring a certain person as my servant;[151] but he has changed his mind and gone over to Brabant, though he intends to return before Christmas. If I go over there myself, which is to take place a little after the first of November, I shall leave John wherever he chooses. But if I don't, will he kindly allow the boy to stay with me until my aforesaid servant returns, to keep me from changing my servant too often within a short time? Perhaps you can persuade him to do this. But if he totally refuses this request, though I'm sure he will allow it without much reluctance, he is to do as he pleases. I won't be unduly distressed at the waste of kindness on my part, inasmuch as I have bestowed my assistance on *good* talents in this case. Farewell, my dear Roger, and write to me occasionally.

P.S. It has just occurred to me why I should seem to yon fellow the only one suitable to teach, clothe, and feed his son at my own expense: the boy has had less drudgery to undergo than he'd have had at your place! He has been treated as a gentleman and done no writing for me. I haven't either fed or clothed him meanly, or given him perfunctory teaching either. Had he been as eager to learn as I was to teach him, he would have no need by now of any junior master or grammar school usher, complete with cane. And I do think my reputation for letters ought to be considered at least equal to those of the general run of teachers. I don't say this because I'm unduly upset by the money involved, but because I, of all men, should seem fit to receive such treatment and then to be robbed of my servant without a sign of thanks.–However, more about this, and at greater length, another time.

LETTER 31 • ERASMUS TO GONNELL

(Cambridge, October, 1513)

Things here are just as before; so I am thus far undecided whether I ought to rush back to join you. Once again there has been a death not far from the college,[152] and Bont[153] the physician has died, out in

[151]Allen suggested that this "person" was Stephen Gardiner, then a law student, age seventeen, at Trinity Hall.

[152]*Non longe a collegio.* Erasmus was still at Queens'.

[153]Dr. Bont, the Dutch physician in whose care Erasmus placed himself when he first came to Cambridge.

the country, as has his little daughter at home. Therefore please oblige me by not changing the beds for four days. If I come, I'll come with our friend Watson.[154]

LETTER 32 • ERASMUS TO GONNELL

(Cambridge, October, 1513)

I can't talk to this monster; you must give him to understand that I've been more than a father to the boy, looking after him as I did in mind and body alike; and that he has *not* wasted his time, but made progress, better progress than he'd have made in any school whatsoever.

If my horse needs shoeing, see that this is done, for he may possibly have a rather long journey to face when he leaves me. There is a piece of business which looks like keeping me here, little as I wish to stay. On Wednesday I'll arrive with Watson. Goodbye, and for my sake show some courtesy to this donkey of a man.

P.S. If Humphrey[155] has time, I'd like him to put the gist of the following into English and send it to me by John's hand for my signature:

To my esteemed friend Robert Smith, greetings.

I have still no definite prospect of a servant, for the one I thought, at the time, I could rely on has changed his mind and gone overseas. However, because I've resolved to conform entirely to your wishes, I am sending John to you, John to whom I have been exactly like a father, or better than a father, in caring for his body and mind. Since his talents deserved good treatment like this, I don't regret having given it. He hasn't completely wasted his time. Although the boy's progress is not at once apparent, he possesses more of good Latin than he would have gained in three years at Roger Wentford's school.[156] As for his escaping beatings, he hasn't deserved these at my hands, and a fine-spirited pupil is far better led than dragged. If you have found a more suitable master for him, I myself am glad, both for the boy's sake and yours (his parents') since this boy's natural endowments are good enough for the services of a first-class tutor. You may find a more learned, but never a more affectionate one, though you search the country through. My good wishes to yourself, your excellent wife and all your house.

"On Wednesday I'll arrive with Watson": Erasmus did make

[154]John Watson of Peterhouse.
[155]Probably Humphrey Walkden of Queens'.
[156]St. Anthony's, Threadneedle St.

another visit to Landbeach, then, in October. He wrote from there to Colet on the thirty-first.

LETTER 33 • ERASMUS TO COLET

(Landbeach), October 31 (1513)

I'm inexpressibly full of congratulations to you on recovering your quiet.[157] I wonder what the Suffragan[158] means; since he knew, at the time when he was given the responsibility for paying my pension, that these deductions had been made chargeable upon it, and yet he said not one word at the time about sharing the burden of the tenths.

I feel you're a little vexed that I've once again left London without paying my respects to you; and you twit me for impatience. Well, that's my particular affliction; I don't deny it myself; but nothing of the kind you suspect took place then. First of all—I had no business to see you about; and your William[159] frankly cautioned me that you were very busy writing letters, so that I shouldn't disturb you (though I hadn't come for this either, but to receive from your William the letters consigned to me). Also—I was in such haste to get away from London for fear of plague, that I decided not to enter even my private room.[160] Thus too, when I was making my return visit for the removal of my books, I got together all my books and my gear in complete solitude, and having done this (by which time, also, it was quite late) I hied myself away from the spot and never slept in my own bedroom; the business of bringing the boxes over I entrusted to Josse. Such were my motives for failing to call upon you.

On the thirty-first of October I got your letter written on the seventh; I too, had written a second letter to you on the same subjects.[161] If my *Matthew*[162] is not in your possession, it must be at the Bishop

[157]*Quies.* This, and the last paragraph of the letter, in which Erasmus notes that Colet has begun to preach again after a "brief interruption" (*cessatiuncula*), mark the end of Bishop Fitzjames' suspension of Colet from preaching, probably pronounced in July.

[158]The Suffragan was John Thornton of Dover, rector of Aldington since July 1512. For this controversy, see p. 147.

[159]Allen suggested that this was William Dancaster, a dependant of Colet (*E.E.*, I, 536).

[160]Where was this "private room"? Either *chez* Grocin or More, one supposes.

[161]None of these letters has survived.

[162]Erasmus' Latin version of Matthew's Gospel, which he had first made in England in 1506 and was now revising. He had lent the manuscript to Fisher.

of Rochester's (this was what I rather guessed anyway); but he failed to add it to the others because I'd given them to him separately. If it's lost, I'll blame myself and punish myself by the tedium of work done over again, as a penalty for being obliging.

Everyone is running away from Cambridge in all directions; I myself have already withdrawn to the country, but perhaps the want of wine will drive me back to Cambridge!

I congratulated you in my last; and now congratulate you again for having returned to the holiest, most beneficent task of all—preaching! Yes, I think that brief interruption will even be turned to good account; men will listen more thirstily to one whose voice they have missed awhile. May the Supreme Lord Jesus guard and keep you.

Erasmus presumably returned to Cambridge at the end of the first week in November (though the first definite date we have is November 26: Letter 36). The following letter to Gonnell is placed by Allen as probably written from Cambridge in the first part of November.

LETTER 34 • ERASMUS TO GONNELL

(Cambridge, first part of November, 1513)

There's no reason for you to be much perturbed at the death of one or two people, unless the scourge begins to spread in all directions; especially when, as things are in England at present, changing one's domicile means simply changing, and not escaping from, one's danger. Avoid the contagion of a crowd as much as you can; live temperately, as you're doing; and keep the members of your household from contact with crowds in the same way. Winter's upon us now; and winter commonly cures troubles of this sort.

I believe you're far too deeply vexed, almost to the point of despair, over the loss of your treasure-chest and the little cash that was in it. In the first place, what has the Muses' nursling to do with money, or Apollo to do with Midas? Next, what concern of a young man are the cares that beset the old? And lastly why should the loss of such a very tiny sum affect the spirits of a Gonnell? Why, when I was on the point of returning to France fifteen years ago I lost money to the value of twenty pounds on Dover beach—shipwrecked before I even got aboard![163] I'd lost all I had in the world at once, but I was so undismayed that I went back to my books all the keener and fuller of energy; and presently, a very few days after this, out came my *Adages*.[164] Make the Muses your delight, Gonnell, and fortune will somehow give you back that money of yours—and with interest, too. Meanwhile, you are to reckon my bit of money, however paltry it is, as being yours for the sharing. If you miss me, I miss you just as wretchedly; but fortune won't be cruel to us for ever!

I was greatly put out at first when my servant John left me. However, my mind is quite inured to this now; so much so that I'd rather he *didn't* come back; for what's the use of obliging people who don't comprehend? "Nothing is so utterly lost as what is bestowed on the ungrateful;" yes, but the loss is far worse when the recipients can't understand what's given. Where the ingrate covers himself by pretences, the uncomprehending man doesn't even feel obligation!—If you should begin anything new, please let me know of it. When there's chance of a talk, I'll tell you about something which (I hope) will give you some pleasure and be of some use to you in your studies.

P.S. Will you please give my kind regards to that most gracious lady your mother and to the rest. I'm surprised Lupset does not write at all; I long to hear how he is and what he's about.

Ammonio had returned from the Low Countries to London at the end of October. He wrote to Erasmus on November 25. The following is an extract from his letter:

[163]This episode was (quite naturally) a hurtful memory to Erasmus. It had taken place at the end of January 1500; the restriction on the export of currency had been imposed by statute in the reign of Edward IV and re-enacted in 1499. He described the incident fully in 1523: "I embarked at the port of Dover, but before I put to sea all my money had suffered shipwreck. A small sum it was, but great to me, as I had nothing left. It was done by the chief, I had almost written thief, of the port, and in the King's name, though More and Mountjoy had assured me there was no risk, unless I carried English coin; and I had none that was English, or gained or received in England. I found out however at the port, that it was unlawful to take out of the country any money, though it might be of iron, beyond the value of six angels. So much it cost me to learn one English law." (Tr. Nichols, I, 227). Six angels were about £2. Erasmus told his tale to James Batt, who wrote to Mountjoy about it: "I felt bound to say something to comfort his trouble, but he reproved my tears with a smile, and bade me be of good cheer. He did not regret, he said, his journey to England, his money had not been lost without the greatest profit, since he had gained such friends, as he would prefer to the wealth of Croesus." (Nichols, I, 229.) The friends especially named were Colet and More.

[164]Paris, June 1500.

LETTER 35 • AMMONIO TO ERASMUS

(extract)

London, November 25 (1513)

As soon as I reached English soil I proceeded to enquire into your whereabouts, since you had written to say you were running away from the Cambridge plague. Eventually Sixtin, and he alone, told me that you had indeed left Cambridge because of the plague and withdrawn somewhere or other; but that since you were in difficulties, he said, because of the shortage of wine, and you thought the want of that was worse than the plague, you had gone back to Cambridge and now were there. Ah, what a mighty champion of Bacchus thou art, who has refused to desert thy Captain in direst danger! Wherefore I send thee from thy Great Commander's hand a gift of Cretan wine; small is the vessel, yet it containeth that which Jupiter, in the days of his childish nurture, in that very Isle, piss'd from his own little penis—mysterious product of mingled milk and nectar!

If you repair early to my London house, you'll be privileged to enjoy far ampler draughts of it. . . .

LETTER 36 • ERASMUS TO AMMONIO

Cambridge, November 26 (1513)

I'm already looking for those glorious deeds of generalship; next, how much booty was brought away under the belts. I wrote to you more than once by the hand of Monsieur John of Lorraine when you were living in camp. Meanwhile I was carrying on as bitter a struggle with blemishes in Seneca's and Jerome's text as you were with the French! Though I've never been in camp, the Bishop of Durham has given me ten French gold crowns out of the Gallic spoils. But more of this when I see you; meanwhile I'm waiting for your campaign letters.

P.S. It's unnecessary to ask you to do what you always do on your own initiative; still, I do beg you, if ever you have a chance, to help my interests by saying some words of commendation. I have made up my mind to "cast a holy anchor" in a few months' time. If this goes well, I am ready to pretend that this country, which I have chosen in preference to Rome, really is my own, but if not, I'll cut myself loose from it and go off, it doesn't much matter where, at least to die elsewhere. I will call all the gods to witness to the honesty with which you-know-who has ruined me. But if I had in three words promised what he has undertaken so often and with such splendid-seeming expressions (I know what I'm promising; I'll fulfil it to the letter), may I be undone if I'd not rather die than desert a man who depended on me. You have my congratulations, Ammonio, because I hear fortune is smiling kindly on you and not behaving spitefully all the time, as she does to me.

LETTER 37 • ERASMUS TO AMMONIO

Cambridge, November 28 (1513)

If anything that has happened this year gave me more delight than your letter,[165] I wish the Graces, together with Charm and Wit—in a word, the Muses, and Literature at large—may curse *me* with the same high displeasure as they do Carmiliano! (Which is an oath you'll certainly deem to be as binding as if Jupiter were to swear to you "by his Stygian brother's streams.") It's the only letter I've had, the earlier one not having been delivered. I'd have overwhelmed you, too, with more frequent letters, except that there was no possibility that they'd reach you; but as soon as your Master John offered the chance, the nicest thing I could do at that moment was to have a "talk" with you by the only available method. Remembering me in the enormous welter of your affairs; attending so conscientiously to my trifling business—there's nothing new in your doing all this, but I keep marvelling at the sincere friendship, and have a profound respect for the care for me, that it reveals in you. I'm just as grateful as if I had actually received the wine. However, I'm surprised that you entrust anything of that kind to rascals like these, after more than one experience of their dishonesty. The carrier who delivered the letter says he was not given any flagon.

The Bishop of Durham has replied, but irrelevantly and *rien à propos*; and when I pressed him with questions, he said (looking as though he would be glad to abandon that particular topic of conversation), "I think the Bishop of Winchester[166] has it, but I'm not certain"

[165]Of November 25 (Letter 35), which Erasmus had received on the twenty-seventh.
[166]Richard Foxe.

—and quickly picked up the thread of talk he'd interrupted. He was quite evidently hostile to Baptista,[167] though I gave him no opportunity. But these are dire secrets.

The reason why it's unlikely I shall go to London before Christmas is partly the plague and partly highway robberies—there's a crop of the latter in England at present. The day before your letter was delivered to me, I wrote by the hand of Bryan,[168] who has written a history of these French in the space of a volume. I saw Carmiliano's[169] epitaph, and when I read *pullulare*, with a false quantity, I said "Here's a disfigurement"—and when I asked, and they told me it was Carmiliano's, I replied: "Quite worthy of him too." Some people understood this to mean "worthy of the Scottish King"; and the more supercilious fellows amongst them smiled! But come, aren't you being just a little *too* kind-hearted when you seek to defend that monster? I swear I'd have given a great deal to induce you to say nothing.

I'm surprised that you leave such a great blank in your letter on the subject of Baptista; for Bullock's imminent arrival is being announced. Come, you call me "most holy"; but here you do *some* injustice to the Pope; though what adjective would fit a campaigning and conquering soldier better than "doughtiest"? Even though your "trifles" may be measured in waggon-loads and not merely in sackfuls, you won't be able to glut my mind's avidity once I get a chance to talk to you.

I see that your Master John—no, our Master John—has been most assiduous in looking after our letters. So I hold him in still higher esteem, though I was fond of him before. He says he is aiming at no small elevation, but—a bishropic, no less! I wish him all success, for I think he has a warm and friendly heart.

I have been living a snail's life for several months now, Ammonio; enclosed and bottled up at home, I mutter over my studies. Everything is very deserted here, most people being away for fear of the plague; though even when all of them *are* present, it's a lonely place for me. Expenses are impossibly high, and I don't receive a penny of profit (imagine that I have just sworn this to you by all that's holy). I've been here for less than five months so far, but in this period I've *spent* about sixty nobles; while I've *received* just *one* from certain

[167]John Baptista Boerio of Genoa, physician to the king, who had in the autumn offered Erasmus a room in London; his sons (Erasmus' former pupils) were now in England.

[168]John Bryan of King's.

[169]Pietro Carmiliano. The epitaph was on James IV of Scotland, killed at Flodden in September. Ammonio pointed out the false quantity to Carmiliano, before publication by Pynson (Nelson, *John Skelton*, 36).

hearers of my lectures, and I took that under strong protests and with a display of unwillingness. I've determined to leave no stone unturned and in fact to "cast a holy anchor," as they say. If this is successful, I shall then find myself some retreat; but if it fails, I've made up my mind to fly away from here, I don't know where. If nothing else, at least I'm certain to die in some other spot.

The next epistle, the longest Erasmus wrote from Cambridge, is a reply to a lost letter from Ammonio.

LETTER 38 • ERASMUS TO AMMONIO

Cambridge, December 21 (1513)

You philosophized quite beautifully, in your letter, about the Muses and wealth. And to me our friend Pace[170] seems deliberately to affect to forget his good literary training and to attempt a style that's calculated to please the Midases rather than the Muses. If the way to wealth is, as you tell me it is, for a man to be divorced from the Muses, certainly Erasmus won't be one of the very last, even in Carmiliano's opinion. For it's obvious that you are openly jesting when you place yourself in this category. Further, I interpret those magnificent phrases, "the Muses' darling" and others of the same sort, as signs that you're either deluded by fondness for me, or else generously giving me, out of your warm-heartedness, praise I don't deserve; or else again (and I think this is nearest the truth!) you wish to raise the spirits of a friend who's out of luck, and console him, by pocket panegyrics like yours. However this may be, I am either indebted to you for taking an interest in me, or appreciative of your characteristic generosity, or filled with regard for your practical kindness.

Just see how vain I am about my *Adages*, thinking nobody knows them but myself, since I had a notion you'd forgotten the proverb "rien à propos"! But what encouraged me to make this mistake was your addition of a pronoun and (if I remember correctly) omission of

[170]Richard Pace (c. 1483–1536) was an Oxford cleric who had studied in Italy in the first decade of the century and had met Erasmus at Ferrara. At the present time (from 1509 to 1515, in fact) he was at Rome, in the household of Cardinal Bainbridge, Archbishop of York (and sometime Provost of Queen's College, Oxford). Pace was later Secretary of State (1516), Colet's successor as Dean of St. Paul's (1519), Dean of Exeter (1522) and also of Salisbury. See Jervis Wegg, *Richard Pace*, London, 1932.

a preposition in the original language of the proverb. Your letter couldn't have been at hand when I wrote, because I was ready to guess that you meant to give ὑπόκρινεν as ἀπέκρινεν. I'm glad your previous letter and Baptista's were not delivered; glad at least to the extent that I've been spared the anxiety and grief that the announcement of his illness would have brought me, while at the same time I'm not cheated of the benefits of happily hearing he's better, combined with self-congratulation on having stayed at home! I was more afraid of *that* enemy than I was of the French, however dubious the issue of a war may be. I'm grateful that he, good fellow, is offering to share his roof and his table with me. I see he's changed his mind entirely since he sent for his sons.

As to Carmiliano: not only do you make a successful apology for him, but I admire your patriotism when, defending your country's honour, you overlook his rascality! All the same I wish you could remove all the fellow's faults (if you did this you'd do still better for your country's reputation!)—I mean "take away all that's accursed."

I'm most surprised that you can be angry with your man Thomas, who's such a sensible and wide-awake servant—he looks after your interests better than you do! Please don't blame *him* but *my* bad luck.

Now I come to your *Panegyric*,[171] whose judge and critic you make —of all people—myself! and give me all the power Homer gives to Zeus, viz. to nod approval or disapproval on anything I choose and pronounce sentence of doom whenever I feel like it. For my part I don't claim to have enough ability, or learning either, to be able to correct or criticize what you write. I will frankly say that there's nothing which emanates from your pen that I don't heartily admire; this may be a result of critical judgement (for even rather poor craftsmen can sometimes pass judgement on first-rate work), or again it may result from a kind of instinctive feeling for genius. Certainly my opinion isn't distorted by friendship, since it was on my admiration for your written works that this very friendship was founded! However, as different eyes are pleased by different beautiful shapes and as different food delights different palates, so I think there is also a certain lack of uniformity in taste—a latent kinship or antipathy, so to speak—between minds. A long time ago our friend Holt[172] showed me some brief pages on trivial subjects you'd written quite casually; a

[171]A Latin poem in praise of Henry VIII.

[172]John Holt, who had been a Fellow of Magdalen, Oxford, in the early 1490's, and then was a distinguished school-master at Oxford and Chichester. His *Lac Puerorum* (1510?) was among the first Latin grammars in English.

taste of them awoke in me at once an admiration and indeed a love of your genius, which I took with me to Italy. And again I recognized the same inspiration in Mountjoy's letter, even though here your handwriting was completely missing. There you have my opinion of your writings as a whole: I am glad they give pleasure, not only to men of learning (who, unless they're utterly soured by envy, can't help applauding them enthusiastically), but also to those in high places, the Dean of York[173] in particular. It's impossible for me to say you've achieved success by having earned the critical plaudits of the learned world, but I'd be justified in calling you *most* successful when you impress *that* particular person so much! Yes, you owe an enormous debt to Fortune.

But now you've been insisting for quite some time on a more detailed critique, crying out that I'm making flattering speeches, not judging your work. Well then, so that I shan't seem disobliging towards a friend, no request from whom I could conceivably refuse, I shall now "put on the lion's skin"—also the critic's scourging rod and frown!

When you urge me to *solicit* favours from Fortune, I acknowledge the sincerity and the friendly spirit in which you advise me; and I will try it too, though my judgement protests sharply and prophesies no successful or happy outcome. If I had previously exposed myself to Fortune's hazards, I'd be obeying the rules of the game and taking rebuffs in good part, knowing that it's Fortune's sport to elevate some men and turn others away at her whim; but I thought I had taken steps to see I had nothing to do with so wanton a mistress, when Mountjoy brought me into harbour and made me fast there. On my oath, I'm not the least bit tortured by the thought of Fortune's indulgence to others, however unworthy they may be; your own success and that of other men bring me on the contrary a true pleasure, of no ordinary sort. And if, finally, I were asked to sum up and assess the merits of the case, I believe my own fortune is more than I deserve—for I measure myself by my personal yardstick and not by those compliments of yours! There is just one thing that grieves me: being defrauded by the man I so supremely trusted. And again, though poverty may be a very harsh burden, especially "on the toilsome threshold of eld," still I'm more deeply influenced by a sense of honour than by want. All the same, I must quell this anguish as well and strip off all shame; if this is the destiny I was born with, who am I to quarrel with Heaven?

I'm very glad, my dear Ammonio, that *your* interests are being

[173]Thomas Wolsey, who had become Dean of York in February.

promoted by "a favourable wind and tide"; glad that this is happening not only to a friend but also to one who thoroughly deserves it. Still, what has Fortune so far given you that is good enough for literary talents and a character like yours? I'd be somewhat afraid of flattering your good luck if I weren't aware that you well know my disposition, a disposition which makes me unwilling to be compliant even to rulers; but either you are destined for very high office, or my judgement misleads me.

Your narrative of events is so good that I couldn't have gained a fuller knowledge of them from anybody's memoirs. First, how the bandits were cut off; next how the enemy unsuccessfully tried to surround the king; and again how on the resumption of the fight they fled in disgraceful rout, once their leaders were included amongst the prisoners. Also the capture of Thérouanne, the Scots meanwhile cut down almost to a man in two engagements; and besides, the capture of Tournai under a sky so cloudless that, as if by celestial encouragement, it clearly invited action. To crown all, the intimate atmosphere of His Imperial Majesty's arrival in camp. Some would have it that a poem is not a poem unless you summon up all the gods in turn from sky, sea, and land, and cram hundreds of legendary tales into it; but personally I have always liked verse that was not far removed from prose (albeit prose of the first order). Just as Philoxenus delivered the opinion that the sweetest-tasting fish were those that were not fish, the most delicious flesh that which was not flesh; and reckoned, again, that the most delightful sea-voyages were those close to the shore and the most delightful land walks those by the sea-side; so do I gain peculiarly intense pleasure from an oratorical poem, in the verses of which the oratorical style can be detected, or from a poetical orator in whose prose we can see and appreciate poetry. And whereas some other men prefer more exotic elements, my own very special approval goes to your practice of depending for your effects on the bare narrative and your concern for displaying the subject rather than your own cleverness.

In a few lines only, I think you should have adopted a rather less harsh style of composition; but this often happens either when the author has no time to rewrite the same passage again and again, or when we overlook these things in our pursuit of higher qualities. There's one line that seems to me unduly pedestrian:

> That you may dash out both the Frenchmen's eyes.

(If already I appear to make these points too freely, you must blame yourself for forcing me to play the critic!) The following passage I liked very much indeed:

> Whilst thou, far-sundered from the English realm,
> Breakest, in distant fields, the Frenchmen's power,
> And where thou goest, victorious e'er dost range.

It brought the situation perfectly before my eyes, anyway. Already I seemed to see Alexander the Great rampaging in arms even beyond India and, after crossing the Ocean, looking for a second world to conquer, wandering far and wide with his all-conquering army through all tribes on earth; I seemed to see the capture, the conquest, the surrender of everything he met.

A few people have found a genuine difficulty about the verse,

> Prince of our Kings in fact as much as name.

The copyist, Vaughan[174] (a learned man and an honest one), having changed "our" to "all," I suggested "no Kings," but this didn't find favour. Again I suggested "foolish Kings"—with a similar result! Then I tried "not in fact but in name"—it was rejected; and "neither in fact nor in name"—which they turned down. Conclusion: since neither what you wrote nor what I have substituted is acceptable, it's up to you to decide what you'd like set down.

The following verse ("He who of late the narrow crown did loose") also pleased me, since investigators of the hidden properties of matter maintain that gold has the faculty of loosening and dilating tightly bound substances. Similarly, I liked the line "Came, by a happy omen, to thy camp"; gold *is* the "one omen" that is best, particularly to a man in difficulties! There are numerous other things worth marking with an asterisk: if I point them out, adding some explanatory notes on your poem, will there be any reward? I add my prayer that you may be as lucky as you are learned, and clever, in your work of flattery. There you are: the Great Critic has finished delivering his critique on your poem, and I now command you in your turn to sit in judgement on the judge.

From Pace's letter I understand you to have written a historical account of the brush with the Scots; I'll read this when I come. I'm most glad that Pace is so friendly disposed to you; there's nothing on earth more affectionate, more upright, than he is. I too wrote a squib some time ago on the flight of the French, but an absolutely uninspired one; I'm enclosing it, and it can't annoy you more than once, for it's extremely short. The fellow who burdened you with my letter

[174] John Vaughan of Queens'.

did not do as I'd have wished: he himself had brazenly asked to be given letters to everyone, boasting that he'd go anywhere and practically tramp England through to deliver them. If there's a convenient opportunity, send it back; but if there isn't, I'd rather you'd throw it on the fire than be embarrassed by the charge of it. About the letter I said I hadn't received, I had no further doubts; all the same I'm glad your suspicion has produced dividends, for the relief your letters bring is quite remarkable, especially when life is so irksome. We're shut in by the plague and beset by highway robberies; instead of wine we drink stale lees and worse than lees, and our coffers are emptying; but "Hurrah for Victory!"—that's what we sing, being the world-conquerors we are. Even here, on all sides your poem is being snatched up, recopied, and praised by everyone for its learning and cleverness.

I've had a bad time at the hands of those publishing fellows in the business of the *Adages*. A certain person printed them at Basle,[175] but so much in imitation of the Aldine edition that to a careless eye it might seem identical. I'd sent an emended and enlarged text to Francis, who has had a virtual monopoly in the importing of books to England, intending him to hand it over to Bade, or to another publisher at the latter's recommendation. That worthy immediately carried it off to Basle and put it in the care of the man who had already printed it—so he'll publish this edition only when he has sold all the copies of his own, i.e., ten years from now! Also there are several books translated from Plutarch and Lucian which I'd entrusted to him to give to Bade, to be added to the previous books he has in his possession; and I suspect he's given these also to the other fellow, and now he's asking me to send more of them! There's German honesty for you! But there's a way in which I can get my own back: a copy of the *Adages* (rather more comprehensive, too, than the copy *he* filched) has been kept—I'll give a Roland for his Oliver yet.

[175]The Aldine edition of the *Adages*—that is, printed at Venice by Aldo Manuzio —had been published in September 1508. The "certain person" at Basle was John Froben, who had reprinted the Aldine edition in August 1513. Erasmus had been preparing at Cambridge an enlarged edition for Josse Bade, in Paris, and had given the manuscript to Francis Berkman, the German bookseller and literary agent, who, in defiance of Erasmus' instructions, took it to Froben at Basle. Berkman was to be caricatured as a confidence trickster in the Dialogue "On Speaking Untruthfully," published in 1523. "I concern myself in all manner of business, I buy, I sell, I receive, I borrow, I take pawns. . . . And in these affairs I entrap those by whom I cannot easily be caught . . . I sow discord between those that live at a great distance one from another"—as, for instance, "Pseudocheus" says, England and Basle. For the identification of Berkman with the character, see Preserved Smith, *A Key to the Colloquies of Erasmus,* 1927, 18.

Immediately after Christmas I'll rush to join you in London, unless the weather keeps me at home. Please give my greetings to Mr. Larke,[176] the most courteous man and the truest friend of all my English acquaintance. I request you to be so good as to add a note in your next letter to Pace, asking him to tell you what has happened to the books I left behind at Ferrara. His silence looks rather suspicious to me; not that I've any doubt about his good faith, but because I fear something may have happened to my notebooks, which neither of us would like to see.

Erasmus was still in Cambridge at the beginning of January 1514. There exists a preface to a Latin translation of a work of Plutarch, dated Cambridge, January 4, and addressed to Wolsey, who was named Bishop of Lincoln at the New Year (*E.E.*, 284). As the next letter, Allen prints the following note to Warham, which was certainly written from Cambridge but is undated. In a letter written from London in March Erasmus referred to an attack of stone, in terms very similar to those of the Warham letter: "not long ago, in consequence of the scarcity of wine, I was nearly killed by stone, contracted out of the wretched liquor that I was forced to drink."[177] Erasmus had certainly left Cambridge by the second week of February—left it for good. So this letter to Warham may be placed as belonging to January 1514, and becomes his last Cambridge letter—a sad postscript to the last two and a half years! His Cambridge sojourn ended, as it had begun, with "bad luck."

LETTER 39 • ERASMUS TO WILLIAM WARHAM

Cambridge (January, 1514)

A dangerous grapple with the stone, the worst he has ever suffered, has befallen your friend Erasmus. He has got into the hands of surgeons and apothecaries, alias butchers and harpies.

[176]Thomas Larke was, like Ammonio, Canon of St. Stephen's Westminster, and royal chaplain.

[177]Erasmus to Anthony of Bergen, London, March 14, 1514 (*E.E.*, 288; tr. Nichols, II, 121).

I'm still in the throes of labour: the pest is still lodged inside my ribs,[178] and when or what the issue will be is unknown. I suspect that this sickness of mine is due to the beer which, for the lack of wine, I've been drinking for some time. Of course—these must be the first-fruits we are to acquire from the glorious war with the French! I have merely dictated this letter, and, even so, with some discomfort; be sure to look after your own health to the utmost, excellent patron.

[178]*In costis.*

LETTERS CONCERNING CAMBRIDGE

Erasmus was in London by the middle of February 1514. He stayed in London until the first week of July, for about five months, that is. During that period he wrote three letters to William Gonnell.

LETTER 40 • ERASMUS TO GONNELL
(extract)

London (c. February 14, 1514)

Since coming to London I have paid my respects to my patrons, the Archbishop and Mountjoy; I had intended to approach a few of my friends with a small present, among them his worship the Almoner (now Bishop of Lincoln),[179] but I met an obstacle in that it is still unsafe to go about in London because of the plague, so I postponed this to a later date. The King was ill while I was there (i.e., at Richmond), last Saturday; but his physician's word was that he was now out of danger. . . .

I have sent back the horse; do be instant in urging your father to look after him well. I have something by me that I think you'll like, but there's a fantastic shortage of copyists here. Give my greetings to Dr. Green.[180]

LETTER 41 • ERASMUS TO GONNELL
(extract)

London (c. April, 1514)

I am much distressed by the prevailing state of affairs, my dear Gonnell. The plague is kindling sparks everywhere in London, and looks like becoming a roaring blaze any day now; war, with its sea of troubles of every sort, is looming close. In addition, I'm being tormented by certain personal embarrassments, besides which a new devil has raised its head at me—a sort of minute creature which, though it's very tiny, is so filled with poison that a viper, or even an asp, would appear poison-free in comparison with this one. Please

[179]Wolsey was appointed Bishop of Lincoln by papal bull on February 6, though he had been assigned to the office at the end of 1513, when the then Bishop (who died on January 2) was ill (*E.E.*, I, 548).

[180]Dr. Thomas Green, Master of St. Catharine's and commissary to the Chancellor.

write to me by Watson and give me word how my Pegasus fares; or better still, how you yourself are; also your most obliging host—and Madam, who is the pattern of goodness. Be sure to give my salutations to Commissary Green, the friend—or, to speak more truly, the patron—of both of us.

LETTER 42 • ERASMUS TO GONNELL

(extract)

London, April 28 (1514)

Your news about the horse delights me; in which respect, too, you're being characteristically yourself, as I acknowledge, dear Gonnell.

The *Cato*, with the other things I've added to it, has long since been finished; but for want of transcribers I possess only a single copy. I've added to my former collection a great number of parables from Pliny; I think they'll be most useful to you and your people, but there's no one to make a fair copy of them. Among the Britons the avoidance of hard work is so prevalent and the love of ease so great, that they can't be roused even when the dawn rises on a prospect of "deceitful cash"! If you come *here*, I'll be delighted to put these things, and all the others, at your disposal. It's for you to decide whether this would be to your advantage; since, while your visit will bring the utmost pleasure to me at least, yet the plague is still "kindling sparks" (to use our friend Green's expression) in several districts of London, and recently has even had the effrontery to force its way into the royal palace itself, causing two or three deaths. But if you are planning a flying visit, you must hurry: for I'm preparing to take wing myself in forty days' time, unless some new piece of fortune should befall me (and I can't yet see even the least hint of this). I've put the latest news in a letter to Green.

P.S. Even I had almost forgotten the thing you most wished to know, namely the identity of the "devil" that confronted me lately! It's a kind of creature which, though very tiny, contains more poison and plague than anything reared in sea or on land, for it's made of the pure essence of poison, capable of infecting friend and foe alike, even at a distance. This scourge was sent us by Liguria, which is a more fertile source of such-like poisons than even Spain. If you wish to know its *name* too, it's very different from John the Baptist's[181] *character*—

[181] John Baptista Boerio of Genoa. See Letter 37.

I had (being an unduly open and straightforward sort of man) struck up with this creature an intimacy that was next to brotherly; however, the poison once tasted, I recoiled: whereas he, in grief at my slipping away from him, continues to spit his nastiness in my direction and to make my distant self the target of his poisonous tongue. I'm comforted by two considerations: one, that I am personally blameless; two, that nobody believes him—a man so universally detested that he is loved neither by his brother nor his children, and is an enemy to his wife.

At the end of the first week in July 1514 Erasmus crossed the Channel to Calais.

On July 8 he wrote from the castle at Hamme (where he was the guest of Lord Mountjoy) to the prior of Steyn, who had been inquiring about his return to the monastery; Erasmus had not been there since a visit in 1501. The prior was a man slightly Erasmus' junior—Servatius Rogerus (c. 1470–1540). There is a slight irony here, for Rogerus as a youth had inspired in Erasmus (when he first entered the monastery in 1487) a particularly intense and romantic friendship. Mr. Nichols wrote that Erasmus "formed a devoted attachment to one of his own sex, which not being returned with equal fervour, was a source of pain to himself, and of some annoyance to the object of his affection" (I, 44). It is perhaps fortunate that Erasmus (whether by nature or necessity) was on the whole not sentimental: "love," he wrote at that time, "is the passion of a vacant mind" (*cum amor sit animi vacantis passio*).[182] And Cupid, as Folly was to observe, is "as blind as a beetle."[183]

Three sections from his *Apologia* to the Prior are quoted here.

LETTER 43 • ERASMUS TO SERVATIUS ROGERUS
(extracts)

Hamme, July, 1514

I have never been a slave to pleasures, though I was once inclined to them; as for drunkenness and carousing, I've always been revolted by these, and have avoided them. But every time I debated about

[182] *E.E.*, no. 6.
[183] *Praise of Folly*, Wilson translation (Ann Arbor ed.), 31.

joining your establishment again, I used to be visited by thoughts of how so many would grudge it, how everyone would despise me for it; of the vain and foolish conversations with no savour of Christ, the dinner-parties so profane in their spirit—in a word, the whole tenor of life such that, if the pomp and show were removed, I don't see what would be left that was desirable. Finally I thought of the weakness of my flesh, now increased by old age, sickness, and toil, which makes me on the one hand unlikely to please you, on the other hand certain to kill myself. For several years now I have been a prey to the stone, a most troublesome and dangerous ailment; and for several years I have drunk nothing but wine, and only selected wine—unavoidably, because of my infirmity. I can't stand every kind of food, or even any and every climate; for this sickness of mine recurs so readily that I have to be extremely temperate in my habits, and I know the Dutch climate; also I know your Dutch theories about diet, to say nothing of your excesses in practice. If, therefore, I had returned to you, I'd have achieved nothing but to bring trouble on you and death on myself.

There isn't a bishop in England but rejoices to be greeted by me, desires to have me as his guest and would be glad if I joined his household. The King himself sent to me (shortly before his father's death, when I was in Italy) a most affectionate letter written in his own hand, and he still speaks often of me, with as much admiration and devotion as anyone else. Whenever I go to meet him, he receives me with most courteous attention and the friendliest looks; clearly therefore, he really feels the high regard for me that he expresses in conversation. Also he has repeatedly commanded his almoner to look out a benefice for me. The Queen has tried to gain my services as her tutor. Everyone is aware that, if I would only stay a few months at the King's Court, I'd heap upon myself as many benefices as I cared to; but I put my present leisure and the work of my studies before all else. The Archbishop of Canterbury, Primate of All England and Chancellor of this realm, a learned and worthy man, is so devoted to me that he could be no more loving if he were my father or my brother; and I can prove to you he's sincere, for he gave me a benefice of about a hundred nobles in value, and, when I resigned it, commuted it for a pension of a hundred crowns; in addition to which, he's made me gifts amounting to more than four hundred nobles within the last four years, even though I have never asked him for anything. Once he gave me a hundred and fifty nobles in a single day! From other bishops I've received more than a hundred nobles, offered freely out of their generosity. Lord Mountjoy, a baron of this realm, formerly my own pupil, yearly gives me a pension of a hundred crowns. The King and the Bishop of Lincoln[184] (who is all-powerful with the King at present) are showering me with splendid promises. There are two universities here, Oxford and Cambridge, and both of them are endeavouring to have me; since I taught Greek and Divinity for a great number of months at Cambridge—always free, however: I've made up my mind never to depart from this practice. In this place are colleges in which there's so much religion and so marked a sobriety in living that you'd despise every form of religious regime in comparison, if you saw it.[185] At London there is Mr. John Colet, Dean of St. Paul's, a man who has married profound learning to wondrous piety and exercises much influence in all quarters; and, as everyone knows, his love for me leads him to prefer nobody's company to my own. I omit countless others, in order to avoid being doubly tiresome (*a*) because I'm boasting and (*b*) because I talk too much.

Now to tell you something about my books. I think you've read the *Enchiridion*:[186] many men confess it has fired them with religious enthusiasm. I claim no personal credit for this; I give thanks however to Christ, if of His gift any good thing has accrued through me. I do not know whether you've seen Aldus' printing of the *Adages*; it's a profane work, of course, but most helpful for the whole business of

[184]Wolsey.

[185]This judgement became well known. Bishop Jewel was to refer to it in 1561: at Cambridge and Oxford "the manner is not to live in these within houses that be inns, or a receipt for common guests, as is the custom of some universities; but they live in colleges under most grave and severe discipline, even such as the famous learned man Erasmus of Rotterdam, being here amongst us about forty years past, was bold to prefer before the very rules of the monks" (*Works*, Parker Society, III, 110). William Harrison wrote in *Description of England* (published 1577): "the manner to live in these universities, is not as in some other of foreign countries we see daily to happen, where the students are enforced for want of such houses, to live in common inns, and taverns, without all order or discipline. But in these our colleges we live in such exact order, and under so precise rules of government, that the famous learned man Erasmus of Rotterdam, being here among us fifty years past, did not let to compare the trades in living of students in these two places, even with the very rules and orders of the ancient monks; affirming moreover in flat words, our orders to be such as not only came near unto, but rather far exceeded all the monastical institutions that ever were devised" (Bk. II, chap. VI).

[186]*Enchiridion Militis Christiani* (Antwerp, 1503; reprinted 1509, 1515, 1516, 1517, 1518 (by Froben), 1519, 1535). English Translation, 1533, "The Manual of the Christian Knight," printed with a translation of the 1518 Preface (*E.E.*, no. 858); the translator may have been Tyndale. Excerpts in Nugent (ed.), *Thought and Culture of the English Renaissance*, 181–8. New translation, with the title "Handbook of the Christian Soldier," by F. L. Battles, in *Advocates of Reform*, ed. M. Spinka (Library of Christian Classics, 1953): abridged.

education, while to me personally it represents an expenditure of untold effort and laborious nights. I have published a book entitled *De Rerum Verborumque Copia*, which I dedicated to my friend Colet; it's a useful handbook for future preachers, but such things are scorned by the scorners of all good literature. In the last two years I have (among many other things) revised St. Jerome's letters; I have slain with daggers the corrupt and interpolated passages, while I have elucidated the obscure parts in my notes. I've revised the whole of the New Testament from a comparison of the old Greek manuscripts and have annotated over a thousand places with some benefit to theologians. I have begun a series of commentaries on Paul's Epistles, which I'll finish when I have published this other work. For I have made up my mind to die in the midst of Holy Writ. These then are the concerns upon which I am bestowing my leisure and my busy hours alike.

It only remains for me to explain to you about the habit I wear. Up to now I'd always worn the garb of canons, and when I was at Louvain I sought and received permission from the Bishop of Utrecht to make free use of the linen scapular instead of a robe all of linen; also a black cassock instead of a black pallium, after the fashion of Paris. But when I went to Italy, and everywhere on my travels saw canons using the black habit with a scapular, I there began to assume the black habit with scapular in order not to give offence by the strangeness of my habit. Afterwards the plague arose at Bologna; and *there* those who attend to persons sick of the plague customarily wear a white linen scarf hanging from the shoulders, and they try to avoid meeting people. So, when I was visiting a learned friend one day, some ruffians drew their swords and made as if to attack me, and would have done so, had not a certain honourable lady cautioned them that I was a clerical person. Another day, too, when I was on my way to see the Treasurer's sons, men carrying clubs rushed at me from all sides and assailed me with a horrible uproar. This is why I fell in with the warning of decent citizens and concealed my scapular, and requested Pope Julius II for permission either to use the habit of my order or to refrain from using it, at my discretion, provided only that I dressed like a cleric. And by the letter in question, a full pardon was accorded to me for any faults I had previously committed in this respect. Accordingly, while I was in Italy, I remained in clerical garb, so that nobody should be offended by the change. But after I returned to England I decided to assume my usual habit. And having invited to my house a friend who is eminently distinguished for his life and learning, I showed him the dress I had decided to adopt, and asked him whether it was acceptable in England. He approved, and I went forth thus attired. But at once I was admonished by some other friends that that form of habit could not be tolerated in England, and that I ought, rather, to cover up my habit! I did so; and since it can't be hidden in such a way as not to be detected at some time and so give rise to offence, I've stowed it away in a chest, and so far, have made use of the Supreme Pontiff's previous dispensation. Papal decrees excommunicate one who has thrown off the religious habit in order to mingle more freely with the laity. But in my own case, I was obliged to put it aside in Italy to save my life; and afterwards was obliged to put it aside in England because it couldn't be tolerated—though personally I'd have preferred to use it. But *now* it would cause greater offence to assume it once more than I caused by the initial change.

From Hamme, Erasmus went to Saint Omer, Ghent, Antwerp, Louvain, Liège, Strasbourg, Sélestat; and so to Basle, which he reached by the end of August. And in September the task began of preparing for publication the work of his Cambridge years. In a letter of September 23 Erasmus wrote: "My book of Adages is being so enriched that it may be thought another work. The New Testament is being prepared, corrected and illustrated with our notes. A revised edition of the *De Copia* is being brought out, and a book on Similes is also to be published. My translations from Plutarch are already printed; and I am preparing with great pains an emended edition of Seneca."[187]

In 1515 Erasmus made his fourth visit to England; this lasted for less than a month. He left Basle at the very beginning of May, travelling as far as Frankfurt with some book-dealers going to the fair; he was in London by May 7 and left at the end of the month. This trip was probably occasioned by his wish to do some checking and research on the London manuscripts of the New Testament and the Jerome; by his "natural restlessness and desire for change of air;"[188] and, of course, by the wish to visit his London friends. He did not visit Cambridge, so far as we know.

[187]*E.E.*, no. 307.
[188]*E.E.*, II, 67.

The next year, 1516, he made another four-week visit to England in August, perhaps to see Ammonio about the dispensation proceedings, now coming to a head.

The *Novum Instrumentum* was published in March 1516, the four volumes of Jerome Letters in April or May, and the *Education of a Christian Prince* in June. Erasmus was in Basle until the middle of May; then he travelled north, reaching Antwerp by the beginning of June. He stayed for a time at the monastery of Saint Omer. Then, apparently, he went down with fever and had to postpone his channel crossing. He sent Peter Meghen on ahead, taking to England presentation copies of the New Testament and the Jerome. He was well enough to travel by the end of July and probably made the crossing in the first week of August; we know that he was in London on the ninth.

At the end of July—probably on the twenty-ninth—St. John's College had been officially opened, over five years after the charter of foundation. Fisher went to Cambridge for the ceremonies.

Erasmus had intended to visit Cambridge this time. Indeed he had already mounted his horse to go there, when he was told that Fisher had returned to London; and Erasmus "loitered" in the City for several days, waiting to see him.[189] Then Fisher invited him to stay at Rochester for ten days. For one thing, he wanted Erasmus to give him help with his Greek! So Erasmus went down to Kent: "but more than ten times over," he wrote to Ammonio, "I have repented of my promise."[190] Rochester was *en route* to Dover, and by August 27 Erasmus was back in Calais. He stayed in the Low Countries for the rest of the year.

A group of letters concerning Fisher is printed next.

LETTER 44 • JOHN FISHER TO ERASMUS
(extract)

Rochester (June, 1516)

Hindered as I am by the volume of business (I am making ready to go to Cambridge for the long-delayed opening of the college), still

[189] Letter 49.

[190] *E.E.*, no. 252; tr. Nichols, II, 320.

I did not wish your servant Peter to go back to you lacking a letter from me. You have placed me enormously in your debt for the New Testament, translated by you from the Greek, of which you made me a present. As soon as I received it, and noticed in several places annotations in which you praise your patron of Canterbury with lavish encomiums. I went to him and pointed out those particular places. When he read those notes, he promised to do a great deal to help you; and he besought me, whenever I should write to you, to urge you to return.

This may be compared with a letter of Fisher to Erasmus a year later, also concerning the New Testament.

LETTER 45 • JOHN FISHER TO ERASMUS

(extract)

Rochester (c. June, 1517)

In the translation of the New Testament, made by you for the common profit of all, no man of sense could find offence, when you have not only enormously clarified countless passages in it, by means of your learning, but also furnished a most full commentary to the whole work, so that it may now be both read and understood by anyone with much more edification and pleasure than before. But I do entertain some fear that the printer may have slumbered rather often. For, as I rehearsed myself in reading Paul, just as you prescribe, I found the printer had very often omitted expressions and sometimes whole sentences in the Greek. This too I owe to you, Erasmus, that I can to some extent guess where the Greek does not exactly correspond with the Latin text. I should like to have been permitted to have you as my teacher for a few months.[191]

Two later tributes of Erasmus to the Chancellorship of Fisher are also most conveniently given here.

[191]By the 1520's Fisher appears to have been quite at home in New Testament Greek. He referred to the Greek vocabulary in his 1526 St. Paul's Sermon against Lutherans, and in his *Defence of the Sacred Priesthood* (1525; tr. P. E. Hallett, 1935, 46, 50, 62, 80, 105); in the *Defensio* he also invoked Erasmus' Latin as against "the old translation" (105).

LETTER 46 • PREFACE TO *ECCLESIASTES*
(De Ratione Concionandi)
(extract)

(August, 1535)[192]

This raw material for a work (for so I would like to call it, rather than a finished work) I had—not indeed promised, but—just silently purposed to dedicate to John Fisher, Bishop of Rochester, a man of unexampled piety and learning, with whom I am joined in an old and close friendship. For it was he, more than anyone, who instigated me to undertake this task, when he told me that he was setting up, in the famous university at Cambridge, of which he is the permanent protector (this they call a "Chancellor"), three colleges[193] out of which could proceed theologians not so much fitted for battles of words as equipped for the sober preaching of the Word of God. He himself was endowed with remarkable charm in his discourse, and in consideration of this used to be highly regarded by the paternal grandmother of the same King Henry who now rules England. Into that woman, God had infused a mind most unlike a woman's. For while other queens are wont to bestow sumptuous expense on the building of monasteries, and that too more for the sake of ostentation (I fear) than of piety, she had devoted all her attention to the holiest pursuit of all, one that even now lives and flourishes; while so little did she seek popular acclaim for doing so, that she did it almost by stealth. She placed in a great number of posts, with exceptionally good salaries, whomsoever she had found fit to instruct the people in the wisdom of the Gospels; for which purpose she handed over a huge sum of money to Bishop John, who being a perfectly upright man spent all of it either in promoting churchmen or in helping those in need—being so far from converting any of it for his own use, that he even generously added to it out of his own resources.[194]

Rightly did this holy heroine, and this Bishop who is the supreme

[192]Fisher had been executed in June.

[193]St. John's, Christ's, Queens'.

[194]For the Lady Margaret, see Fisher's "Remembrance" of her, printed by Wynkyn de Worde in 1509; edited by Thomas Baker, 1708, reprinted 1840; also in *The English Works of John Fisher*, ed. J. E. B. Mayor, 1876. Wynkyn de Worde had printed in June 1508 Fisher's seven English *Sermons on the Penitential Psalms*, preached before the Lady Margaret: very fine, with a sort of succinct strength (in J. E. B. Mayor; selections in Nugent (ed.), *Thought and Culture of the English Renaissance*).

pattern of true piety, judge and decide that there is nothing of more moment in improving public morals than the sowing of the seed of instruction in the Gospels through fit and proper preachers. For how does it come about that Christ now grows so cold in the hearts of the multitude, or should I say has quite been expelled from them? And how is it that under the name of Christianity so much paganism flourishes—but from the reason that faithful churchmen are lacking? It has seemed to me that even the population of Italy (I will say nothing of her princes) could be taught piety, if it were not for the want of teachers.

LETTER 47 • ERASMUS TO ALONSO DE FONSECA[195]

(extract)

Freiburg, May, 1529

John, Bishop of Rochester in England, head of the University of Cambridge . . . at great expense has established three colleges in which the things to be taught are not those which fit men for sophistical contests, making them dull and witless in serious matters, but studies such that from them they may proceed forth well versed in true learning and in sober discussion, men who can preach the Word of God in a serious and evangelical spirit, commending it to the minds of learned men by well-nigh irresistible eloquence; men such as the Bishop himself has long made himself for the service of Christ's Church, both by his discourse and his writings and the uprightness of his life—this he has done with the authority and blessing of William Warham, Archbishop of Canturbury and Primate of all England, whose suffragan he is by the rank he holds, and whose most dear brother in the Lord he is by the depth of his piety and the worth of his virtues.

Erasmus' English trip in 1516 had spurred his correspondence with two Cambridge friends, Henry Bullock of Queens' and John Watson of Peterhouse, though he did not see either of them on the visit.

[195]Alonso of Fonseca (1477–1534) a leading Spanish disciple of Erasmus, Archbishop of Toledo and Primate since 1524. He founded colleges at Salamanca (his birthplace) and Santiago, and was a generous patron of the University of

LETTER 48 • JOHN WATSON TO ERASMUS

(extract)

(Cambridge, c. August 13, 1516)

On the eleventh of August I received the letter you had written to me on the fifth of June;[196] believe me, my dear Erasmus, most beloved teacher, it gave me vast happiness to know by it, both that you were safe and sound and that you had won favour and influence with your own prince, Charles. Great was the service you did me when you sent me a letter; for upon my life, my feelings towards Erasmus are such that two or three short pages inscribed by him to myself are of nearly the same worth to me as a benefice, yea, the richest benefice. —But you'll say laughingly, "Why, you do well to add 'nearly'!" I frankly confess I don't altogether despise those extraneous advantages! But I don't cleave to them, either, so ardently as to prefer them to good literature and the friendship of learned men, provided I have enough for the sustaining of life. Certain it is that I so esteemed and valued your letter that, if my wealth kept in step with my situation and my desires, I should give a gold piece in return for every letter of that letter!

It is to me a daily-increasing marvel how Erasmus grows greater as his years accumulate, and how each day he shows himself writ larger, and ever fresh. All over Italy, and most of all among learned men of the first rank, your praises are being sung. You'd hardly credit the enthusiasm shown by men of this class everywhere in devouring your *Copia*; also your *Praise of Folly*, which they view as just the very crown of Wisdom. . . .

. . . Both by emending the New Testament and by your notes upon it, you have shed marvellous light on Christ, and placed mightily in your debt every student of Our Lord. May God recompense you a hundredfold, together with the gift of eternal life; for, in my judgement, you could have done no work more worthy of a Christian professor. A few days ago I came upon the small *Cato* that you have furnished with explanatory notes; and you'd be more than amazed to

Alcala—and of the publication of Erasmus' works in Spain; he renewed the attempts to bring Erasmus to Spain, more especially to Alcala. The great period of Erasmian influence in Spain began in 1526; but the idea of a religious reformation in that country, to be inspired by Erasmus and encouraged by the Emperor Charles, faded after 1533. See Marcel Bataillon, *Erasme et l'Espagne*, 1937. For the Fonseca family, see Allen, *Erasmus*, 184–8. The present excerpt is from the Dedication to Erasmus' edition of Augustine.

[196]The letter has not survived; Erasmus was then at Saint Omer.

know what delight these same notes have given me, while I marvelled at the view of a harvest so sweet and so rich garnered out of a field so modest in extent. Please, I beg of you, cause to be attached to some one of your books a list of all your works; for as I was not aware of the existence of this little book, so I fear there may be others again about which I do not know. We shall come forward to welcome your Jerome with open arms, and hearts full of good wishes, ready to express our gratitude to Jerome's enthusiastic champion and restorer.

I am very fond of Peter Falk, the Swiss,[197] whom we Englishmen have nicknamed "the Great." He was, too, the most unwearying of hosts, and in addition the most delightful of companions, to foreigners like us. . . .

. . . If you stay there until Michaelmas, I shall visit you, if God of His goodness wills it; but if in the meantime you shall be pleased to come here, which I should like best of all, no one will so eagerly look forward to your arrival as I. We shall spend a most delightful holiday together; and whatever I have that will serve for pleasure or use, shall be yours.

LETTER 49 • ERASMUS TO JOHN WATSON

Brussels, January 13, 1517

Watson, my excellent fellow, what's this that you are telling me? Am I to understand that I have journeyed abroad with you even as far as Syria? Well, that's just how I carry about with me in my own heart all my friends, particularly my dear Watson: wherever on earth I go, I shall remember those most pleasant days when we were bosom companions and the evenings we spent in perfectly delightful talk—not a single boring word. This, too, gave me pleasure: that you have refreshed my memory of old friends with whom I kept company at Venice. The man whose name you had forgotten is Marcus Musurus.[198] I know the kind hearts those fellows possess; they so load Erasmus with their praise that, ye gods, there are some who even envy him—something I had never expected to happen, and which I can

[197]Falk had travelled to the Holy Land in the same ship as Watson (*E.E.*, III, 316). The pilgrimage left Venice in July 1515. Watson went with John Reston (B.A. 1506), later Master of Jesus, 1546–51 (*E.E.*, III, xxvi).

[198]Musurus was actually to die in this year of 1517. A Cretan, who had taught Greek at Padua, he became an assistant to Aldo Manuzio in Venice, where Erasmus met him in 1508.

scarcely now believe true. I am not displeased that you, i.e., a man both upright and learned, approve of my New Testament; yet in connection with it, I myself would not dare to venture any assertion, save that I have tried as well as I could to recommend Our Lord's wisdom to well-disposed intellects by such small efforts as I could command. I highly approve of *your* attitude, my dear John, when you can explore the mazes of the Scotists without at the same time despising these cruder and more straightforward enquiries of my own, so that in equal measure you give satisfaction to *them*, and, nevertheless, enjoy the exercise of your private judgement. This suits your own character, which is pious without arrogance, gay without levity, strict without sourness. But I must stop, or else this will appear to be "not praise, but emulation in flattery."—Peter Falk, a man of the highest esteem among his countrymen, has returned home to write a great deal about "two Englishmen," forgetting their names I think. At once the thought occurred to me, "Why, this is my friend Watson;" for I had heard that you had set out on your journey.

I'd already mounted my horse to go to Cambridge, when suddenly someone announced that the Very Reverend the Bishop of Rochester, Chancellor of your University, was to be in London that very day; as I waited for him from day to day, I loitered for several days in London, and your letter was not delivered to me until several months later. As for your request for a list of my works, one had already been prepared, unknown to me, by Adrian of Baarland,[199] a man who possesses great charm of mind and a markedly elegant fluency in conversation; so I am sending you his very letter. Will you please greet all my friends in my name, even though I don't rehearse their names to you for the purpose?

LETTER 50 • JOHN WATSON TO ERASMUS

Peterhouse (April, 1517)

My most gracious teacher, you do a kind and friendly act when you deign to write some lines to me, who have no means of returning your services to me, either by a good deed which may give pleasure or by a compensating kindness, but can enter the lists only with feelings of responsive goodwill. I am very grateful to you for not only refraining from adverse criticism of my letter, in order to avoid discouraging me from writing, but even praising me so as positively to beckon me

[199] 1486–1538; at the time a professor at Louvain. Baarland is near Flushing.

to write—albeit in a manner as though you were giving me a cuff upon the ear to prevent my being high-minded! For when you call me a Scotist, if my notion is correct you are upbraiding me "darkly" (σκοτίως) and obscurely for misapplying my studies. I confess frankly, I am not so good a Scotist as I'd wish to be, though I have decided not to be so any more than I am, so far as I can look ahead, since I've taken a most solemn resolve to devote all the remainder of my life to sacred and mystical literature exclusively. However, to confide in you, my friend and second father, as beseems my lowly condition, I am not a Scotist, nor yet a Thomist: neither one nor the other but a mere nothing, a lifeless stock. If only I might show myself a true and sincere Christian!

I congratulate you on your good fortune; and I shall rejoice still more when the hope at present deferred, which vexes your mind, shall reach the haven of present reality. That this may come about, shall be my constant prayer; especially will I pray that you may attain some fortune worthy of yourself, in order that you may be in a position to adorn this kingdom and to be of service to your many friends in this place. I have obtained a living less than seven miles from Cambridge.[200] It has a fine house and is reasonably adequate to maintain a livelihood; moreover it is worth twenty English pounds after subtraction of all yearly dues, though in this present year about half of this sum will be expended in repairing the house. If this can give you any pleasure or be of any service to you, it shall be yours and you shall share it with me; so also shall be whatever else I possess. I wish you'd decide to visit me here as soon as your occupations permit; if I were not enmeshed in a great quantity of affairs, I'd fly at once to join you in London, for the enjoyment of your company.

I hear Bullock is sick,[201] but do not know what his ailment is.

Bullock, also, had hoped that Erasmus might visit Cambridge in August 1516.

LETTER 51 • HENRY BULLOCK TO ERASMUS

Cambridge, August 13 (1516)

Most learned teacher, your return to England, while it gives unbounded pleasure to all your friends at Cambridge, gives by far the greatest pleasure to myself, even more than the rest, inasmuch as I am

[200] Elsworth.

[201] See Letter 53.

far more closely bound to you than anyone else. For this reason, I should be most delighted to see you at Cambridge, so that, even if it were not given to me to return your manifold acts of kindness to me in the manner I should wish, yet at least I might reveal what is practically all that my means will allow me to display, namely my forwardness in affection; for I am filled with eagerness to see you and to stay unceasingly in your company. But I am kept away by fate and by the fortune which still treats me a little grudgingly; otherwise wherever on earth you went, I'd resolve on following you there.

Here at Cambridge, men are devoting themselves ardently to Greek literature. They profoundly wish you would come; such persons hold in great favour this newly published work of yours upon the New Testament: great gods, how clever it is, how clearly reasoned, and to all men of sound judgement how pleasing and how indispensable!

But enough of these matters. There is a certain young man here—his name is Edward Pollard—who by continual requests has at length prevailed on me to recommend him to you. He is of a blameless character and most devoted to yourself; and he has made up his mind that he would be in heaven if he might be admitted within your household. So you will act according to your own high principles, and in a way to oblige me very much, if you would write in reply to say whether you wish to have him, and make it known (albeit in the briefest manner) that I have recommended him to you; otherwise he will not believe I have fulfilled my frequent promises to write to you. Farewell, glory of this modern age.

Erasmus replied to this letter from Rochester.

LETTER 52 • ERASMUS TO HENRY BULLOCK
(extract)

Rochester, August, 1516

From your letter I see clearly enough that mine, which I left at Thomas More's house in London, hadn't yet reached you. I'm delighted to recognize, dear Bullock, your old familiar affection for myself, and I embrace it joyously, hoping that we may at some time return to our former intimate companionship, both in living and—greatest of delights by far—in studying together. I intend to pass the winter at Louvain. Meanwhile you must look carefully to see what suits your interest.

I'm very pleased that the New Testament, restored by our labours, is approved at Cambridge by all the best scholars, indeed by everyone whose taste, as you put it, is sound. Even so, certain quite trustworthy people have told me there is one college there, a "most theological" one, that has perfect Areopagites in it; they've passed a full-blown Resolution to prevent anyone from bringing "that book" within the august walls of the said college "by horse, ship, waggon, or porter." I ask you, Bullock my learned friend, is this something to laugh or weep at?. . . .

Are they afraid their own schools will be deserted if the youth are enticed away to these studies? Why don't they rather consider how at Cambridge, about thirty years ago, nothing was taught but Alexander and the so-called "Small Logicals" (*Parva Logicalia*) and those ancient Aristotelian rules, with the *Questions* derived from Duns Scotus; how, subsequently, good letters were added, and a knowledge of mathematics,[202] and a new, or at least refurbished, Aristotle; and how the command of Greek was added, with a host of authors whose very names were once unknown even to those lofty pundits themselves. Now tell me, what has been the effect of all this upon your university? Why, it has blossomed forth so as to rival the leading modern schools, and now contains men of such quality that, in comparison, those of the old time appear mere shadows of theologians rather than the reality—a fact which would not be denied by the fair-minded element among the older generation, who congratulate others on the good fortune they share even while deploring the ill luck that belongs to themselves. Or does this class of men *grieve* that more people are henceforward to read the Gospels and the apostolic Letters, and read them more attentively too? And are they pained by the waste of even such a short time as this upon studies to which every single moment could properly be devoted? Would they prefer a man's whole life to be spent on the trifling subtleties of the *Questions*?

Still, precisely for this reason I don't exactly repent of my sleepless labours. I have discovered that hitherto there have been some theologians whose previous neglect of the very reading of Holy Writ was

[202]A lectureship in mathematics had been endowed in Cambridge about 1500: a post—like the Lady Margaret Professorship of Divinity—which stood outside the basic system of lecturing by resident M.A.'s (such lecturing being a requirement for higher degrees). In theory arithmetic and geometry, part of the quadrivium, were studied for the Master's degree: the "mathematicals." But in fact mathematics was a neglected study in Tudor Cambridge, though there were individual mathematicians of some note. Erasmus' reference in the present letter is understandable: Bullock held the mathematics lectureship.

such that they scarce could turn the pages, even of the *Books of Sentences*, and in fact never touched anything but the riddles of the *Questions.* Isn't it some benefit for such persons to be recalled to the true sources? My own wish, dear Bullock, is that the labours I have undertaken (surely in no small quantity) for everyone's sake should bear fruit for everyone. It is to Christ Himself I look for the payment of my reward, and then only in so far as I deserve it; but if it is not my destiny to find favour with everyone, I am consoled for the present by the reflection that almost universally I am well regarded by those who themselves are best regarded; and I hope that at some not distant time that which now pleases the best of men will come to please the majority of men. The quality of novelty, which has served to recommend other books, has given rise to hostile feelings in the case of this one; however, I believe the final result will differ similarly, for whereas the lapse of time has diminished their reputations, it may be that the same factor will add to *mine*. At least I do prophesy that posterity will be kinder to my works, such as they are.

Still, I have no cause to complain even of my contemporaries, who allow me more credit, I do not say than I should like, but than I deserve or can continue to support; for though mortal men's judgements are so very diverse and so prone to carp, especially in literary matters, yet nobody at all has hitherto attacked my writings—writings which are not blasphemous, merely deficient in learning by comparison with other men's—except those few critics who are either so peevish as to approve nothing at all save their own products, or else so stupid that they lack perception altogether, or else so mentally lazy that they fail to read, even, the thing they are pulling to pieces, or so starved and greedy for fame that they wish to gain distinction for themselves in impugning the work of other men. In this category also are those who condemn and reject publicly what they read and approve of in private. Perhaps it is a sign of modesty to dissemble one's debt to those on whose shoulders one climbs, but if so, such modesty is of an ungrateful, ungenerous kind; and to tear apart in public the reputation of men by whose toil and sweat one is privately aided surely is diametrically opposed to the whole principle of civility. However, one who would enrol under the banner of Christ must swallow even this bitter experience.

As to your preaching, I applaud your course of action in doing this and offer my congratulations on its success; especially since you teach Christ in purity and make no boast or show of merely human subtleties.

I will briefly answer your point about the boy:[203] really I have enough and to spare as things stand, and certainly I'd not wish to be burdened with more than one.

Please be sure to convey my greetings to the friends whom I take about with me in my heart—Dr. Fawne, the learned John Bryan, the ever kindly John Vaughan, my very good friend Humphrey, and my host of old time, Garrett the bookseller; for I am told Watson is away.[204]

LETTER 53 • HENRY BULLOCK TO ERASMUS

Cambridge, May 1 (1517)

Just lately, when Bryan (whom on many counts I am fonder of than all other men, yourself only excepted) was chatting with me as usual, at sermon-time with the friars commonly called Preachers, he told me among other things that you had returned safely to England,[205] which (I swear by the Muses) consoled my heart vastly; and I'd have written you a letter and entrusted it to his care, had he not left us so suddenly. As it is, I now have to make use of another man's hands, as I am afflicted with a serious sickness which (accompanied by a good many kinds of distress) has attacked me so cruelly that I gave up hope of life, and for several days it was rather the physician than I that judged me likely to live; but now, Heaven be thanked, I am a little better. Yet the violence of my illness was in some degree worsened by an unexampled sort of ingratitude, prevalent in this day of ours, that accords so grudging a recognition to the services of men of learning, and to yours in particular. If only those who have both the knowledge and the desire to employ these services might attain to greater wealth! But, as things are, those who have the power to do so, granted the will were not absent, are so remarkably close that you'd sooner expect iron to desert steel than a penny to part from *their* pockets, unless one

[203]Pollard (mentioned in Letter 51).

[204]In a letter to Bullock in February 1518, Erasmus asked to be remembered to John Vaughan, Humphrey Walkden, John Bryan, John Watson, and "my host Garrett" (*E.E.*, no. 777); and in a further letter of April 1518 he especially saluted Vaughan, Walkden, and Bryan (*E.E.*, no. 827).

[205]Erasmus was back in Calais on May 1; he had arrived in England during the first week of April, perhaps to see Ammonio concerning the Dispensation granted in January. This visit to England in 1517 was his sixth and last.

begs importunately and shamelessly, or becomes one of two things: a greater flatterer than Gnatho or a greater liar than the Cretans. And these are vices from which my own disposition, at least, recoils so much that I'd rather starve like a hero than acquire by shameful and evil tricks, at the sacrifice of my very liberty, some wretched little sum of money that scarcely would suffice even to cover life's necessities.

For several months past I have been lecturing on St. Matthew's Gospel, in which task those masterly Brief Notes of yours have helped me more than the most extended Commentaries of certain people, especially in considering the harder puzzles. I chanced to obtain a very old copy of the text, which agrees with you in almost all the passages where you maintain that such was the reading in the older MSS.; and this I have even shown to my class. In the daily services, so long as I was well, I did what was but right for a pupil, bound to you by so many acts of kindness, to do: I made mention not only of yourself but of all those whom I know to have been your partisans in the past, or to be so still. I pray Almighty God that you may continue well, in length of days and all happiness, O pattern and paragon of learned men.

LETTER 54 • HENRY BULLOCK TO ERASMUS

Cambridge, May 4 (1517)

Pshaw! Come now, I've never heard of anything more ridiculous. God forbid that I should behave so disgracefully as to refuse to let my letter see the light, albeit it's hardly Latin, and less carefully written than I'd wish; for you replied to it with a very long one,[206] as friendly as long, and (as everyone considers) not only most clever but also most brilliantly phrased. To say the truth, my learned teacher, I was so far from displeased with it that I'd have given a great part of my tiny store of fortune's goods to buy anything of the kind; and I'd have proved this in doing the very thing I've mentioned, if my abilities had not failed to second my desires. Nay, I was rather astonished at a generosity unexampled in history, together with your own sort of exquisite modesty, inasmuch as you did not disdain to share the dazzling and undying lustre of your reputation with myself, the least distinguished of mortals, and were ready to lighten my darkness with your brilliance. For when I reflected upon that merest shadow of

[206]Letter 52.

learning to which I have attained, scarcely able to use more than a single eye, by means of those tiny Greek letters and at the expense of losing my health, and then thought of that wondrous encyclopaedia of all branches of study which you have long since brought to completion, I seem to myself, compared to you, to be proportionately what a small stream's trickle is, when compared to the mighty ocean. But this lie has been concocted by some rather spiteful person, who is annoyed that so much honour has befallen myself. There are some people who take delight in lying, even though they attain to no advantage by it; others there are also, whom envy prompts to play the detractor's part; but I know you are too wise to believe the one sort, and too level-headed to be upset by the other. Never will anyone separate this lowly heart of mine from you. I have no more ardent daily wish than to attain a fortune sufficient to allow me to display the quality of my feelings towards you.

My sickness is slowly diminishing; and that which struck me so swiftly and precipitately is now holding a kind of serious and most unprecipitate debate as to whether it is going to leave me even yet. Farewell, choicest adornment of the Muses.

The next group consists of four brief excerpts relating to Cambridge in letters which Erasmus wrote in 1517 and 1518.

On December 6, 1517 Erasmus wrote from Louvain to Basle two letters containing references to Cambridge. The first was to the Swiss theologian Louis Ber, a native of Basle, Doctor of the Sorbonne, and former Rector of the University of Basle (1514) and Dean of the Faculty of Theology (1514–15).

LETTER 55

I am not disturbed by the monstrous words these men of Paris employ; you'll see that sort of nonsense exploded, for the most part. Cambridge is a changed place. This university now abominates those vain quibbles, which conduce rather to quarrelling than to piety.

The second was to Wolfgang Koepfel (Capito, 1478–1541), a native of Alsace who had gone to Basle in 1513 and was now Dean of the Faculty of Theology.

LETTER 56

In this place, these subtleties already are earning condemnation; while at Cambridge they are quite banished.

The third and fourth excerpts concern the appointment, late in 1517, of Richard Croke as lecturer in Greek at Cambridge.

LETTER 57 • ERASMUS TO BULLOCK[207]

(extract)

Antwerp (February, 1518)

I must first say how delighted I have been to hear that you have not been attacked by the wicked plague. I congratulate Croke, and indeed your University too, which besides the other honourable studies in which it has long excelled, has now obtained this further distinction.

LETTER 58 • ERASMUS TO RICHARD CROKE[208]

(extract)

Louvain, April 23, 1518

I congratulate you, my Croke, on that splendid Professorship; an appointment not less honourable to you than fruitful for the University of Cambridge; in whose welfare I take an especial interest on account of the hospitality I have enjoyed there.

The next letter contains some references to Oxford, which should be explained. On March 1, 1517, Richard Foxe, Bishop of Winchester and Master of Pembroke College, Cambridge, signed the foundation charter of Corpus Christi College, Oxford. The royal patent was dated November 26, 1516; and the original licence had been issued in March 1512. Negotiations for the property, and some of the building, had been going on since 1512, and the front quadrangle was ready to live in by the end of 1517. The first President and some of the Fellows came from Magdalen, Foxe's probable Oxford college. Foxe's statutes for Corpus were

[207]Translation by Nichols, III, 295. [208]Translation by Nichols, III, 355.

of great importance, if only because Corpus was the first English college officially to provide for a lecturer in Greek. He was to lecture in the College Hall at 10 A.M.: the grammar of Gaza to be expounded on Monday, Wednesday, and Friday, and Greek authors on Tuesday, Thursday, and Saturday. These lectures were open to the whole university; the lecturer was also, each week, to give three private lectures in Corpus on grammar and literature. The public lectures were compulsory for members of the college. There was also a lecturer in Latin literature; and one in Divinity, who was to base his lectures on the Latin and Greek fathers.

Now, in the spring of 1518 Cardinal Wolsey, Archbishop of York, visited Oxford (he was a Magdalen man). That was the time when students of Greek were liable to be attacked in the streets by the so-called "Trojans," opponents of the "new learning." Wolsey announced his intention of founding six lectureships at Oxford: in Greek, Latin, Divinity, Mathematics, Civil Law, and Philosophy, it seems. Until Wolsey's plans for a new college came into effect, these men were to be resident in Corpus; and apparently the Greek, Latin, and Divinity lecturers could be the same as the Corpus lecturers. Those who were "public lecturers of the Cardinal" and also "in Corpus Christi College" included John Clement, a much-loved member of More's household, and, from 1520, Thomas Lupset, who lectured in both Latin and Greek (the intention of Foxe had been to have separate lecturers, but apparently this was not always so in practice).

To continue the story beyond the date of Erasmus' letter: in July 1525, a royal licence was issued for the foundation of Cardinal College, which Wolsey had been engineering actively since 1523. Wolsey intended a foundation of about 180; a Dean, sixty senior canons, forty petty canons (junior scholars), six college lecturers, sixteen choristers, and servants, and he imported scholars from Cambridge to improve the teaching. The Hall was ready for use by 1527. But when Wolsey died in 1530 the college had only thirty members; and it was suppressed, a new college being established by Henry in 1532—which was transformed into Christ Church in 1546, the year of the foundation of Trinity College, Cambridge.

LETTER 59 • ERASMUS TO WILLIAM BLOUNT, LORD MOUNTJOY

(extract)

Antwerp, May, 1519

In particular your universities show this: in age they rival the oldest, in fame the most illustrious. I am very fond of the Reverend the Bishop of Winchester, who has expressly, and at his own expense, dedicated a most splendid college to the study of good literature; even more do I embrace with affection the noble, indeed god-like, disposition of the Most Reverend Cardinal Lord Archbishop of York, by whose wise provision Oxford University is presently to be adorned, not only with languages and studies of every kind, but at the same time with moral training suitable to the highest studies. As for Cambridge University, it has long been flourishing with extreme distinction under the presidency of the Very Reverend the Lord Bishop of Rochester, who in no single respect omits to play the part of a distinguished prelate.

LETTER 60 • ERASMUS TO JUAN LUIS VIVES[209]

(extract)

Louvain (June, 1520)

Still I often privately wonder, when almost all universities in the world are coming back to their senses, so to speak, and composing themselves into a sober frame of mind, how it is, that among the teachers at Louvain, and them alone, there are those who so stubbornly continue in resisting the better sort of literature—especially when they are not even very distinguished in their own sophistical variety of learning. Three years ago a man, uniquely worthy of the bishopric he holds and of the profession of a theologian, told me how it stands in the University of Cambridge, of which he is the permanent

[209]The Spaniard Vives (1492–1540) met Erasmus in 1517 at Brussels. He had been educated at Valencia and Paris; and visited England in 1517, 1522, and 1523, on which later visit he was incorporated in the University of Oxford (October) and lodged in Corpus Christi College. He stayed in England—apart from brief trips to the continent—until 1528, lecturing for some of the time at Oxford.

Chancellor (for so they name their supreme and permanent head): at Cambridge, he said, instead of sophistical refinements, sober and sound discussions are held nowadays among the theologians; and from these they depart not only more learned, but better men. In the University of Oxford, at first, some attempt at resistance was made, for which certain monks were responsible; but by the authority of the Most Reverend the Cardinal, and of the King, those who exhibited hostility to these great benefits towards a very distinguished and very ancient university were restrained. Need I mention Italy, where these studies have always been supreme, though almost isolated, if one excepts medicine and law? Alcala University has achieved a famous name from no other source than the welcome it has accorded to language and literature;[210] and its especial glory is that famous old

[210]The University of Alcala de Henares (about twenty miles north-east of Madrid) was founded by Cardinal Ximenes de Cisneros (1436–1517), Franciscan, since 1495 Primate of Spain (Archbishop of Toledo); a Reformer "au premier rang des promoteurs de cette *Philosophia Christi* pour laquelle va s'enthousiasmer l'Europe" (Bataillon, *Erasme et l'Espagne*, 2). Ximenes laid the foundation stone in 1498; the first students were admitted in 1508; instruction was properly under way by 1509. Ximenes' aim was the provision of a learned clergy: "de la grammaire aux arts libéraux et des arts de la théologie vivifiée par l'étude directe de la Bible, telle est la voie droite et royale pour les jeunes gens que Cisneros voudrait voir affluer à Alcala, de tous les diocèses d'Espagne, et retourner au plus tard à ces diocèses pour constituer les cadres d'une Eglise plus digne du Christ" (Bataillon, 14). It was originally intended to have eighteen colleges, headed by a theological college, with six of the other seventeen being for grammar. The theological college was opened in 1508; by 1514 there were two grammar colleges, each for seventy-two Latin students (of whom twelve were also to study Greek, which was taught at Alcala from 1513). Hebrew was taught from 1512; and there was instruction also in philosophy and medicine (but not civil law).

Alcala is most justly famous for the edition of the Bible prepared there, a printing of the Hebrew and Greek text together with the Vulgate Latin: *in academia Complutensi noviter impressum.* (The Roman name for Alcala was Complutum: hence the awkward description of Ximenes' project—the "Complutensian Polyglot".) This was begun in 1502, when Ximenes gathered a group of scholars at Alcala. The New Testament, double-columned, Greek to the left, Latin to the right (as in Erasmus' edition of 1516), was printed at Alcala in January 1514—when Erasmus was on the verge of leaving Cambridge. The printing of the Old Testament, in five volumes, was complete by July 1517; Ximenes died in November. However, though printed, the six volumes were not published until 1522; the sheets had been left unbound pending the authorization of publication. Six hundred copies of the Alcala Bible were printed. Of the ten now in Cambridge, the Corpus copy was presented by Parker, the Pembroke copy by Whitgift, and a University Library copy by Tunstall.

For all this, see the first chapter of Bataillon's book, headed "Cisneros et la Préréforme Espagnole"; James Lyell, *Cardinal Ximenes*, 1917, which has photographs of the Bible; and Allen, *Erasmus*, 140–4, 179–84.

man, quite worthy to outlive many Nestors, namely Antonio of Lebrija.[211] In Germany there are almost as many universities as towns; and of these there is scarcely one that does not attract professors of languages by means of large salaries. (By some ill luck it has happened that the humaner studies have never been esteemed at Cologne; this is because, as I am told, swarms of Dominicans and Franciscans hold sway there.) Certainly it has always been possible for anyone who wished, to profess a subject freely and even to accept fees for doing so.

LETTER 61 • ERASMUS TO NICHOLAS EVERARD[212]

(extract)

Anderlecht (October) 1521

Both at Paris and at Cambridge the study of theology is flourishing as it never flourished before. What's the reason? Why, that theologians are adapting themselves to the age, which was turning itself in another direction; that they don't repel, as if they were enemies, this better literature which tries to break in even by force, but welcome it genially, like hosts. The fact that the school at Louvain is cold and deserted —for some people complain of this—cannot be blamed upon myself, who never have, even by a single word, turned anyone aside from it; but the ravings and the boorish abuse emanating from quite a small number of persons tend to alienate honest minds. Furthermore, what is done by few men is attributed to all by the mob, when it sees this happening so often and receiving punishment so seldom—when they

[211]1444–1522. See the account by M. Bataillon, *Erasme et l'Espagne*, pp. 27–41: "Il incarne, au seuil du XVIe siècle espagnol, l'effort autonome de l'humanisme pour restaurer l'antiquité toute entière, profane et sacrée" (27); "Lebrixa, Colet, Erasme, communient dans un même esprit" (29). He had been to Italy (1460); he compiled a Spanish-Latin dictionary (1492); he edited many school-books, including the *Disticha* of "Cato"; and he was the Spanish heir of Lorenzo Valla in his approach to Biblical scholarship. From July 1513 he was Professor of Rhetoric at Alcala, lecturing on Pliny, Aristotle, and Augustine; and he then was officially associated with the Alcala Bible. Lebrija is in southern Spain, between Cadiz and Seville. See also Allen, *Erasmus*, 187. At the time of Erasmus' letter, Antonio was 76.

[212]Nicholas Everard (1462–1532), ecclesiastical lawyer, born at Middelburg, educated at Louvain; Chancellor to Henry of Bergen, Bishop of Cambrai, in whose service Erasmus was for about a year (1494–5). From 1509 he was President of the Council of Holland, Zeeland, and Friesland. (*E.E.*, IV, 237.)

have made such a great fuss over a single small word spoken by a professor of Greek, without (nevertheless) any disparaging meaning or intent towards anyone.

The final group of letters, written thirteen years after Erasmus left the University, is a postscript to his Cambridge work on Seneca. His research assistant then had been the "smooth-tongued young man," Robert Aldrich of King's, who had gone on the pilgrimage to Walsingham; and together Erasmus and Aldrich had collated Seneca manuscripts from the libraries of King's and Peterhouse. One King's MS., which Erasmus thought valueless, contained the Letters (*Epistulae Morales*) which Seneca wrote to his young friend Lucilius, procurator of Sicily, of which 124 survive. A Peterhouse MS. also had these letters, among other things. The second King's MS., much more reliable in spite of some absurd interpolated commentaries, included the moral essay *De Beata Vita* and some aphorisms attributed to Seneca. This second manuscript volume, as Erasmus remembered after thirteen years, was in the "lesser library"—the smaller of the two rooms in the Old Court of King's which housed the nearly four hundred volumes belonging to the college. It was an unchained book and could be borrowed. None of these manuscripts survives today.

Erasmus' edition of the works of Seneca was published at Basle in the summer of 1515. Unfortunately, Erasmus had left the town in March, leaving the final stages to the editorial staff of the Froben press, who badly botched the book. In 1525 Erasmus set himself to preparing a revised edition, which was finally to be printed in Basle in March 1529. And at the end of 1525 he wrote to Aldrich to do some checking for him in the libraries of King's and Peterhouse. Aldrich took a whole year on the job; and unfortunately in his researches at King's he worked entirely on the bad MS. and did not consult the second one, so that his work was in fact useless. Mr. James Cargill Thompson has suggested that the second MS. was out on loan at the time, and therefore escaped Aldrich's attention.[213]

[213]W. D. J. Cargill Thompson, "Notes on King's College Library, 1500–1570," *Transactions of the Cambridge Bibliographical Society* (1954).

LETTER 62 • ERASMUS TO ROBERT ALDRICH

Basle, December 25, 1525

If you remember our early acquaintance and still have the same character you had in those old days, I'd like you to do me just one service, which you may perform without any expense to yourself. There is in King's College a manuscript, done on parchment, of Seneca's works. Having used it as a source for numerous annotations in my own copy,[214] I then entrusted the publication to a certain German,[215] whom I took to be a quite faithful friend. In my absence, he has behaved in a most untrustworthy manner in the printing of the book; and, to prevent detection, has taken away the best part of the manuscript. This is the scandal I must repair; and therefore I am asking you, my dear Aldrich, to be so kind as to take the volume of Seneca's works printed by Froben,[216] and to entrust it to some reliable persons, for the purpose of noting afresh in the margin the points where variant readings occur. Will you please send the MS., marked in this fashion, to Thomas More, so that he may forward it to me. As for the books of the *Naturales Quaestiones*, I am aware that they have been published;[217] I will personally carry out the latter collation. Seneca deserves this attention. You too have some debt to pay to public studies, while to me you owe nothing save our mutual affection. I shall repay to the last farthing whatever you may spend on this business, and will furthermore see to it that you shall not appear to have sown the seed of those good deeds of yours in an unproductive plot. I should like to be with you as soon as possible. Please give my greetings to my old companions Fawne, Humphrey (Walkden), Vaughan, also Garrett (Godfrey), Nicholas (Spering), and John Siberch, all booksellers. Peace and prosperity attend you.

P.S. There are some very old MSS. at Cambridge, especially at Peterhouse. Do give Froben and myself any help you can; you won't be able to stir up the *ungrateful* by doing them kindnesses!

[214]That is, an earlier printed edition (not by Erasmus) of Seneca.

[215]Allen identified this editorial culprit, of the house of Froben, as a certain William Nesen (*E.E.*, II, 51).

[216]The 1515 edition.

[217]Best rendered as "Inquiries into Physical Science"; a substantial work in seven books, written about 63 A.D. and first printed in Venice in 1490; re-edited by Erasmus for the 1515 volume; and printed afresh by the Aldine press in Venice in 1523. Milton was to have it on his assignment sheet for his proposed "Academies" (*Of Education*, 1644).

LETTER 63 • ROBERT ALDRICH TO ERASMUS

(Cambridge, c. December, 1526)

The excellent and learned Erasmus will have just cause to be surprised that his own former scholar, whom he treated with an affection far beyond his deserts, is postponing so badly the execution of a single request (quite a small one too, and not hard to fulfil) that it could well be in doubt whether he intends to perform it or quite refuses to do so. But may God preserve both myself from being disposed to dream of failing you, and you from believing that I could fail to carry out that which has but once been enjoined by so great a teacher upon so insignificant a disciple. For, to speak the truth and speak it frankly, those six months of reading I enjoyed when you took me to your side and bade me attend on you—while you were my constant occupation, myself having meanwhile made the acquaintance, among other employments, of the diversions afforded by literature—have profited me more than many years of study would otherwise have done.

Therefore I do beg you not to think that I am refusing to do what I merely postponed; and furthermore I beg you to think that, in view of the opportunity afforded by circumstances, I have not in fact postponed it. Always, day by day, my hand was ready to seize its book on the instant; but what could I accomplish with no one at hand, or available, to read along with me?[218] The terrible plague, among other things, has so harassed our University since the beginning of March that almost all of its scholars have taken flight, with the intention of safeguarding their health in the countryside, and there was nobody left at home whom I could induce by any reward to assist me when I set myself to read. Once I *had* secured qualified and trustworthy collaborators, I used never to let a day slip by without using it to accomplish as much of the task as I could.

I used the following method in pursuing the task. The manuscript which is kept in our library at King's College[219] contains only the *Epistles to Lucilius*, and the same are contained in the book at Peterhouse; and the borrowing of the latter from the said library would, I believe, never have been permitted save by the authority of Erasmus alone—for so the College ordains, out of a deep concern for the safe custody of books. Well then: while I am going through the *Epistles to Lucilius*, I keep comparing Froben's printed edition with those two

[218] I.e., to read aloud.
[219] This was the valueless MS. Aldrich misunderstood Erasmus' letter.

very ancient manuscripts. When I record variants in the margin, I distinguish the two MSS. one from the other by means of appropriate signs: variants in the King's College MS. I mark by adding the sign θ, and those in the Peterhouse MS. by adding the sign $>$. When these two MSS. are in agreement, but differ from Froben's edition, I append the variant readings without any distinguishing mark. I have nowhere omitted any instance of a variant reading so long as the passage made any sense; and even where I thought what appeared in Froben's printed text was much better, yet I added the variants, for two reasons: first because in your letter you seemed to desire this, and secondly in order to ensure that Erasmus' far-famed perspicacity might not be deprived of any opportunity to put forth its power and "recognize the lion by its claw;" for your intellect is skilful at reconstructing damaged and mutilated phrases, reducing to order things disarrayed, replacing interpolated and corrupt passages with the true and authentic text, and bringing sound sense out of no sense at all.

This quick readiness in judgement—or rather, a power of divination that surpasses the Delian oracle or the Sibyl—is something I came to appreciate in you at the time when I personally read with you some books by Seneca and Jerome, at Queens' College, Cambridge. It will daily be appreciated afresh by anyone who is neither blind nor besotted with malice, when he examines with eyes free from impiety, or else hears with the ears of a fair-minded man, your emendations and annotations upon all that sacred literature and upon that horde of good authors. But how ungrateful the men of our own day are; if it weren't for the ignorance that might excuse them! Most piteous generation, in which men without the power of judgement pass sentence on the greatest judges of letters and (which is even more to be regretted) their pronouncements receive popular acclaim! Yet is it matter for surprise that a vulgar taste does not displease the mob? There are assemblies to raise an uproar, congresses to mutter dislike, and dining tables to resound with it; nay, even sermons fail to keep silent, saying, "Erasmus corrupteth good and blessed literature;" inasmuch as he is replacing some old, though long since corrupt, phrases with others newly substituted! And this happens, as I conjecture, simply because some men are so poor of eyesight or else possess such baleful eyes (I mean the *inner* eye which constitutes discernment), that they cannot or will not see how much they are gaining from him who replaces mud and filth with gold and pearls. This single consideration ought to spur them, even if nothing else will, to spare Erasmus and to be well inclined towards his reputation (provided they are not determined to be harder than flint); recognizing that it was for their sakes and all men's, that he took upon himself all those intolerable labours.

For (most eminent Erasmus) I will take my oath that even from this distance I can savour the nature of the treadmill in which you live and move when you are not cursorily reading (as I do) but thoroughly revising so many works of literature. For when I am but reading and comparing with others a single work of Seneca's, and not even the whole of that work either, how often, without being so very tired myself, do I exhort men tired with reading to persevere and to consume the tedious task by the aid of pleasant memories! It is thus I ponder alone, and thus I cheer others: "Great God, how many toils does *Erasmus* overcome, how many dull tasks devour, what drudgery endure! He reads so many authors, and not only reads but at the same time probes error and corruption of text, seizes upon faults and corrects whatever is faulty. He knows how long he must linger, here on the words and there on the meaning, in order to restore to its pristine freshness and fullness that which he found in a meaningless condition." And it is my habit to say, "If so light a task of reading overwhelms and distresses us, what distress does not that prince of literary men endure, when he is tortured in so many ways besides—nay, in doing so is nailed to his own cross? For from those he serves well by all this labour he gets no gratitude at all; and whether I am to call this *his* loss or that of literature is for those to decide who, as they defame men of letters, would hinder the increase of letters, were not those who are schooled in good letters too courageous to be capable of yielding to evil tongues." You, Erasmus, as you are the most cultivated in letters, so must surely be the most courageous of men in bearing all adversities. We, that is to say all who desire letters and learning, beg you to persevere in the advancement of good literature, both for your welfare and with an eye to your old age, and we at least shall be at your command. For indeed you may command as your subjects both all men of learning and all who are desirous of knowledge; among whom I (who am the least) now hasten to do your bidding.

I have assembled and compared the books you wished. Of the Epistles there were two copies, which you mentioned to me.[220] Of the rest, that I have noted, the sole copy was that at Peterhouse. Of those which have not been marked, I could not find any ancient copy, either in the places you mentioned or elsewhere. I have sent the marked

[220] At King's and Peterhouse.

copy, as you desired, to Thomas More on the eleventh of May, begging him earnestly to have it forwarded to you as speedily as possible. Which indeed he undertook to do at Easter, when I met him at his house and was received by him in a most courteous manner, for he is a man who is exceedingly prone to kindness; and I know he gave me much finer entertainment for your sake, as soon as he learned that I was an old and trusted friend to you. You will oblige me very much if you see fit to recommend me to him again in your letters, whenever you please.

Even if I had refused to give this help to *you*, for whose sake I have wished there were a still greater debt to repay, yet (as you write) the noble Seneca himself was worthy of that help; for his aphorisms are the best builders of character, and those of them which refer to Nature (the *Naturales Quaestiones*) hold, unless I am mistaken, the leading place in natural philosophy—if indeed there *are* any others, in Latin at least, that are worth the reading. Even though it is to him we are obliged to yield first place for his excellent instruction on the secrets of Nature, and for training and enriching our characters, to you by the same token we shall have to allot the second place, inasmuch as you are restoring him in such a fashion that we are able to learn each of these subjects in a perfect form.

As for your remark in your letter that I owe something to public instruction but nothing to yourself save our mutual affection, the fact is that I owe *everything* to you just *because* of that public instruction, which you do so much to foster and to extend; to you I owe my very self, all the more profoundly so because you deem me worthy to be included among your friends, and remind me of our old acquaintance which I shall not cease to remember until I forget myself. And so there is no need for you to think of repaying anything either to me or to my studies, except by continuing to hold me in friendship.

I have conveyed your greetings to Nicholas, Garrett, and Siberch the booksellers. As for Fawne, he is being cherished in the bosom of the Bishop of Winchester's[221] household, and is already perfectly happy there, I hear. Fortune has taken away Vaughan; I know not whither; it was shortly after you departed. And death has restored Humphrey[222] to the common mother of us all. I greet yourself and our friend Froben, with a wish for the longest of life and the best of fortune.

[221]Foxe.
[222]Probably Humphrey Walkden.

LETTER 64 • ERASMUS TO ROBERT ALDRICH
(extract)

Basle, March 24, 1527

About the time of Quadragesima,[223] I at length received your Seneca. It wasn't necessary to send the book; everything could have been put down on slips of paper. The librarians at King's College have misled you. They possess, in the smaller library, another manuscript volume, written on parchment. In order that you may recognize it, it had the aphorisms arranged in groups under their initial letters, and in the middle space each aphorism was reproduced in a couplet, though a barbarous one. The volume also contained initial letters illuminated in colours, and gilded.[224] Also, in the essay *De Beata Vita* it contained many of my past emendations. If you had the time to do it, you'd be able to note the variant readings from it, marking by number the lines of Froben's edition, and adding the reading which the manuscript volume gives; the rest of the work, I should do. I am sorry you have undertaken so much toil without much result. I was aware that the manuscript which contained the books of the Epistles had no value. I would not presume to make further use of your kindness: but if you could stomach the drudgery, you'd oblige me very greatly, and you will not have spent your services on the ungrateful, if you will show me how I may repay the favour. I took some pains to recommend you to Thomas More.

[223]That is, since the first week in March.

[224]Erasmus described this second King's MS., or at least that section of it devoted to the Aphorisms, in a note in the 1529 edition of Seneca: "I came across this small work at Cambridge, accurately transcribed on parchment, with initial letters picked out in colour and gold—but execrably! Commentaries had been added, and good God, how absurd they were! A hexameter couplet had been appended to each of these commentaries, explaining the aphorism again, in other words—to show off an abundant vocabulary, one supposes! . . . With such depressing fripperies," continued Erasmus, "the natural abilities of boys are perverted" and "the humanities are turned into literary puzzles." (*E.E.*, no. 2132.)

APPENDIXES

BIOGRAPHICAL REGISTER

ROBERT ALDRICH (c. 1495–1556)

Born at Burnham, Buckinghamshire, Aldrich went to Eton in 1503 and on to King's in 1507. He commenced B.A. in 1512; in May of that year Erasmus took him, and others, to Walsingham.

From 1512 to 1515 Aldrich was Fellow of King's College; from 1515 to 1521 he was at Eton as Headmaster (some say he introduced the study of Greek there); in 1521 he went back to King's (having taken the degree of Bachelor of Divinity in 1517) and was ordained deacon in 1522. In 1523 he was a University Preacher; in the academic year 1524–5, when Henry Bullock was Vice-Chancellor, Aldrich was Proctor. In 1530 he succeeded Thomas Lupset in the living of Cheriton, Hampshire. By that time he had deserted Cambridge for Oxford.

A supporter of the Royal Supremacy, Aldrich became Archdeacon of Colchester in 1531, Canon of Windsor in 1534, Provost of Eton in 1536, and Bishop of Carlisle in 1537. In the reign of Mary, though, he was a commissioner for the suppression of heresy, such Cambridge men as Edward Crome, former Fellow of Gonville Hall (1507), and John Rogers (B.A. Pembroke 1526) coming under his jurisdiction.

He died in Lincolnshire in March 1556.

ANDREA AMMONIO (1478–1517)

Ammonio was originally a citizen of Lucca; though his family came from Arena, about twenty miles down the river Serchio from Lucca—Polydore Vergil of Urbino was to call him *harenarius*: prize-fighter.[1] Like Giovanni and Silvestro Gigli, also of Lucca, and Vergil, and Pietro Carmiliano of Brescia, Ammonio originally came to England in the papal service. He probably arrived in London about 1504. He appears to have visited Cambridge at some time in the next few years.

In June 1515 Leo X appointed Ammonio deputy-collector of papal revenue in England, in succession to Polydore Vergil, who had held that office since 1502 (except for the years 1509 to 1512, when Pietro Griffo was deputy-collector). Vergil had been imprisoned in April 1515 because he had written to Adriano Castelli (the Collector, in Rome) some letters attacking Wolsey. It has been suggested that the key to these intrigues was the ambition of Ammonio. "The means Ammonio adopted to secure these ends indicate how violently he coveted the post: he arranged that Vergil's correspondence be intercepted."[2] It is certain that Vergil and Ammonio were on bad terms; and that Ammonio personified the "new" humanist group encouraged by Henry VIII, as against that for which Henry VII had been patron—Vergil, Carmiliano, the Frenchman Bernard André.

[1]Denys Hay's translation, *Polydore Vergil*, 12. The dictionary has "gladiator."

[2]Hay, *Vergil*, 11. For an example of Ammonio's italic hand, as Latin secretary to Henry VIII, see Plate 15 of A. Fairbank and B. Wolpe, *Renaissance Handwriting*, 1960.

Ammonio was carried off by the sweating-sickness in less than eight hours in August 1517 at the age of thirty-nine. His will was dated August 17. In it, he wished to be buried in St Stephen's; he left about £40 to his cousin and assistant Pietro Vanni of Lucca, who was to succeed him as Latin secretary and later became Dean of Salisbury;[3] the rest of his money went to his mother Elizabeth, who still lived in Lucca; the executors were two Lucca merchants.[4]

More wrote to Erasmus about Ammonio's death on August 19, 1517.[5] Erasmus wrote from Antwerp asking that Pietro Vanni should collect all the Ammonio-Erasmus correspondence and send it to him; also that "the letters and draft letters relating to the dispensation may be destroyed, so that they may not go astray into the hands of those whom I would not like to have them."[6] "What is there worth anything," said Erasmus to Pietro, "that has not been lost in him?"[7]

WILLIAM BLOUNT, LORD MOUNTJOY (1478–1534)

Pronounced "Monjoy." Born at Burton (Staffordshire), William became fourth Baron Mountjoy in 1485, at the age of six. He studied at Cambridge in the 1490's. The University was later to write to him, appealing for money: "whereas it is to your parents that your Lordship owes your nobility of blood, it is (as you yourself are wont to say) to this University of ours that you owe the nobility of your mind": and "to his teachers every man owes a debt."[8] It is likely that he was at Queens'; for when he went to Paris to study in the spring of 1498, his chaplain was Richard Whitford, Fellow of the College. By that time he had married Elizabeth, daughter of Sir William Say, at Easter 1497. The first of four wives, she died in 1506. Erasmus was to write for Mountjoy's amusement a rhetorical exercise in praise of matrimony, which Thomas Wilson of King's (Scholar 1541) was to translate in his *The Art of Rhetoric* (1553).

Erasmus' first letter to William was in November 1498: "well named Monjoie."[9] At the beginning of 1499 Mountjoy invited Erasmus to live in his house in Paris; Erasmus accepted the invitation in March. In May Mountjoy mentioned the possibility of Erasmus' visiting England (he had been thinking of going to Italy). And a month or two later Erasmus in fact crossed the channel with Mountjoy—the first of his six visits to England.

A little later—probably in 1500—Mountjoy was appointed one of the tutors to the young Prince Henry, whom Erasmus had met (taken by More) in 1499.

Erasmus dedicated his *Adages* to Mountjoy (first edition, June 1500). And Mountjoy was one of his three most permanent patrons, the other two being Henry of Bergen, Bishop of Cambrai, and William Warham, Arch-

[3]For Pietro Vanni, see W. Bullock in *Italian Studies*, November 1938, 53–5.

[4]D. Hay, *Italian Studies*, February 1939; from a partial transcript of the will in Cambridge University Library MSS.

[5]*E.E.*, no. 623; tr. Nichols, III, 2.

[6]*E.E.*, no. 655; tr. Nichols, III, 43.

[7]*E.E.*, no. 656; tr. Nichols, III, 40.

[8]*E.E.*, I, 613; tr. Thomson.

[9]*E.E.*, no. 79.

bishop of Canterbury.[10] "Lord Mountjoy . . .," wrote Erasmus in 1514, "formerly my own pupil, yearly gives me a pension of a hundred crowns."[11] But in fact—and this is one of the themes of the Cambridge letters—it was often slow in coming. Erasmus later described Mountjoy as "more friendly than munificent": *amici verius quam benigni.*[12] This was part of his general grumble: "Some yearly allowance was promised, nothing was sent—that is the fashion with Princes."[13]

In July 1509—within three months of Henry VIII's accession—Mountjoy was appointed "Master of the Mint in the Tower of London, the realm of England, and the town of Calais."[14] By 1512 he was also Chamberlain to Queen Catharine, with a salary of £66 13*s.* 4*d.* a year.[15] In the Parliament which met in February 1512 he was named as one of the fourteen triers of "petitions from Gascoigne and beyond sea."[16] He was a Comissioner of the Peace for Hertfordshire in 1512,[17] and for Hampshire in 1513 and 1514.[18] So, while Erasmus was at Cambridge, Mountjoy had much to occupy him in England. In London, he lived at Mountjoy House, which was in Knightrider Street, three or four minutes' walk from St Paul's down towards the river. The street, according to John Stow, was "so called (as it is supposed) of knights well-armed and mounted at the Tower royal, riding from thence through that street, west to Creed Lane, and so out at Ludgate towards Smithfield."[19]

But Mountjoy's main responsibilities were not in England but in Flanders: in "your town of Calais and the marches there under your obeisance" (to use the statutory phrase addressed to the King). In October 1509 Henry had appointed him Lieutenant of the Castle of Hamme, for twenty years "and afterwards during pleasure."[20] Mountjoy held the position until 1531. Hamme, "in Picardy and the marches of Calais," was a hundred miles east of Calais, fifteen miles south-west of Antwerp; it was one of the four English garrisons in the Calais region—Calais itself, Guisnes (just south of Calais), and Rysbank being the other three. At this time the English government maintained about five hundred permanent troops in these frontier outposts—a "colony" which cost over £10,000 a year.[21] Hamme was less important than Calais (with its Staple) or Guisnes: Mountjoy was paid 1*s.* a day, as against the 2*s.* a day paid to his equivalents there. He had under him about forty soldiers, and a general retinue—all of whom were to be English, except gunners, crossbow-makers, beer-brewers, armourers, and smiths.[22]

[10]So said Beat Bild (Beatus Rhenanus) in 1536 (Nichols, I, 24).
[11]Letter 43.
[12]*E.E.*, I, 50 (Compendium Vitae, 1524); tr. Nichols, I, 10.
[13]*Ibid.*
[14]*Letters and Papers Henry VIII*, I, no. 299.
[15]*Ibid.*, no. 3197.
[16]*Ibid.*, no. 2082.
[17]*Ibid.*, no. 3102.
[18]*Ibid.*, nos. 4159, 4676.
[19]Stow (ed. Kingsford), *Survey of London*, I, 245.
[20]*Letters and Papers Henry VIII*, nos. 618, 1306.
[21]*Ibid.*, no. 4635.
[22]*Ibid.*, no. 617.

From 1529 until his death, Mountjoy was High Steward of the University of Cambridge, being preceded in the office by Thomas More and succeeded by Thomas Cromwell.

Erasmus' last surviving letter to Mountjoy was written in 1531.

JOHN BRYAN (1493–1545)

A London boy, Bryan went to Eton about 1505 and thence to King's in August 1510, when he was seventeen. Erasmus mentioned him first in a letter of May 1512. He commenced B.A. in 1515 (with John Skipp of Gonville Hall and George Joye of Peterhouse). In 1513 he became a Fellow of King's and remained at the College until 1526, having been ordained in 1517. His university lectures were said to be in the new style: the textual Aristotle, not the scholastic gloss. After leaving Cambridge he took a living in Essex and was a country priest until his death.

HENRY BULLOCK (c. 1487–1526)

The best of Erasmus' Cambridge friends.

He was an undergraduate at Queens' in the very first years of the sixteenth century, commencing B.A. in 1504. He was elected Fellow in 1506, when he was about nineteen, and stayed there until his death. If Erasmus came to Queens' with the royal party in 1506, he probably met Bullock then. They met again after 1509, when Erasmus returned to England from Italy. Bullock was well known in the Colet-More-Grocin circle in London. When Erasmus went to Cambridge in 1511, Bullock was the only friend he knew there.

By the spring of 1512 Bullock was studying Greek, one of the members of Erasmus' small class. His personal library included a copy of Theodore Gaza's Greek Grammar, as printed by Aldo Manuzio at Venice in 1495; this copy later belonged to Thomas Smith (who went up to Queens' in 1526) and is now in the Cambridge University Library, "Magister Bulloke" written on the front cover. From about 1512 Bullock was University lecturer in mathematics; by 1516 he was also lecturing on Divinity.

In 1517 he became B.D., in 1520 D.D. When Wolsey visited Cambridge in 1520 (and lodged in Queens', which had been cleaned and in part white-washed for the occasion) Dr Bullock delivered the official oration, which was printed in Cambridge by John Siberch in 1521. Siberch also printed Bullock's Latin translation of a work of Lucian—another enthusiasm Bullock had acquired from Erasmus. He was Vice-Chancellor 1524–5.

Bullock was out of sympathy with the Lutheranism which began to be popular in Cambridge in the last years of his life. Thomas Fuller (another Queens' man) was to account him "an opposer of the Protestant religion."

He bequeathed twenty-four books to Queens', including the Erasmus New Testament, the Jerome, the 1519 *Annotations*, and the *Adages*.

JOHN FAWNE (born c. 1475)

Dr Fawne (D.D. 1510) had commenced B.A. in 1493, and he proceeded to the degrees of M.A. in 1497 and B.D. in 1503. He was elected Fellow of Queens' in 1497 and became Vice-President in 1507, when Fisher was President. From the autumn of 1512 until 1514—the second half of Erasmus' Cambridge period—he was Vice-Chancellor. He succeeded Erasmus as Lady Margaret Professor of Divinity and held the chair until 1521. He then seems to have joined the household of Bishop Richard Foxe of Winchester, where, according to Robert Aldrich in 1526, he was "perfectly happy."[23]

RICHARD FOXE (1448–1528)

Erasmus first met Foxe—an ecclesiastical statesman of the type of Wolsey—in 1500, Foxe then being Bishop of Durham, member of the Privy Council, and Keeper of the Privy Seal. A Lincolnshire man, he appears to have been an undergraduate at Pembroke, Cambridge, in the early 1470's; earlier, he was at Oxford, and later, at Paris. He was Chancellor of Cambridge from 1500 to 1501 and Master of Pembroke from 1507 to 1519; but it is unlikely that he visited Cambridge during Erasmus' stay there. From 1501 until his death he was Bishop of Winchester. In 1506 Erasmus dedicated to him one of his Latin translations from Lucian: a dialogue on friendship.

In the story of English humanism, Foxe is best remembered as the founder of Corpus Christi College, Oxford, in 1516.[24] So far as Cambridge is concerned, he should be noted for his help given to Fisher in the founding of St John's, and, later, for the commissioning of Barnard Flower, the royal glazier, to do the glass for the Chapel of King's (1515–17), though Flower in fact died after finishing only four windows.

William Harrison quoted a piquant remark of Foxe's, in a passage concerning those who go to seed after taking the degree of Doctor (which took about twenty years after matriculation): "after this time, and forty years of age, the most part of students do commonly give over their wonted diligence, and live like drone bees on the fat of colleges, witholding better wits from the possession of their places, and yet doing little good in their own vocation and calling. I could rehearse a number (if I listed) of this sort, as well in one university as the other. But this shall suffice instead of a large report, that long continuance in those places is either a sign of lack of friends or of learning or of good and upright life: as Bishop Foxe sometime noted, who thought it sacrilege for a man to tarry any longer at Oxford than he had a desire to profit."[25]

[23]Letter 63.

[24]There are translated extracts from the foundation statutes in Nugent (ed.), *The Thought and Culture of the English Renaissance*, 31–5, from the full translation and Life by G. R. M. Ward (1843).

[25]*Description of England* (1577), Bk. II, chap. VI.

STEPHEN GARDINER (c. 1495–1555)

Gardiner was to be Chancellor of the University from 1539 to 1547 (succeeding Thomas Cromwell) and again from 1553 to 1555, succeeding Northumberland. He was Master of Trinity Hall, 1525–52; Bishop of Winchester, 1531–51 and 1553–5; and Lord Chancellor, 1553–5.

His career before the 1520's is difficult exactly to chart. He was born in Bury St. Edmunds, his father being a cloth merchant. In 1511, when he was about fifteen, he was staying in Paris with an Englishman called Eden, a friend of his father; there he met Erasmus, who was Eden's guest in the spring of that year. The next fact we have is that in 1518 he took at Cambridge the degree of Bachelor of Civil Law. It was possible to do this without going through the usual course in arts; William Harrison tells us that at both universities "a man may (if he will) begin his study with the law or physic (of which this giveth wealth, the other honour) so soon as he cometh to the University, if his knowledge in the tongues, and ripeness of judgement, serve therefore; which if he do, then his first degree is bachelor of law or physic."[26] Such a candidate, who did not have the M.A., had by statute to study for seven years before being eligible for the degree of Bachelor of Law.[27] So Gardiner probably matriculated in Cambridge at the Michaelmas of 1511—the very time that Erasmus began to lecture there.

In 1526 Gardiner, then Master of Trinity Hall and secretary to Wolsey, wrote to Erasmus: "Of course, that power of memory you have is applied and devoted by you to the most careful retention of all matters that are of supreme worth; nevertheless, if it isn't a sin to recall that memory to the past for a quite trifling reason, do you remember that sixteen years ago when you were the guest of a certain Englishman named Eden, who was making a short stay at the time in the quarter of Saint-Jean in Paris, at the time when you first published your *Praise of Folly*, if I mistake not, and already had obtained for yourself a great number of books both Greek and Latin; there was with this Eden a little boy to whom each day you gave instructions to prepare for you lettuces cooked with butter and olive oil, and that you used to declare that dish was garnished by him for you more skilfully than ever was done before? That same boy am I, Stephen Gardiner, your most loving friend, and to this day, in spite of absence, steadfast in loyalty to you; but now so reft away from you finally by duties at court that, while I may always be (as I am) fond of you, yet I fear I may never at any time enjoy that sweetest converse with your writings. Alas for my deep misfortune that I had no chance to accept the situation which you offered me through Garrett the Cambridge bookseller—if indeed he spoke me truth—of entering your service. For in that case, instead of your silent writings, that I have sampled as best I could, I should have had the active power of your living intellect as my instructor."[28] This reference to a "situation" is

[26] *Ibid.*

[27] In fact, some scholars seem to have been granted the degree after six years, or even less. William Petre went up to Oxford in 1520, when he was fourteen, and became Bachelor of Civil Law when he was twenty (F. G. Emmison, *Tudor Secretary*, 2–3).

[28] *E.E.*, no. 1669, lines 18–36; tr. Thomson.

usually taken to apply to the period at the end of 1513 when John Smith, Erasmus' servant-pupil, had for the moment returned to the bosom of his awful family. Erasmus wrote in October 1513: "I was almost sure of acquiring a certain person as my servant; but he has changed his mind and gone over to Brabant."[29] Gardiner was then about seventeen.

There are no appropriate Trinity Hall records surviving from the early sixteenth century, but it has been assumed, almost certainly correctly, that Gardiner was a student there. Trinity Hall had been founded in 1350 by the Bishop of Norwich as "a perpetual College of scholars of the Canon and Civil Law."

GARRETT GODFREY (died 1539)

Cambridge stationer and bookbinder, born in the south-west of modern Holland (the province of Limburg), Godfrey was living in Cambridge by 1503, and he lived there until his death. As *stationarius* he had a close connection with the University; in 1503 he was named in a covenant between Town and Gown as among those to be accounted a "common minister and servant" of the University, and therefore to be under the protection of its privileges. In 1534 he was to be one of three University stationers, appointed by letters patent: the other two being his kinsman Segar Nicholson (a Fleming who had studied at Gonville Hall in the early 1520's) and Nicholas Spering. Their duties included the binding, repairing, and chaining of books. Some of Godfrey's bindings are illustrated in G. J. Gray's *The Earlier Cambridge Stationers and Bookbinders* (Oxford, 1904). Godfrey was an important figure in the life of the parish of Great St Mary's, being churchwarden in 1516 and again in 1521. His gifts to the church show that he was reasonably affluent.[30] In his will he left three presses to his apprentice; and also a "fox-furred gown," which may have been supplied him by the University. He was buried in Great St Mary's and left a widow, Agnes.

He acted as a messenger for Erasmus, taking his letters down to London. And it was from Garrett Godfrey that Roger Ascham got his story of Erasmus riding his horse around the Market Hill. On two occasions after leaving Cambridge Erasmus referred to Godfrey as "my old host."

WILLIAM GONNELL (c. 1490–1560)

The name of Gonnell first appeared in Erasmus' correspondence in November 1511.[31] William was a school-master whose parents lived at Landbeach, five miles from Cambridge. A Gonnell, perhaps William's father, had graduated from Cambridge in 1485. William knew, or came to know, such Cambridge friends of Erasmus as Thomas Green, John Watson, and Thomas Lupset; and he also knew Roger Wentford, the Headmaster of St. Anthony's

[29]Letter 30.
[30]Foster, J. E. (ed.), *Church Wardens' Accounts of St. Mary the Great*, index under "Garrard."
[31]Letter 15, to Roger Wentford.

School in the City of London. The Gonnells lent Erasmus a horse, which William took charge of when it was at Landbeach.

In September 1517 William became rector of Conington, a living in the gift of the University, ten miles north-west of Cambridge (near the Huntingdonshire border). He held the living until his death on August 28, 1560.

Also in 1517 (probably) Thomas More chose him as one of the tutors to his children, probably on Erasmus' recommendation; so he must have spent most of his time at the More House in Bucklersbury, Cheapside. A letter of More to Gonnell, written about 1518, has been preserved:[32] "my dear Gonnell, I have often begged not only of you, who would do it out of affection for my children, of your own accord . . . but all my friends, that they will warn my children to avoid the precipices of pride. . . . And this your prudent character will so enforce, so as to teach virtue rather than reprove vice." Gonnell became well known as a teacher of Latin and Greek. John Palsgrave, a Corpus man, tutor to the natural son of Henry VIII, consulted Gonnell on these matters in 1529; the other two people whose advice he asked were William Horman of Eton and John Rightwise, once (on Erasmus' recommendation), Under Master of St Paul's, and now High Master.[33]

THOMAS GREEN (c. 1468–c. 1529)

"Commissary Green," as Erasmus called him in his letters to Gonnell. The Commissary was appointed by the Chancellor, as a judge representing him. The Commissary's Court dealt with cases concerning members of the University below the rank of M.A.: an inferior court, that is, to the Chancellor's (or Consistory) Court, which met weekly in term time, the Vice Chancellor being the usual chairman, to consider cases concerning any graduates, or persons enjoying University privilege. One could appeal from the Court of the Commissary to that of the Chancellor.

Green was Master of St. Catharine's from 1507 to 1529, having previously been a Fellow of Jesus. A range of buildings facing Queens' Lane was to be named after him. A Cumberland boy, he had gone up to Cambridge in the early 1480's, at about the same time as Fisher, and had taken his M.A. in 1490 (a year before Fisher). He became B.D. in 1503 and D.D. in 1512. He was to be Vice-Chancellor in the year 1523–4 (preceding Henry Bullock)—the first member of St. Catharine's to be Vice-Chancellor.

THOMAS LUPSET (1495–1530)

Lupset was a Londoner; his father was a prosperous goldsmith, and the family had some Cambridge connections—the parents were to be benefactors

[32]Number 63 in *The Correspondence of Sir Thomas More* (ed. Elizabeth Rogers), Princeton, 1947. Abridged translations in W. E. Campbell, *More's Utopia and his Social Teaching*, 1930, 129–31, and in E. M. G. Routh, *Sir Thomas More and his Friends*, 1934, 128–30.

[33]Rogers, 404.

of St. Catharine's. Thomas was educated at the old school attached to St Paul's, and attracted the attention of John Colet, who became Dean of St Paul's in 1505 and shortly thereafter took Lupset into his household. By the time he was fifteen Lupset had made the acquaintance of Linacre, More, and Erasmus.

It seems most likely that he went up to Cambridge in the autumn of 1511—at almost the same time as Erasmus. He left the University in the autumn of 1513. His college appears to have been Pembroke. In the summer of 1513 he was helping Erasmus with the Jerome and the New Testament; Erasmus wrote to Colet and More about the youth at that time.[34]

In the autumn of 1515 he was in Italy, with Richard Pace, and he stayed there until the following summer. Then he studied for two years in Paris—mostly Greek. But again, he did not take a degree. In Paris he helped Gilles de Gourmont with the second edition of More's *Utopia* (November 1517) and with two of Linacre's translations from Galen.

In 1519 he went to Corpus Christi College, Oxford (founded in 1516 by Foxe), as lecturer in Greek. He also gave lectures on Greek and Latin to the University at large, on a foundation established by Wolsey in 1518. He remained in Oxford until 1523.

Then he returned to Italy, arriving in May 1523 and going first to Venice to see Pace. In November he moved to Padua, where Reginald Pole was living. At this period he was tutor to Wolsey's natural son, Thomas Winter (b. 1509). At the beginning of 1525 he was in Venice again, helping with the first printed Greek edition of Galen, a five-volume project, produced by Andreas Torresanus, father-in-law and successor of Aldo Manuzio. He left Italy in the autumn of 1525, and lived again in England until his death, except for about nine months in 1528, when Wolsey sent him to Paris to keep an eye on Thomas Winter.

On December 27, 1530 he died of consumption at his mother's house in London. News of his death reached Erasmus in June 1531.

His works include "A Treatise of Charity" (1533), "An Exhortation to Young Men persuading them to Walk in the Pathway that leadeth to Honesty and Goodness" (1535), and "A Compendious Treatise teaching the Way of Dying Well" (1534). He may also have been the author of the English translation published in 1531 of Colet's Convocation Sermon of 1512. Dr. J. A. Gee of Yale, author of a commendable biography (1928), considered that the best English prose written before 1530 was that of Lupset.[35]

THOMAS RUTHALL (died 1523)

An Oxford man, Ruthall was incorporated as Doctor of Divinity at Cambridge in 1500 (the year before Fisher took that degree); and he was Chancellor of the University for the year 1503–4, preceding Fisher. From 1499 he had been Secretary to the King and Privy Councillor; Henry VIII

[34] Letters 26 and 27.
[35] *Life and Works of Thomas Lupset*, 1928, 137.

continued Ruthall in these appointments, and in 1516 he was to be Keeper of the Privy Seal. When Henry VII died Ruthall was also Bishop-elect of Durham (having been for the previous four years Dean of Salisbury). He was consecrated Bishop in the first summer of the new king's reign and held the see until his death. Thus, like Wolsey, Warham, and Foxe, Ruthall was in the first rank of influential ecclesiastical statesmen; and his position as royal secretary made him especially close to the King.

Erasmus probably first met Ruthall in 1505, during his second visit to England; he dedicated to him one of the translations from Lucian, published in 1506.[36] And he was to dedicate to him the edition of Seneca, published in 1515.[37] So far as actual correspondence goes, there survive only two very short letters from Erasmus to Ruthall, one in 1516, the other in 1519,[38] and no letters from Ruthall to Erasmus.

RICHARD SAMPSON (c. 1484–1554)

Sampson took the degree of Bachelor of Civil Law in 1507. Thus he probably went up to Cambridge about 1500. He was attached first to St Clement's Hostel, south of St Clement's Church, and then to Trinity Hall. He took the degree of Doctor of Civil Law in 1513, by which time he had become a friend of Erasmus.

By April 1514 he was in Tournai, which had been captured by the English in the previous September; he went there on Wolsey's behalf—Wolsey having been nominated Bishop of Tournai by Henry, an appointment which occasioned much controversy in the city and the diocese. He had entered Wolsey's service with the condition that he be allowed time to study further in civil and canon law.[39] He was still in Tournai at the beginning of 1518, when Erasmus met him there; Erasmus paid tribute to that "sweetest possible friendship" which he had enjoyed on that occasion, as he had previously enjoyed it at Cambridge.[40]

By 1518 Sampson was also Dean of the Chapel Royal and Dean of St. Stephen's, Westminster. Later, he was Dean of Windsor (1523–36), Dean of Lichfield (1533–6), Dean of St Paul's (1536–40), Bishop of Chichester (1536–44), and Bichop of Lichfield and Coventry (1543–54). He was also much employed by the government on embassies abroad. We know also that he was very fond of claret.[41] In 1538 he took part in the heresy proceedings against John Lambert (Fellow of Queens' 1521), who was to be burnt in that year; Sampson published tracts against Lambert, on the subject of the Real Presence.

[36] *E.E.*, no. 192.
[37] *E.E.*, no. 325.
[38] *E.E.*, nos. 437, 974.
[39] *Letters and Papers Henry VIII*, I, no. 5251. For Sampson in Tournai in 1514, see also nos. 4982, 4983, 5006, 5251.
[40] *E.E.*, no. 806.
[41] *Letters and Papers Henry VIII*, I, no. 5418.

JOHN SMITH (born c. 1500?)

Erasmus' servant-pupil at Cambridge from November 1511 to October 1513. The son of Robert Smith, a Cambridge citizen, John was first educated by William Gonnell; he entered Erasmus' service as an alternative to going to St. Anthony's School in London. In spite of the trouble concerning him in 1513, John re-entered Erasmus' service and went to the continent with him in the summer of 1514. He stayed with Erasmus until March 1518, at which time, his mother thinking him unsafe out of England, he returned home and probably entered the service of Thomas More. More's words concerning his "boy," John Clement—who sat in on the conversation between More, Peter Gilles, and Raphael Hythloday in 1515—give a hint of the value of such a relationship: "whom I suffer to be away from no talk wherein may be any profit or goodness (for out of this young-bladed and new-shot-up corn, which hath already begun to spring up both in Latin and Greek learning, I look for plentiful increase at length of goodly ripe grain)."[42]

NICHOLAS SPERING (died 1546)

Stationer and bookbinder in Cambridge from 1505 to 1546. Nicholas belonged to a family of Netherlands stationers, and before coming to Cambridge he had worked at Lille and Antwerp; he may have been born in Lille. Like Garrett Godfrey, he lived in the parish of Great St Mary's, probably in the High Street. He was elected churchwarden in 1517 and 1522 (on both occasions succeeding Godfrey), and he was buried in the church. His son William married Elizabeth, the sister of John Cheke. In 1534 he and Godfrey and Segar Nicholson were appointed official stationers to the University. Some of his bindings are illustrated in G. J. Gray's *The Earlier Cambridge Stationers.* One of the books he bound was Siberch's 1521 edition of Erasmus' *De Conscribendis Epistolis.*

JOHN VAUGHAN (born c. 1480)

Vaughan became B.A. in 1500 and M.A. in 1503, in which latter year he was appointed Principal of Garrett Hostel (also known as St William's Hostel), which was on the present site of the east wing of the Trinity Bishop's Hostel, and the name of which is preserved in Garrett Hostel Bridge and Lane. (Bishop's Hostel was originally a rebuilding of Garrett Hostel, financed by Bishop Hackett in 1669.) The position of Principal of a Hostel, usually held by a young graduate, was like that of Head or Tutor of a residence hall in many British and American universities today. In 1504 Vaughan was elected Fellow of Queens'; he was bursar of the college from 1505 to 1507, and Dean from 1507 to 1509. He seems to have resigned his Fellowship on 1519 and left Cambridge. Robert Aldrich wrote in 1525: "Fortune has taken away Vaughan; I know not whither."

[42] *Utopia* (Everyman ed.), 8.

HUMPHREY WALKDEN (c. 1484–c. 1525)

B.A. 1504; M.A. and Fellow of Queens' 1507; B.D. 1517; D.D. 1520. Like Bullock, Walkden was a lecturer in mathematics before 1520. Erasmus asked to be remembered to him in letters to Bullock in 1516 and 1518; and also in a letter to Aldrich in 1525—to which Aldrich replied with the news that Walkden was dead.

WILLIAM WARHAM (1450–1532)

A former Fellow of New College, Oxford, Warham became Bishop of London in 1501, and Archbishop of Canterbury and Lord Chancellor in 1504. From 1506 he was also Chancellor of the University of Oxford.

Erasmus first met Warham at a dinner party at Lambeth at the beginning of 1506. He gave the archbishop a manuscript copy of his Latin translation of the *Hecuba* of Euripides, to be printed by Bade in Paris later that year. "I was received by him before dinner with a few words, being myself by no means a talkative or ceremonious person; and again after dinner, as he also was a man of unaffected manners, we had a short conversation together, after which he dismissed me with an honorary present."[43]

During his Cambridge period Erasmus wrote, in private letters, two extended tributes to Warham, both in February 1512 (when he was on a trip to London). "The Archbishop of Canterbury, who not only is primate of England in rank and title but also clearly holds the first place for learning, honour, courtesy, and meekness, regards me (undeserving as I am) with the greatest good will. He, I may say, is second-to-none in his devotion to the See of Rome: though indeed this Kingdom of England has to her a very warm affection."[44] (On that latter theme, note the judgement of a modern historian, G. R. Elton: "throughout the fifteenth century and later, the English Crown maintained the friendliest relations with Rome, and England was the most papalist of countries."[45]) "If you have any wish to hear how I'm situated, the fact is that Erasmus is now almost entirely turned into an Englishman; so notable is the kindness with which he is being treated by a host of people, among them in particular the Archbishop of Canterbury, that unrivalled patron of mine—no, not of mine, but rather of all scholars: among whom I hold the lowest, if indeed any, rank. Immortal god, what a well-endowed, fertile, alert mind the man has! What address, in disposing of affairs of the utmost moment; and what distinguished scholarship too! And also, what unheard of kindness to everyone, and how delightful to meet! Consequently, by a truly royal trait, he sends nobody away unhappy. In addition, how generous and prompt his liberality is! And finally, how totally absent is any arrogance, in spite of the eminence of his rank and estate. He gives, accordingly, the impression of being himself the only one who's unaware how great a man he is. Nobody is trustier or more steadfast

[43]*E.E.*, I, 5; tr. Nichols, I, 393.
[44]To Robert Guibé, February 8, 1512. *E.E.*, no. 253; tr. Thomson.
[45]*New Cambridge Modern History*, II, 228.

in cherishing friendships. To sum up, he's truly a Primate, not only in title, but in every praiseworthy quality of person: and when this is the man whose favour I enjoy, how can I avoid deeming myself uncommonly fortunate, even without any further advantage?"[46]

A month after these letters were written, Warham presented Erasmus to the rectory of Aldington. And Erasmus later said that between 1510 and 1514 Warham had given him money gifts amounting to about £150; once he got £50 as a single gift.[47]

JOHN WATSON (c. 1477–c. 1537)

From 1501 to 1516 Watson was a Fellow of Peterhouse, under Henry Hornby (Master 1501–18), secretary to the Lady Margaret, and among those who "represented the Renaissance in Cambridge."[48] Watson had commenced B.A. in 1498, and therefore probably went up to Cambridge about 1494. He was Proctor for the year 1504–5; curate of Little St Mary's, 1510; bursar of his college, 1509–13; and B.D. 1513. It is possible that Hugh Latimer was one of Watson's Peterhouse pupils.

In 1515 Watson travelled on the continent with John Reston (B.A. 1506, to be Master of Jesus 1546 to 1551). The two looked up some of Erasmus' friends in Venice; from which port they sailed in July for the Holy Land.

He became rector of Elsworth, seven miles from Cambridge, in 1516—a living worth £20 a year. And in 1517 he was elected the fourth Master of Christ's; Fisher no doubt thought highly of him.

Watson was Master of Christ's for fifteen years. He became D.D. in 1517 and Vice-Chancellor in 1518, 1519, and 1530—when he wished to require all graduates in Divinity to take an oath repudiating the errors of Huss, Wycliffe, and Luther. For Watson was a hammer of the Lutherans; in 1528 he had been among the judges of Robert Barnes, the advanced Prior of the Cambridge Augustinian Friars.

He resigned the Mastership in 1531 or 1532, when he was in his mid-fifties. For the last years of his life he seems to have been a Fellow of King's Hall, one of the colleges that went to the making of Trinity in 1546.

ROGER WENTFORD

Erasmus met Wentford in 1505 in London. He wrote to him from Paris in June 1506: "Among the many delightful friends with whom Britain has made me acquainted, you, my dear Roger, are one of the first to come to my mind. Your love has been so constant, your society so delightful, your services so useful, that to whatever quarter of the world my fates may lead me, I shall carry with me the most agreeable rcollection of my Roger. I wish your fortune had allowed you to accompany us to Italy. You would

[46]To Anthony of Bergen, Abbot of St. Omer, February 6, 1512. *E.E.*, no. 252; tr. Thomson.

[47]Letter 43.

[48]H. Butterfield, *V.C.H.*, 336.

then be in entire possession of your Erasmus, whom you have already in many ways made most thoroughly your own."[49] Wentford was Headmaster of St. Anthony's School, Threadneedle Street, which had been founded by Henry III and re-endowed by Henry VI. Like St Thomas', the other prominent London school in the first decade of the sixteenth century, St Anthony's was at once a Hospital ("of thirteen poor men," wrote John Stow) and a "college, with a free school for poor men's children." The hospital was suppressed in the reign of Edward VI; the school by the end of Elizabeth's reign was "in some sort remaining, but sore decayed."[50] The school was near the site of the present Stock Exchange. Thomas More had been educated there; and its Tudor alumni also included John Whitgift.

There seem to be no records relating to Wentford's own education.

RICHARD WHITFORD (1470–c. 1555)

Born of a landed family in North Wales, Whitford was a Fellow of Queens' from 1495 to 1504. He probably went up to Cambridge in 1488. In March 1498 he was given leave of absence by the college to accompany Lord Mountjoy to Paris; Whitford was twenty-seven, Mountjoy eighteen. In Paris the two met Erasmus. Whitford was incorporated as B.A. in Paris in 1498 and as M.A. 1499. Erasmus wrote him a short note in February 1499: *Ricarde candidissime*.[51] He returned to England with Erasmus and Mountjoy in the summer of 1499.

In 1504 Whitford left Queens' to become chaplain to Bishop Richard Foxe of Winchester. Concerning this period, William Roper was to bring Whitford into his *Life of More*. The story went that Henry VII had imprisoned More's father after More had spoken in the House of Commons against the King's financial demands. "Shortly hereupon it fortuned that this Sir Thomas More coming in a suit to Doctor Foxe, Bishop of Winchester, one of the King's Privy Council, the bishop called him aside, and pretending great favour towards him, promised him that if he would be ruled by him, he would not fail into the King's favour again to restore him, meaning, as it was afterwards conjectured, to cause him thereby to confess his offence against the King, whereby His Highness might with the better colour have occasion to revenge his displeasure against him. But when he came from the bishop, he fell into communication with one Master Whitford, his familiar friend, then chaplain to that bishop, and after a father of Sion, and showed him what the bishop had said to him, desiring to have his advice therein; who, for the passion of God, prayed him in no wise to follow his counsel, for my lord my master, quoth he, to serve the King's turn will not stick to agree to his own father's death."[52]

Erasmus dedicated to Whitford one of his translations from Lucian in 1506.

The next year, 1507, Whitford entered the Abbey of Syon, on the Thames, between Islesworth and Brentford. This was a community unique

[49]*E.E.*, no. 196; tr. Nichols, I, 413.
[50]Stow (ed. Kingsford), *Survey of London*, II, 143.
[51]*E.E.*, no. 89.
[52]Roper, *Life of More*, 2–3.

in England, consisting of sixty Bridgettine nuns, and about twenty priests who acted as their spiritual directors. David Knowles writes that the Bridgettine brethren formed "a group without parallel in Tudor England; men who combined personal austerity of life with theological or devotional competence, and who by their books, by their direction of a fervent and aristocratic nunnery, and by their influence as counsellors and confessors of leading laymen, were a power to be reckoned with in a religious world which contained all too few centres of enlightened piety."

The house of Syon "was distinguished not only by its good observance, but by its informed devotional life, based largely upon the spiritual writers of the later medieval period, including the English mystical writers of the fourteenth century; it possessed a magnificent library, particularly rich in modern devotional works." It was "an orthodox Port Royal."[53] Compare William Tyndale in 1532: "our hirelings have no God's word, but trust in the multitude of words, length of babbling, and pain of body, as bond servants: neither know they any other virtue to be in prayer; as ye may see by the ordinances of all foundations. King Henry V built Syon, and the Charterhouse of Sheen on the other side of the water, of such a manner that lip-labour may never cease. For when the friars of Syon ring out, the nuns begin; and when the nuns ring out of service, the monks on the other side begin; and when they ring out, the friars begin again, and vex themselves night and day, and take pain for God's sake; for which God must give them heaven."[54]

During the last thirty years of the house, at least six Cambridge dons joined; including Richard Reynolds, another friend of More, who was a Fellow of Corpus when Erasmus was in Cambridge, and was executed in May 1535.

While at Syon, Whitford translated or wrote about fifteen works, including *Exposition of St Augustine's Rule* (1525); a translation of the Martyrology "after the use of the Church of Salisbury and as it is used in Syon";[55] and a version from the Latin of *The Imitation of Christ*, published in 1531,[56] but perhaps written as early as 1510. The previous English *Imitation of Christ* (1503), had been made, partly by the Lady Margaret, from the French. The *Imitation* was one of the three devotional books recommended by More in 1532 to "nourish and increase devotion", the other two being the *Scale of Perfection* by the Augustinian canon Walter Hilton, first printed in 1494, and Bonaventura's *Mirror of the Life of Christ* (Caxton, 1486).[57]

Syon was dissolved in November 1539. Whitford received a pension, and joined the household of Charles, Lord Mountjoy, son of William.

[53]Knowles, *The Religious Orders in England*, III, 212, 213, 215.

[54]*Exposition of Matthew V–VII*, *Expositions* (Parker Society), 81.

[55]Edited 1893 by F. Procter and E. S. Dewick.

[56]Modern reprint, Mount Vernon, 1947. Extracts in Nugent (ed.), *Thought and Culture of the English Renaissance*, 376–82.

[57]*Confutation*, 182.

BOOKS CITED

ALLEN, H. M. (ed.). *Letters of P. S. Allen*. London, 1939.
ALLEN, P. S. *Erasmus: Lectures and Wayfaring sketches*. Oxford, 1934.
ASCHAM, R. *English Works* (including *Toxophilus* and *The Schoolmaster*). Ed. W. A. Wright. Cambridge, 1904.
AYLMER, G. E. *The King's Servants*. London, 1961.
BALDWIN, T. W. *William Shakespeare's Small Latin and Less Greek*. 2 vols. Urbana, Ill., 1944.
BALL, W. W. R. *A History of the Study of Mathematics at Cambridge*. Cambridge, 1889.
BARNES, R. *Works*. London, 1572.
BATAILLON, M. *Erasme et l'Espagne*. Paris, 1937.
BOLGAR, R. R. *The Classical Heritage and Its Beneficiaries*, Cambridge, 1954.
BROWN, J. H. *Elizabethan Schooldays*. Oxford, 1933.
CAIUS, J. *The Annals of Gonville and Caius College*. Ed. J. Venn. Cambridge, 1904.
CAMPAGNAC, E. T. *The Cambridge Platonists*. Oxford, 1901.
CARDWELL, E. *Documentary Annals of the Reformed Church of England*. 2 vols. Oxford, 1839.
CLARK, D. L. *John Milton at St. Paul's School*. New York, 1948.
CLARK, J. W. *The Observances in Use at the Augustinian Priory at Barnwell*. Cambridge, 1897.
CLARKE, M. L. *Classical Education in Britain 1500–1900*. Cambridge, 1959.
COLET, J. (transl. and ed. by J. H. Lupton).
—— *On the Sacraments of the Church*, London, 1867.
—— *On the Hierarchies of Dionysius*. London, 1869.
—— *Lectures on Romans*. London, 1873.
—— *Lectures on I Corinthians*. London, 1874.
—— *Lectures on the Mosaic Account of the Creation, etc*. London, 1876.
COOPER, C. H. *Annals of Cambridge*. 5 vols. Cambridge, 1842–1908.
COSTELLO, W. T. *The Scholastic Curriculum at Early Seventeenth-Century Cambridge*. Cambridge, Mass., 1958.
CRANMER, T. *Remains*. Ed. J. E. Cox (Parker Society). Cambridge, 1846.
CURTIS, M. H. *Oxford and Cambridge in Transition, 1558–1642*. Oxford, 1959.
DICKINSON, J. C. *The Origins of the Austin Canons*. London, 1950.
DUFF, E. G. *Fifteenth Century English Books*. Oxford, 1917.
EDWARD VI. *Journal*. In J. G. Nichols, *Literary Remains of King Edward VI*. 2 vols. London, 1857.
EMDEN, A. B. *A Biographical Register of the University of Oxford to A.D. 1500*. 3 vols. Oxford, 1957–9.
EMMISON, F. G. *Tudor Secretary: Sir William Petre at Court and Home*. London, 1961.

ERASMUS, D. *Colloquies*. Transl. N. Bailey (1725), ed. E. Johnson. 2 vols. London, 1878.
—— *Ten Colloquies of Erasmus*. Transl. C. R. Thompson. New York, 1957.
—— *The Education of a Christian Prince*. Transl. L. K. Born. New York, 1936.
—— *Enchiridion militis christiani, which may be called in English, the Handsome Weapon of a Christian Knight* (with the 1518 preface). London, 1534, 1905.
—— *An Exhortation to the Diligent Study of Scripture*. 1529.
—— *Inquisitio de fide* (1524). Transl. C. R. Thompson. New Haven, 1950.
—— *Paraphrases upon the New Testament*. 2 vols. London, 1548–9.
—— *The Praise of Folly*. Transl. J. Wilson (1668). Ann Arbor, 1958.
FAIRBANK, A., and B. DICKINS. *The Italic Hand in Tudor Cambridge*. London, 1962.
FISHER, J. *The Defence of the Sacred Priesthood* (1525). Transl. P. E. Hallett. London, 1935.
FORTESCUE, J. *De laudibus legum Anglie*. Transl. S. B. Chrimes. Cambridge, 1942.
FOSTER, J. E. (ed.). *Churchwardens' Accounts of St. Mary the Great, Cambridge*. Cambridge, 1905.
FRITH, J. *Works*. In. vol. III of *Works of the English Reformers*, ed. T. Russell. London, 1831.
FULKE, W. *Answers* (to Stapleton, Sanders and Martiall). Ed. R. Gibbings (Parker Society). Cambridge, 1848.
FULLER, T. *The History of the University of Cambridge* (1655). Ed. M. Prickett and T. Wright. Cambridge, 1840.
GEE, J. A. *The Life and Work of Thomas Lupset*. New Haven, 1928.
GODET, M. *La Congrégation de Montaigu 1490–1580*. Paris, 1912.
GOLDSCHMIDT, E. P. *The First Cambridge Press in Its European Setting*. Cambridge, 1955.
GRAY, G. J. *The Earlier Cambridge Stationers and Bookbinders and the First Cambridge Printer*. Oxford, 1904.
GRAY, T. *Letters*. Ed. D. C. Tovey. 3 vols. London, 1900–12.
GRINDAL, E. *Remains*. Ed. W. Nicholson (Parker Society). Cambridge, 1843.
HAY,D. *Polydore Vergil*. Oxford, 1952.
—— *The Italian Renaissance in Its Historical Background*. Cambridge, 1961.
HECKER, J. F. K. *The Epidemics of the Middle Ages*. Transl. B. G. Babington. 2nd ed. London, 1846.
HEYWOOD, J. *Early Cambridge University and College Statutes*. London, 1855.
HOSKINS, W. E. *Local History in England*. London, 1959.
HUIZINGA, J. *Erasmus of Rotterdam*. Transl. F. Hopman (1924); with a selection from the letters (transl. B. Flower). London, 1952.
HYMA, A. *The Devotio Moderna, or Christian Renaissance, 1380–1520*. Grand Rapids, Mich., 1925.

JEWEL, J. *Works*. Ed. J. Ayre (Parker Society). 4 vols. Cambridge, 1845–50.

KAY, M. M. *The History of Rivington and Blackrod Grammar School*. Manchester, 1931.

KNIGHT, S. *The Life of Erasmus*. Cambridge, 1726.

KNOWLES, D. *The Religious Orders in England*, vol. III. Cambridge, 1959.

LATIMER, H. Ed. G. E. Corrie (Parker Society).

——— *Sermons*. Cambridge, 1844.

——— *Remains*. Cambridge, 1845.

Letters and Papers of the reign of Henry VIII. Ed. J. S. Brewer, J. Gairdner, R. H. Brodie. 33 vols. London, 1862–1911.

LEWIS, C. S. *English Literature in the Sixteenth Century*. Oxford, 1954.

LEWIS, J. *The Life of John Fisher*. 2 vols. London, 1855.

LUCIAN. *Works*. Transl. H. W. and F. G. Fowler. 4 vols. Oxford, 1905.

——— *Satirical Sketches*. Transl. P. Turner. London, 1961.

LUPTON, J. *Life of Dean Colet* (1887). 2nd ed. London, 1907.
See also Colet.

——— *Erasmus Lives of Vitrier and Colet*. (A translation of Erasmus' June 1521 Letter: *E.E.*, no. 1211.) London, 1883.

MAJOR, J. *History of Greater Britain* (1521). Transl. A. Constable. Edinburgh, 1892.

MALLET, C. E. *A History of the University of Oxford*. London, 1924.

MORE, T. *Utopia*. Transl. R. Robinson. Everyman ed., London, 1951.

——— *The Confutation of Tyndale's Answer*. 2 parts. London, 1532–3.

MULLINGER, J. B. *The University of Cambridge from the Earliest Times*. 2 vols., London, 1873–84. Vol. 3, Cambridge, 1911.

NASHE, T. *Works*. Ed. R. B. McKerrow. 5 vols. Oxford, 1958.

NELSON, W. *John Skelton, Laureate*. New York, 1939.

NORTON, F. J. *Italian Printers 1501–20*. London, 1958.

NUGENT, E. M. (ed.). *The Thought and Culture of the English Renaissance: an Anthology of Tudor Prose 1481–1555*. Cambridge, 1956.

Original Letters: English Reformation. Ed. H. Robinson (Parker Society). 2 vols. Cambridge, 1846–7.

Oxford Dictionary of English Proverbs. 2nd ed. London, 1948.

PARKS, G. B. *The English Traveler to Italy*. Vol. I. Rome, 1954.

Portable Renaissance Reader. Ed. J. B. Ross and M. M. McLaughlin. New York, 1959.

RASHDALL, H. *The Universities of Europe in the Middle Ages*. Ed. F. M. Powicke and A. B. Emden. 3 vols. Oxford, 1936.

Renaissance Philosophy of Man. Ed. E. Cassirer, P. O. Kristeller, J. H. Randall. Chicago, 1948.

RENAUDET, A. *Erasme et l'Italie*. Geneva, 1954.

——— *Humanisme et renaissance*. Geneva, 1958.

REYNOLDS, E. E. *St. Thomas More*. London, 1953.

ROGERS, E. F. *The Correspondence of Sir Thomas More*. Princeton, 1947.

ROPER, W. *Life of More*. London, 1902.

ROUTH, E. M. G. *Sir Thomas More and His Friends*. London, 1934.

SALTMARSH, J. *King's College and Its Chapel*. Cambridge, 1957.

Searle, W. G. *The History of Queens' College.* 2 parts. Cambridge, 1867–71.
Sheppard, J. T. *Richard Croke.* Cambridge, 1919.
Simon, A. *The History of the Wine Trade in England.* 3 vols. London, 1907–9.
—— *Drink.* London, 1948.
Smalley, B. I. *The Study of the Bible in the Middle Ages.* Oxford, 1941.
Stow, J. *A survey of London.* Ed. C. L. Kingsord. 2 vols. Oxford, 1908.
Thompson, C. R. *The Translations of Lucian by Erasmus and St Thomas More.* Ithaca, N.Y., 1940.
Tilley, M. P. *A Dictionary of the Proverbs in England in the Sixteenth and Seventeenth Centuries.* Ann Arbor, 1950.
Turner, W. *A Book of Wines* (1568). Ed. S. V. Larkey. New York, 1941.
Tyndale, W. (ed. H. Walter [Parker Society]).
—— *Doctrinal Treatises.* Cambridge, 1848.
—— *Expositions, etc.* Cambridge, 1849.
—— *Answer to More, etc.* Cambridge, 1850.
Vasari, G. *Lives of the Artists.* Ed. B. Burroughs. New York, 1946.
Watson, F. *The English Grammar Schools to 1660.* London, 1908.
Weiss, R. *Humanism in England during the Fifteenth Century.* 2nd ed. Oxford, 1957.
Whitaker, W. *A Disputation on Holy Scripture.* Transl. W. Fitzgerald (Parker Society). Cambridge, 1849.
Whitgift, J. *Works.* Ed. J. Ayre (Parker Society). 3 vols. Cambridge, 1851–3.
Woodward, W. H. *Desiderius Erasmus concerning the Aim and Method of Education.* Cambridge, 1904.
—— *Studies in Education during the Age of the Renaissance, 1400–1600.* Cambridge, 1906.
Zurich Letters. Ed. H. Robinson (Parker Society). 2 vols. Cambridge, 1842–5.